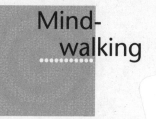

Mind-walking

Mind-walking

Rewriting Your Past to Create Your Future

Nancy L. Eubel

A.R.E. Press • Virginia Beach • Virginia

A.R.E. Press
215 67th Street
Virginia Beach, VA 23451-2061

ISBN-13: 978-0-87604-591-6 (trade paper)

Cover design by Christine Fulcher

In gratitude to my dear husband Frank
for the love and support he gave me during his life
and continues to send from the other side.

Contents

Acknowledgments

This book was a team effort—a team comprised of many individuals— A.R.E. members, clients, friends, family, and volunteers all working together with Spirit on a co-creative basis. We each had our individual tile to add to the amazing mosaic of past-life stories that unfolded.

There are several special people whom I would like to thank for their contributions that placed me on the path to writing this book. The first are my parents, Betty and Sam Greco, who fostered in me a love of education. Then there are Edgar Cayce and Gladys Davis Turner who left a legacy that continues to help and inspire people around the world to this day. My heartfelt gratitude goes to Trula Crosier and the angels who guided me in this process.

Many thanks go to Stephanie Helberg, Rhonda Corbitt, Donna Sturm, and Julie Hilt who are always supportive and lift me when I falter. To Walter Semkiw, MD and Donald Norsic for sharing their own past-life histories and their visions of the potential for positive change that understanding and acknowledging reincarnation can have. My teachers are many, but most important among them are Jack Elias CHT, Founder, Director of the Institute of Therapeutic Learning in Seattle; Dolores Cannon, past-life regressionist, hypnotherapist, President and Founder of Ozark Mountain Publishing; Allen S. Chips, DCH, National Association of Transpersonal Hypnotherapists (NATH) President and President of the American Holistic University, and Michael Harner, PhD, anthropologist and founder of the Foundation for Shamanic Studies.

My appreciation goes to my editor, Stephanie Pope, who untangled the intricate web of my convoluted sentences.

And, of course, to Frank.

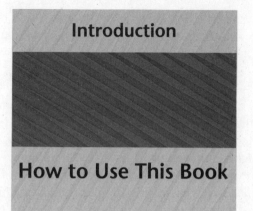

Introduction

How to Use This Book

About Past-Life Regression

Past-life regression is a specific method of hypnotherapy in which a person is lead into an altered state of consciousness to remember his or her own past-life or -lives. There are practitioners who are trained exclusively in past-life regression, perhaps in one specific method, while hypnotherapists are trained in other types of trance work such as positive behavioral change in addition to past-life.

You may choose to do this past-life remembrance on your own using the information in this book, or you may need or desire to find a good past-life regressionist/hypnotherapist to guide you. There are many available. When selecting someone, ask about the person's background and methodology. Also ask about the practitioner's philosophy and make sure that it is in concert with your own. Then use your own spiritual guidance, your internal knowing, as to whether this person is the best one for you.

It may not be advisable to regress yourself if you want to address particularly difficult issues or suppressed memories. The regressions in this book are not intended to replace professional advice you might need, whether that be medical or psychological. If that is the case, you should check with a professional in that field before you proceed.

About the Regression Scripts

Suggested past-life regression scripts are provided in many of the chapters so that you can continue your exploration of your own past-lives even after finishing this book. The first regression in Chapter 1 will take you to a prior time in which you lived a fulfilling and happy life, and the regression follows a traditional format. This will allow you to become familiar with the process and feel comfortable with it. The regressions in the chapters that follow address specific types of goals. Some of them are adaptations of the happy past-life script, but several are unique to their chapter.

The regressions are designed to help you *remember* the origin of negative patterns and then aid you in applying spiritual principles to transform them to more positive ones. As a result, the inductions—initial suggestions for relaxation and setting the stage for the actual regression—have been fashioned in a way meant to disengage the conscious mind, which may attempt to analyze and judge what is happening. This allows you to open to your imaginal abilities to form mental images of information about your past-lives provided to you by the subconscious. Although you may receive the information as pictures in your mind, as many do, it may come to you instead through your other senses. Be open to receiving it in whatever way is best for you, whether that be through your inner knowing, hearing, touch, taste, or even smell. Wait to judge what comes to you until the regression is over. Then your conscious mind has the full picture with which to analyze, if it chooses.

The last regression in the book, to retrieve past-life skills and create a future you desire, is not intended to be spiritually therapeutic as are the others. It engages your co-creative abilities to manifest the life of your dreams. This script and the happy past-life script can be adapted to revisit any of your past-lives you choose to explore.

Energy Work

In some of the reports of the regressions, you will read how energy was released, transformed, or sent into the Light, sometimes to be returned to the person after purification. This type of energy work is typically not part of a past-life regression, but it is part of my methodology so I use it for the person's benefit. Although it is referred to, I have not included ways in which you can incorporate energy work as it is not the focus of this book and would be difficult for you to do on your own without training.

Creating Your Safe Place

Before you try these regressions for yourself, it is important for you to find a quiet place in which to work and create a safe place in your mind. This will provide you with a sanctuary, so to speak, into which you can retreat if you feel the need to remove yourself from a regression experience. Although you are encouraged to view your prior lives as an impartial observer, there may be times when you are reliving the experience. If it feels uncomfortable for any reason, you can visit your safe place or even open your eyes until you are ready to continue.

The safe place you select might be somewhere you have been before that you love and feel comfortable in—a place where you always wanted to be or somewhere that your imaginative mind creates just for you. Wherever that place is, you must feel totally safe and protected there. Be sure to add details to make this a beautiful and comfortable place. Invite the participation of all your senses so that it becomes alive for you.

Higher Self

Your Higher Self is going to be your guide on your journeys through former incarnations. It will also be assisting you for your highest good. Your Higher Self is that part of you that has always been aware of its, and your, connection to the Divine. It knows you on a soul level and sees you as the true, pure being you are. Edgar Cayce told us that it is the aspect of us that is an individuation of God's energy. It is the voice of God within, so look to it for help and assistance, not only in your regressions, but anytime you have need. If you ask, it will always be there. It may appear to you in a human–type body, an energy body, or as a feeling or scent. Even if you are not able to discern its presence with any of your senses, it is always there. It is part of you.

Recording the Sessions

If you want to experience any of these regressions yourself, you can read the script, make any adjustments you desire (including changing the word "you" to "I"), set the intention, enter into a meditative state, and lead yourself through it. You might find that playing soothing or spiritual music may be helpful for you to reach the state of consciousness necessary to access the past.

You may, however, decide to record it for yourself and play it while you go back in time. There are many different types of technologies you can use. Among these are tape recorders, digital recorders, and other types of recorders you can use. You can even record it and play it back on your computer. Since digital recorders are very sensitive, you might want to add an inexpensive software editing program so that you can take out the hissing and scratching noises. One word of warning: do not listen to your recording while you are driving. You might just find yourself transported from the highway to a pasture where you are herding cows!

May Spirit guide you in your adventures!

Nancy Eubel

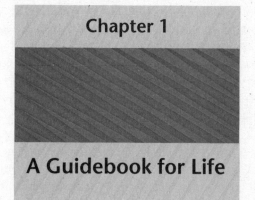

Chapter 1

A Guidebook for Life

Imagine, if you will, a world in which *everyone* believed in reincarnation. Linger with this thought. Explore its possibilities—a world where race, ethnicity, differences of any kind would be irrelevant because we have been or could be in the future: yellow, white, black, red, brown, gay, straight, female, or male. The opportunities for the unique expression of our soul's experience in a physical body are seemingly boundless.

Remembering past-lives is a slice of the topic of reincarnation, a slice of the potential. In the life readings Edgar Cayce gave, he told people of some of their past-lives as a guidebook for this life. They were advised as to whether they had gained or lost in their soul development in those lives and what their weaknesses and their strengths were so that they might use this information for their benefit on their journey home to Source.

Visiting a past-life is like opening a portal in time and space. As P.M.H. Atwater, a near-death researcher, wrote, "A human being not in proper balance physically, emotionally, mentally, and spiritually will

1

subconsciously set up a vibrational 'signal' which will attract to him or her the very diseases, accidents, or incidents necessary for that individual's redirection, rebirth, or death."[1] Through a past-life regression the original cause of a particular recurring pattern or problem, the source of this "signal," is suddenly viewed or relived in context. What we may be experiencing currently as a constant pain in the neck may have resulted from a stab wound by a former enemy; eye deterioration may happen as an awakening of our pattern of having previously refused to see a wrong, or the quivering of our hands may come from a life in which we were disdainful or fearful of getting our hands dirty and manipulated others to do it for us. What value does this knowledge have? Sometimes just revisiting the cause unleashes the energy that has been locked in this former time and change occurs. In other cases spiritual therapy must also happen. Perhaps forgiveness of all those involved, including ourselves, is required. Our very way of being and doing in the world may need to be changed so that we are more expansive and loving, more mindful of the interconnectedness of all beings. Whatever it is that we need do, spiritual assistance is always available if we ask for it.

Are these memories of having lived in former times real? This is an answer you must come to on your own. My purpose is not to try to convince you of the validity of either reincarnation or information acquired through past-life regression or mindwalking journeying. The goal here is to provide you with a catalyst for change by first remembering who you truly are—a spiritual being expressing itself through adventures in and out of matter—and then by affording you the opportunity to make course corrections necessary in your evolutionary process. I would, however, add this to the discussion of the question of whether or not reincarnation is real: in regressing a few of my clients it was quite clear to them and to me that the details of prior incarnations contained information they did not have prior knowledge of. Some even began speaking in foreign languages that they did not know. For others,

---

[1]P.M.H. Atwater, *We Live Forever: The Real Truth About Death* (Virginia Beach, VA: A.R.E. Press, 2004), 42.

it seemed as if the subconscious had used this venue to express itself in a way that it could be heard through symbols rather than through actual past-life memories, similar to the messages in dreams. As a hypnotherapist and past-life regressionist it is not my place to judge. What is relevant is the value that can come from this type of exploration. My focus, and the focus of this book, is to provide a vehicle to assist you in creating your future in a way that aids you not only on your soul's journey but also in adding vibrationally to the shift to higher consciousness on this planet.

Remembering Past-Lives

"... there is no fence or hedge round Time that has gone. You can go back and have what you like if you remember well enough."[2]

Richard Llewellyn

Memories of past-lives can come to us in many forms; some sought after and others unsolicited. Although past-life regression is the most common method of retrieving our memories, it is but one of the many means available for accessing them. Mindwalking is another. It is my own unique process that incorporates the retrieval of past-life memories and the "rewriting" of them during a shamanic journey into nonordinary reality. During the journey neural pathways in the brain are corrected to transform negative life-patterns of the past-life into positive ones. You will read more of this process in Chapter 3.

Psychic readings, dreams, flashbacks, among others, can also bring information about our former incarnations to us. Here are a few interesting examples:

Past-Life Recall in Meditation

In his book *Ancient Egyptian Mysticism*, John Van Auken, a director of the A.R.E., wrote about reliving a past-life in ancient Egypt while in a

---

[2]Richard Llewellyn, *How Green Was My Valley* (New York: Simon & Schuster, 2009) 12.

deep meditative state. It felt to him that this life still existed and that he was a part of it. This was followed by similar experiences in meditation, dreams, and even flashbacks. Sometime after that, John visited Egypt. While meditating in the sacred temple at Abydos, he had the profound experience of finding himself as a participant in an initiation ceremony. He was so deeply engrossed in this event that when the tour leader tried to tell him that it was time to leave, John did not even recognize who he was!

This experience was so profound that it awakened an almost insatiable interest in ancient Egypt, its mysticism, and mythology. In many ways it has shaped his life as he has lead numerous tours to Egypt, speaks at the A.R.E. Ancient Mysteries conferences, writes books about the subject, and continues to delve even deeper into the mysteries of that place and time.

Past-Life Recall During a Near-Death Experience

Near-death experiences (NDE's) are being reported more frequently as medicine and technology are able to save many who would have previously died from their injuries or illnesses. Less common are NDE's in which the person relives a past-life. One such instance was Gretchen's near-death experience that took place while she was laboring to birth her daughter. As the baby was unable to pass through the birth canal because of its position, the anesthesiologist administered sodium pentothal in order to deliver the child. That was when Gretchen began reliving a series of three prior lives in which she had died in childbirth.

In the first recall Gretchen was an English woman married to a planter in Africa. They were attacked by Africans of a tribe different from the ones who worked for them. She was raped, left for dead, and rescued by a native man and woman who lived in a cave. The English woman discovered she was pregnant but was unsure if the father was her husband or one of the attackers. When it was time to deliver the child, she went into protracted labor and was unable to deliver. In her agony she somehow learned to lift out of the body to alleviate the pain and was finally able to drag herself out of the cave. She did not want to die inside the cave because the man and woman who had helped her would have had to abandon it.

After leaving that body, she immediately found herself in a second past-life inside a covered wagon that was being attacked by Native Americans. Again she was pregnant and in the throes of delivery but could not deliver the child because the wagon was bouncing around. She became very angry and rose out of her body, filling the sky with her spirit. She was furious. The horses of the attackers sensed her spirit and would not move. The wagon trains immediately pulled into a circle for defense. When the members of her party checked on her, they found that she was already dead, and no one attempted to save the baby.

Then, through the fog, Gretchen heard the voice of the anesthesiologist telling her to breathe deeper, which she did, and in doing so slipped into a third past-life where she was once more exiting her body during delivery. She was married to a farmer in Britain who had a disability. As the farmer's wife she was very ecstatic to be released from that life, but her husband was distraught. Although her spirit playfully said to him after it left the body, "Don't you know I'll be with you always? I'll never leave you," he couldn't hear her and refused to be comforted. She began to sense the enormity of how bad her decision to leave her body was when suddenly Gretchen found herself back in the present looking down at her body in the delivery room. Gretchen thought in amazement, "I've done it again!" As she watched, a nurse reported, "No detectable pulse, doctor." The anesthesiologist responded, "No discernable breathing," and the doctor said, "Well, let's get the baby out, at least."

As she watched what was taking place, Gretchen felt sad, recognizing that there must be something she needed to work through FOLLOW-ING the birth of a child. That caused her to take a deep breath and immediately return to her body and deliver her daughter.

Gretchen was raised with a very conservative Christian religious upbringing. Reincarnation was not part of that belief system, but this experience caused her to begin a search which changed her life. She subsequently returned to school to receive a Master's degree, divorced her highly dysfunctional husband, met and subsequently married the man who had been the farmer in the third past-life recall (!), and became involved with the A.R.E. The information in the Cayce readings answered her questions and led her to a new spiritual life based on those concepts. All of this occurred because of the very dramatic reliving of three lives in a near-death experience resulting in her making a different choice this time—the choice to stay in the body and birth a new life, not just for her daughter, but for herself.

Past-Life Recall Flashbacks

Past-life flashbacks happen unexpectedly and can by very disconcerting, as this one was for me. My husband Frank and I were in Georgia working as volunteers at a Sports Car Club of America event some years ago. After the event we drove to Washington, D.C. for sightseeing. While still in Georgia, we took one of the exits off the highway to stop for dinner. The road back to the highway was not the same as the one leading to it, and Frank took a wrong turn when returning. We found ourselves surrounded by cornfields. The sun was going down, and we were driving deeper and deeper into the back country. Sitting there in the passenger's seat, I began to panic and quite suddenly found myself in a past-life—as a black male slave hiding from a group of men who were coming to lynch me. The man in charge leading the search was none other than Frank! I was petrified. Frank's voice brought me back to the present when he informed me he had found the highway. I was once again in the passenger's seat, breathing a sigh of relief.

Later when I had time to reflect, I questioned why this very vivid experience had surfaced and looked for the message it contained. I recalled two other flashbacks that had occurred shortly before this one. In the first, someone was placing a black hood over my head just before cutting it off! In the second, I was imprisoned in a pit with an iron door of some kind covering it. Obviously, none of these flashbacks was pleasurable. As a member of an A.R.E. Search for God Study Group (and I still am), the work I had done in the group caused me to look at the pattern these flashbacks reflected back to me. The theme was clear; it was that of a victim. The next step for me was to ask myself how I was acting or reacting as a victim in my current life. Then, I consciously began to observe when I was acting or thinking that way and intentionally changed my response. When I began taking more responsibility for what happened in my life, it changed in very positive ways. Thankfully there were no more victim flashbacks.

Past-Life Dreams

Dreams of another time have a very distinct quality to them that is hard to articulate but also makes them difficult to forget. One of Julio's favorite dreams (and you will meet him again in this book) is a dream of a "lifetime" in which he was either a tree or a flower. In this incursion into the physical he was in front of a meadow watching all the life around him as he felt the breeze. He said that this was great because it was a timeless experience of just being and seeing life. This is very reminiscent of the story revealed to us by Edgar Cayce of our evolution into matter when we first began to experiment in the material world and experience its effect by projecting our spirit into the forms of nature.

Past-life dreams, like many other types of dreams, are sent to us by the soul for a reason. Icléa shared one of hers with me in which she was doing a ritual in Egypt. Before she entered the place that housed the altar where she was going to perform the ritual, she looked at herself in a shield that was highly polished like a mirror. What she saw was a very young woman, very beautiful and very dark. When she looked in the mirror, Icléa just knew that "she" was "me." The altar had charcoal and a fire. Icléa could even smell the fire. Then she reached into a basket, picked up a snake, bit it in two, and threw the pieces into the charcoal. She knew she was "not nice." Icléa woke up trying to clear her throat. The vividness of the colors, the music that was playing, and the intense smell convinced Icléa that this dream was indeed a remembrance of a past-life event.

Sometime later she attended a talk given by the late Betty Bethards, a spiritual healer, meditation teacher, psychic, and mystic. After the meditation, Icléa went outside for a breather, and Betty was there. Betty said to her, "It's okay. We meet again. We knew each other in Egypt, but we were *not very nice*." Then Icléa shared the dream with her. If Icléa had needed any confirmation, Betty's comments did just that. Perhaps this dream was giving her a message similar to the one delivered in her spiritual regression you will read about in Chapter 5.

Past-Life Remembrance

Georgina Teyrovsky and I were introduced at a local meeting of the International Association for Near–Death Studies (IANDS) where I was giving a talk on reincarnation. She shared many stories of her past–life remembrances, especially those of when she was a child. The following is one of her more compelling experiences, which I am presenting in her own words.

"The year was 1939, March 15, and I was fifteen. On that spring day I was in the kitchen in our home in Jahodnice, Prague. When my father came home that afternoon, he called in an excited voice to Mother and me, "Do you know what the news is today?" We answered, "No." "The Second World War was declared today!" he said in a voice filled with apprehension.

Some voice inside me called out, "War, again war! How many wars do I have to live through before people will discover that wars are harming everybody! They bring so much pain and suffering for everybody!" I was stunned! My young personality somehow answered, "How can you say that?" I searched my memory and answered, "You were born in 1924, the First World War ended in 1918, and there wasn't any war in Europe or in our country since then!" But I remembered many wars! I felt these thoughts inside me. I remembered the suffering, the anguish, and the humiliations of lost wars! I even remembered being in the middle of one with the emotional pain of a lost cause.

A vision came to me. I was standing in front of some big gates. I was a strong, enthusiastic man about thirty-years-old. I valiantly held some weapon in my hand, but I knew that the attackers were

*much, much stronger than I. I knew they would win, kill us all, and
kill our just and righteous cause. Death did not scare me, but the
destruction of all that we believed in gave me tremendous pain in
my heart. It was a pain which my fifteen-year-old person or personality had not experienced before. Its depth scared me.*

*Then I came out of my vision and wondered what to make of it.
I lacked any explanation. In conclusion, I decided it had showed me
that I could be a person of courage. I said to myself, "When the
opportunity comes, I know I will be courageous!"*

Our soul speaks to us in its own language of the subconscious. It
prods us through means such as these as it guides us through our lives.

Past-Life Regression Information Quest

In my own past-life regression practice I work in concert with my
client's intention to take him or her back to a former time. This is done
not only for spiritual archeology, but also, more importantly, for spiritual therapy. However, great benefit can often be derived by merely
accessing a prior life and learning the "history" of it. The following regression is such a case. As you read details of Dean's former life from
childhood to death, note the recurring patterns.

DEAN

Dean always talked about being a mountain man, and when he saw the
movie *Jeremiah Johnson*, he knew he had lived a similar life. [*Jeremiah
Johnson* tells the story of a trapper in the mid-1800's who lived a solitary
existence in the mountains of the western United States.] Dean's wife
Samantha gave him a gift of a past-life regression with a well-known
regressionist to explore this feeling that was so strong for him.

After the regression, he said this was a "trip of a lifetime." Here are
some of his own words which he recorded immediately after this epi-
sodic experience.

My parents are leaving in a covered wagon with all of their

belongings, except their children! I have an older brother and
sister and a younger sibling. We are being left in the care of a
couple roughly the same age as our parents. There are other
people leaving with my parents, but no children. It seems that
they are going someplace that is too dangerous for children
and will return for us at a later date.

I must be eight or nine. The man caring for us is a bit of a
tyrant. The land is quite rocky, and my brother and I are trying
to remove rocks from the fields with picks and shovels. There
is no respite from the chores to be done; he works us very hard.

My brother has finally had it and runs away. I try to talk
him into taking me with him. However, he feels I am too small
and leaves without me, presumably following the trail of our
parents. Now I have to do his work as well as mine, and it is
not a pleasant situation. Our "surrogate father" is quite mean
to me.

My dilemma is soon resolved, because my "father" trades
me to a group of Native Americans for something in exchange.
The Native American community is very well organized with
straight streets and well-cleared areas between houses. The
houses are cylindrical in shape with round roofs and are con-
structed of adobe or similar earthen material. There is a school
in the community to which I am allowed to go. There are two
male teachers, one Native American and one white. I am initially pleased with the schooling but later become restless,
wanting to leave and find my brother and parents.

My feeling of being alone and unwanted is very heavy. The
sense of not belonging to anyone is extremely powerful. While
I am initially relieved and pleased to be going to this group of
Native Americans, it is quickly apparent that they don't want
me either. I feel absolutely unwanted by anyone. These second
surrogate parents are very unemotional, and the rest of the
Native Americans couldn't care less. I am extremely unhappy.

One day several soldiers in blue uniforms come with the
word that we must evacuate. No one seems to mind, at least

I'm not aware of any resistance, and we are herded out the gate on to a road. The small, weak, or ill are allowed to ride inside huge military freight wagons, while the healthy are told to walk. After a period of time, we arrive at a military fort. I am removed from the evacuee train (possibly because I'm not Native American) and adopted by a military family at the fort. The military family that takes me in is strict.

Ultimately, I become a flag bearer. I am too young to bear arms. I think my age must be around twelve. My best friend is a young soldier, who is in actuality my friend in this life [although they do not look the same]. He is only three or four years older than I, but he is a real soldier and carries a rifle and bayonet.

The entire troop is ordered out of the fort to march somewhere. We finally engage the enemies in a large swampy area. We are overrun by enemy soldiers. I see that it is a bad situation. I drop my flag and pick up a rifle with a bayonet on it and start hand-to-hand fighting with the enemy soldiers. I am stabbed in the abdominal area with a long knife and lose consciousness. The next image I have is looking up into the face of an army doctor and an orderly as I am being bandaged. I am carried outside the hospital tent and laid down on a blanket. It is very muddy around me, and I roll over and see a pile of human bodies, all dead soldiers. I am horrified to see my best friend among them, and my grief is incredible. (I revisited this scene several times during the regression and was in tears on each occasion.)

I am disgusted with the killing, carnage, and the military, in general. I leave the army. I board a large river boat and head upstream, finally arriving at a sizeable town. It is very early in the morning as I walk ashore, and at this point a tremendous earthquake strikes. I run to a small ridge and watch the destruction take place. A man with a foreign accent runs up to me and grabs my arm, pulling me along with him, telling me that we must help. We clear some of the debris away with the help of others, then go to his store and start cleaning it. He offers me a job on the spot, and I accept. He calls me "boy."

He buys furs and trades goods with the trappers. I make friends with three of them — two are white and the other is a Native American. I want to go West with them, but the store-keeper refuses to let me go at first. Finally when I am eighteen or nineteen, with the blessing of the storekeeper, I leave with them in two large canoes.

Then I see myself alone, paddling a canoe loaded with furs through a narrow canyon. The canyon gradually widens out into a valley with tall trees along the river and mountains in the distance. Soon I see a Native American village on my left, and I turn in toward it. It is home. I get stuck on a sand bar, and several men and women (Native Americans) wade out to free me and to drag the canoe to the shore. Once there, the young men unload the bundles of furs. My mate (my current wife, Samantha, although there is no physical resemblance) feeds me and listens to my adventures. There are some children about, but none are ours.

Sometime after that, my mate and I are walking along a high mountain pass. We are leading our horses and stop to admire the view, which is really spectacular. This is a special moment. The peace and feelings of love for one another and for nature is incredible. I see an eagle soaring toward us and remark that to fly like an eagle must be a special thing. My mate removes some eagle feathers from her dress and gives them to me, and be-hold, I become an eagle and am soaring down the canyon. Soon I return to my mate. She is a "shape-changer." The good feel-ings I have are indescribable.

Later, while walking side-by-side, possibly hunting, my faithful old rifle discharges accidentally and kills my mate. My grief is overwhelming. (I revisited this sequence also, and the grief was again instantaneous.) We are far from the village so I cremate her body. The villagers are incensed and ban me from their lands forever. There is obviously much more to my mate's accidental death than I am aware of. I don't really understand the Native Americans' sudden hostility.

Next, I am beaching a canoe and am attacked by a brave from our village. He runs a spear through me. He cuts off my left ear, then my special pouch, and stabs me again, killing me. Following my death, I arrive as a shapeless entity in an area of light blue coloring, and I become part of the color. It is here that the spirit goes for comfort and healing. It is very soothing and calming.

The regressionist asked if there is anything I would like to leave behind or eliminate from my mind. I suggested that the ill feelings I had toward several people should be left behind — the hatred toward my parents for abandoning me, the "surrogate parents" with whom I was left, the initial group of Native Americans, the army, the enemy soldiers, and, in fact, nearly everyone with whom I had contact. She guided me to concentrate this hatred into one spot in my body, and I selected my head. She and I next "channeled" this element out of my body by using a breathing technique, which was similar to hyperventilating one's self. The process was, then, complete.

Dean also wrote in his notes that when not reliving his past existence during this session, he was drifting around in a "soup" of atomic matter and the sights were unlike anything he had heretofore experienced. The shapes were incredible! Other times he felt as though he were soaring above a layer of clouds. He could climb and dive. Once he even rolled, inverted, and remained so for quite a while. That was what he was doing as the regressionist was asking him to descend into a human body form, and it occurred immediately prior to finding himself in the canyon with the canoe. He actually sensed that he was floating above the stream for quite a while prior to "landing" on a small gravel beach that had a cave containing his canoe.

When I asked Dean about the significance of this regression and if he had gained any benefits from it, he told me that prior to the regression he had an ever-present, foreboding **fear of dying**. That **disappeared**.

He also recognized three **important people in this life** who had **played similar roles in that one**—his wife Samantha, his older brother, and his best friend—and their personality traits were similar to the ones in the pioneer life. As a result, he expects to meet this cast of characters again.

Remembering a Happy Past-Life Regression

Revisiting a happy past–life will set the stage for the deeper work you will be doing during the regressions in the other chapters. This regression contains the elements of creating a safe place and meeting your Higher Self. It will allow you to experience how easy it is to go back in time and remember a past–life.

Happy Past-Life Regression Script

While you are comfortably seated or lying down ... take a moment to breathe deeply and slowly ... and as you exhale, you find that your eyes automatically close ... and you just settle in ... as your body unwinds ... Slowly and gently breathing in and breathing out ... Allow yourself to be in this place of easy relaxation for awhile ... sinking deeper and deeper ... down into that in-between place ... that place of letting go ... no longer awake ... yet not asleep ... a peaceful place ... *pause for several minutes.*

Bring to mind your safe place ... that special space you created just for yourself where you are totally safe and protected ... When you bring it to mind, you find yourself instantly there ... Look around and identify a comfortable spot to sit down ... then sit down and enjoy this place for a moment.

Now it is time to meet your Higher Self ... that part of you that has always been aware of its connection to the Divine ... Just by your asking, your Higher Self will make its presence known, although it is always with you, looking out for your highest benefit ... Ask your Higher Self to join you now in your safe place ... You may see it in a human-body form or as a being of light ... or you may have a sense that it is there with you ... You may even identify its presence by a special scent ... Even if you do not have a direct experience of your Higher Self, it does not matter ... Because you have requested it, it is actively there to assist you as you explore your past-lives as a catalyst for positive change in your current life ... Acknowledge its presence ... If it has appeared in human form, invite it to sit down next to you ... However it has chosen to make itself known to you, take a few minutes to experience your Higher Self fully.

When you are ready to continue, set your intention to visit and re-experience, in some way, one of your past-lives in which you had a very happy and fulfilling life ... one in which you lived your soul's purpose and reached your full potential for that life ... Then ask your Higher Self to guide you back in time ... In response, your Higher Self touches you on your third eye in the middle of your forehead just above the eyebrows ... Instantaneously you and your Higher Self are standing on a path leading underneath a beautiful archway of trees ... This is the path that leads back in time ... The trees are surrounded by colorful flowers, plants, and bushes so that it almost looks like you have stepped into a botanical garden ... Open all your senses to this beauty around you ... As you prepare to start walking down the path, once again bring to mind your intention to re-experience a happy past-life in which you felt loved and that brought you great joy ...

Now, with your Higher Self by your side, take the first step on the path of remembrance ... As you walk, begin counting backwards from 100, either out loud or silently to yourself ... placing one foot in front of another ... Each step taking you further and further back in time ... Walking further and further back with each number ... Feeling more relaxed, more peaceful as you continue to walk this path ... having a sense of anticipation as you come closer and closer to that time ... Continue to walk down the path until you see or experience an opening of some kind in front of you ... Discontinue counting and walk with your Higher Self through the opening into another place and time ...

When you have walked through the opening, orient and ground yourself ... First, notice where you are in relation to your body ... Are you looking out of your eyes or are you looking at yourself from outside? ... Are you above, behind, or to the side of your body? ... If you are not completely in your body, direct your consciousness there, and look out of your eyes ... Feel your feet ... Send a grounding cord from your root chakra at the base of your spine down to the center of Mother Earth and connect there ...

Once you are in your body and grounded ... become aware of what you are wearing, how old you are, what your sex is, and anything else about yourself that is important ... Then take time to look at your surroundings ... Enlist all your senses so that you might fully experience this life ... Notice whether you are inside or out ... Are you alone with your Higher Self or are there other people there with you? ... What is this place like? ... What time of year? ... Are there buildings, and if so, what are they like? Set out with your Higher Self and explore ... Perhaps you even hear someone call your name.

When you are ready, ask your Higher Self to take you to the most significant event for you in this life, whether it be further back or forward time ... to re-experience the event and people that will allow you to recapture the sense of joy, happiness, and fulfillment you felt then ... You will be able to bring that good feeling back with you to this current life ... Take it all in with each of your senses ... Feel, hear, smell, touch, and even taste this life in which you found great joy and satisfaction ... Take in every aspect that will benefit you in your current life ... Spend as much time here as you desire ... Feel it deep within your heart ... Ask to experience all the important events and people of that life that was so fulfilling ... and when you are ready, place your hand on your heart to retain this feeling, and prepare to return ...

With your Higher Self by your side, you easily find the opening in time ... and walk back through it ... back through the archway of trees ... and back into your safe place ... If you choose, take a moment here to dialogue with your Higher Self about the experience ... Thank it for its help, and say goodbye for now ... knowing that you are able to contact and communicate with your Higher Self whenever you desire by setting your intention and asking for that to happen ...

Slowly count from 1 to 5 as you breathe deeply and exhale ... feeling your energies aligned and balanced ... happy and at peace ... remembering everything you experienced ... being able to recall that happy past-life any time you wish just by closing your eyes for a moment and putting your hand on your heart ... When you reach the number 5, slowly open your eyes and smile.

About the Regression Stories

The individual stories reported in the various chapters are descriptions of actual regressions. They are being offered for your benefit by my clients, A.R.E. members, members of the A.R.E. Search for God Study Group to which I belong, friends, family, and volunteers. Some of these people I have known for some time, personally and professionally, while others I met for the first time at their session. I was even fortunate enough to regress several members of the same family, and that gave a unique perspective to their issues. Through their generosity all of these people allowed me to share their experiences in this book. For most of them, their actual first name has been used with their permission, but for some I have used an alias.

I think that you will find great benefit in reading not only the details of their former lives, but how what happened so long ago and under very different circumstances affected them in their current lives. Many are down-to-earth stories of the difficulties that are often faced in our physical existence. Others have expansive themes which will lift your spirits. Regardless of the nature of the regressions, the results of their past-life explorations and healing work were sometimes profound while others were more subtle. Merely knowing the circumstances of a prior life is often sufficient to effect change, as in Dean's case. Other times more work is needed or the person is not ready and must progress more slowly. Regression work provides an amazing opportunity for self-growth, and I invite you to come along on the journey.

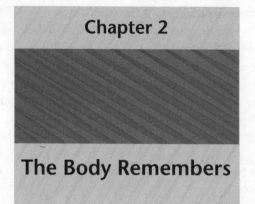

Chapter 2

The Body Remembers

The vessel of our body holds our spirit, and our soul looks out through our eyes. Even though we are spiritual beings, by definition we cannot experience the material world without being in the physical. On Earth we learn what it is to be human and yet be of Spirit. The body acts as a focal point for the immense transitions that will take place during a lifetime. It is the vehicle for our manifestation in this plane of existence, and we must care for it lovingly. If we were not such capable beings, "gods in the making" (699–1) as Cayce told us, this would not be possible.

Our physical form is a product of all we have ever done, thought, and experienced with each lifetime contributing to the totality. Old memories are stored as patterns in the cells of our body. The energetic imprint of life–ending or –threatening injuries and accidents can carry over to future incarnations with their residue showing up as birthmarks or physical ailments. Current illnesses and conditions can be a direct result of something that we did or experienced in a prior life. For example, a person may be obese in this life, and he or she died of starvation in a previous one and made a death vow never to be hungry again. Perhaps the person laughed at overweight people and must now learn how that feels. The current life condition may not always manifest exactly as it occurred when the pattern was initiated. In one Cayce reading a man was told that his stuttering was due to an incarnation in which he had not hesitated in voicing his negative opinions. Another learned that his asthma was the karmic manifestation of previously having pressed the life out of others. Many past-life regressionists believe that *any* challenge encountered in the physical body can be related directly to one or more past-lives.

We are each the direct cause of and are responsible for the physical form we now have. Our bodies are the product of habits begun long ago, often over many lifetimes. The body is a finely-tuned machine that desires love, comfort, nourishment, and care. Spiritual distortions eventually manifest in the physical if they are not corrected, and the body tells us when we are off track. When it is out of alignment, we are meeting self. Pain is a reminder that the physical body has reacted to our thoughts in a way that is in conflict with what the body would want for us. Back pains, for example, can be fear based resulting from our not feeling supported or by trying to hold onto something that does not support us. The nature of the problem points to the very issue we must address. For example, being nearsighted might indicate that our vision of ourselves, others, and the world is too narrow, perhaps too focused on our own ego or personality. An ankle injury could result from fear of moving forward, and cancer is often caused by bottled up anger. As you will read in one of the regressions that follows, intestinal surgery was necessary after the awakening of the memory of someone close to this person trying to eliminate her, mentally, if not physically. Looking at this from the soul's perspective, illnesses and conditions of the body prompt us to take responsibility for our creations and to change our ideals and thoughts to those more in keeping with our higher purpose. By correcting our limiting choices, they can then be expressed in a different form of manifestation. As Cayce said in one of the readings, "All healing, all correcting of the spiritual and of the mental life must come from the Divine within, and the results in the physical being will be in keeping with that which is developed in the spiritual self." (3064-1) Whatever our physical issue, it points to a correction that we must first make on the spiritual level by making our decisions more in concert with God's energy. When we do this, healing can occur on the spiritual, mental, emotional, and often the physical levels.

The Importance of Forgiveness

In order to heal our bodies, we must first understand what is unconsciously motivating us and what message our body is trying to send us. An exploration of our subconscious responses often leads back to one or more past-lives that originated the symptoms we are experiencing. Discovering what happened to our bodies in another time, such as dying in battle from a gunshot wound in the stomach, being tortured for our beliefs, dying from black lung disease after working in a coal mine, or being executed for having killed someone, is the first step in the healing process. Knowledge is potent but not always sufficient to change the imprint that sends energy to our automatic reactions. It is not beneficial to throw up our hands and move on, suffer in silence, forget a wrongdoing, or even entertain the thought that it was our spiritual lesson and therefore somehow okay. We must address the spiritual and mental reasons why this happened and make corrections. It is essential that we learn the lesson this history represents and use it for our own soul growth. Unless we do this, the imprint persists, and the body will continue to send us messages of pain and illness.

Forgiveness plays a key role in this reshaping of our thoughts and in transforming the energy stored in our physical and subtle bodies. Its power is unlimited. When we forgive, we clear the imprint of that negative influence and come once more into alignment with our divine nature. Forgiving a person does not mean excusing, rationalizing, justifying, or condoning his or her hurtful, inappropriate, or unconscionable actions. It does, on the other hand, mean releasing grudges, eliminating negativity, and trying to achieve a positive outcome, even if the other party is no longer alive or this happened thousands of years ago. The willful intention to forgive is what is needed to reap the full rewards for us and to dissolve the destructive energetic tie between us and another person. Without forgiveness we remain stuck in the mold of our negative reactions, responding automatically and unconsciously to what is happening in our lives. We become a prisoner to these patterns.

Our own names should be on that list of those in need of forgiveness. We are often much more critical of ourselves than we are of others who make similar mistakes. It is almost as if our parents (or others who judged us harshly) have taken up residence inside our heads and are always on call to tell us how unworthy or incompetent we are. The Cayce readings tell us that the spiritual error we often make is being harsh with ourselves, not loving ourselves.

Although we may struggle to forgive ourselves and others, we must honor the necessity of forgiving as part of the process of healing. Even when we have done our work, others may not be ready or able to change. Allow them to be who they are. They have chosen this path. Through forgiveness you have freed yourself from the negative bond between you and the other person, and your body will respond.

Over time A.R.E. members have achieved extraordinary results from using the 40-Day Forgiveness Prayer created by J. Everett Irion who served as the treasurer of the A.R.E. for many years. In addition to his administrative role, he wrote several books and gave lectures that were based on information in the readings of Edgar Cayce. The September/ October 1985 *Venture Inward* magazine, published by the A.R.E. for its members, included an article on the 40-Day Prayer written by Irion. Here is an excerpt from that article to provide you with the information you need to put this transformative tool to work for you.

A man in his mid-50s who came to see me during a conference on dream studies told me his doctors had given him only six months to live, and that he knew he was going to hell and there was nothing that could be done about it. He had been having a repetitive dream. This was it:

I am standing alone looking at an empty house. I walk around the house and look in the windows. I back away, wondering why I am here. Hearing a noise behind me, I turn and find a black lamb. It says to me, "You didn't eat the bread." End of dream.

The man interpreted his dream, saying, "I know the white lamb represents Christ and the black lamb has to be Satan, and since I did not eat the bread I am going to die and go to hell."

I asked him what had happened in that house. He replied, "It is the house my wife and I lived in before I divorced her."

He seemed to want to make amends, so I asked if he would consider going to his wife and saying simply, "Thank you." He looked at me in sorrow, slowly shook his head and said, "I can't do that, she is dead."

Did he believe in reincarnation? I asked. He said he did. So I asked if he believed his wife still lived and that only her body had died. Again, he said, "Yes, I do."

So I suggested that he try saying a little prayer to his ex-wife, and then a similar prayer to himself, leaving God out of the prayer because their problem had been at a personal level between them and needed to be handled on that same level—they were jointly responsible for the intimate problems that had divided them. Without knowing what was in the prayer, he agreed. Let's say her name was Mary and his was John. I asked him to say—and to mean—this simple prayer to his former wife.

"Mary, I am praying to you. Thank you, Mary, for doing to me all that you have done. Forgive me, Mary, for doing all that I have done to you."

This idea of thanking her for everything came out of the simple concept that we should be thankful for everything that happens to us. Years ago I had read in *The A.R.E. Journal* an article by a man in the diplomatic service who had adopted the practice of saying, "Thank You, Father," for everything that happened to him, whether it was painful or pleasurable. I have often done this in the belief that whatever happens to us is for the good.

Next, I told the man who wanted to make amends, to say the prayer to himself—to his inner self, his unconscious as follows:

> "John, I am praying to you. Thank you, John, for doing to me all that you have done. Forgive me, John, for doing all that I have done to you."

I asked the man to use this two-pronged prayer once a day for a week. As we talked further, he told me that there were other people he had had problems with. He wondered whether he could use this prayer to reconcile those relationships. I said he could use it for anyone he had problems with. He left shortly thereafter, seemingly in much better spirits.

I heard nothing from him until I received a letter a year later. "I want to thank you for healing me," he wrote, "From the moment I left your office I have had no more pain. The doctors tell me I am completely healed. I have felt better this past year than ever before—it has been the best year of my life."

I had nothing to do with this man being healed, but I'm sure his prayers did. So I thought others might benefit from using that simple prayer. My decision to offer it to them grew out of the problems that people brought to me. As people responded, I somehow connected the prayer to the forty days Jesus spent in the wilderness, the forty years Moses took to reach the Promised Land, and another forty years wandering around, and finally, to the forty days and nights of the flood. I suggested that the prayer be used for forty days in succession.

During the years since, as many have used this prayer, I've learned some do's and don'ts for the results to be helpful. They are:

- After doing the prayer each day, put it out of mind so that the prayer can do its work undisturbed by our wishes and expectations. The best thing is not to expect any results, as the prayer will do its work only if undisturbed by the person doing the praying. Don't tell the person to whom you are praying. Talking about it disturbs the operation of the unconscious at a very deep level.

- Keep track of the forty days on a calendar. If you forget and miss a day, start at the beginning of the forty-day cycle again. Remember Moses made a mistake getting to the Promised Land and had to start all over again.
- In a crisis, the prayer can be used over a shorter period of time. Instead of forty days, use forty hours. Instead of seven days, use seven hours or seven minutes, repeating the prayer accordingly.
- If you need help in diverting attention from the prayer and any possible results, try saying, "Thank you, Father," as often as necessary. This can be said hundreds of times a day if you like.

Some people have to dare themselves to try using this prayer because it says "thank you" to someone we've found difficult or even thought of as an enemy, and it asks forgiveness when the person doing the praying may feel he or she is the one who has been wronged. But many people have reported remarkable results when they dared to try . . . I dare you to try it.[3]

40-DAY PRAYER OF FORGIVENESS
Remember that you are praying to the Higher Selves.

"_____ (person's name), I am praying to you. Thank you,
_____ , for doing to me all that you have done. Forgive me,
_____ , for doing all that I have done to you.

"_____ (your name), I am praying to you. Thank you,
_____ , for doing to me all that you have done. Forgive me,
_____ , for doing all that I have done to you."

---

[3]J. Everett Irion, "The 40-Day Prayer," *Venture Inward* (September/October 1985): 8–9.

Finding the Original Cause

What we hold as our intention and build with the energy of our thoughts will manifest at some point in the physical. This is one of the universal laws often repeated in the Cayce readings. The intensity and frequency of the thought determines how quickly it is attracted into our lives and exhibits itself in our physical conditions. Spirit, mind, and body all work together, and what we build as a result depends upon, first and foremost, the nature of our spiritual intention. That is why we must address all three aspects of our being in order to correct a physical problem. When we identify its cause or its origin, we can change the distorted energetic pattern and activate whatever healing is appropriate at this time—at the soul level, the mental, and perhaps even at a body level. Past–life regressions are an excellent way to accomplish this.

Past-Life Regression to Address the Physical

Weight issues often represent a multiplicity of causes, usually related in some way. Addressing them can sometimes be done in one session but frequently require several, each one stripping away another level of obstruction as the person is ready to release it. Because weight is currently such a major problem in our society, the following regression script is intended to address excess weight. If you would like to use it for other physical conditions or illnesses, simply replace the word "weight" with the appropriate words. It is important to know that you will be viewing this prior life from the vantage point of the soul so that you do not have to feel any of the physical sensations or emotions attached to this experience. This regression allows you to feel the loving arms of Spirit around you as it protects you during your search for and release of the originating cause of your weight concern.

Releasing Weight/Physical Issues Script

Inhale ...and exhale ...Again inhale and close your eyes as you exhale ...Centering your attention in your body ...Feeling your body ...all parts of it, from your head to your toes ...Shrugging your shoulders ...and relaxing as you drop them ...Focusing now on your third eye, above the bridge of the nose ...between the eyebrows ...Relaxing more and more ...Breathing in slowly—1,2,3,4,5—until your lungs are full ...holding for the count of five—1,2,3,4,5 ...and breathing out—1,2,3,4,5.

Surround yourself with the energy of love and light ...Feel yourself being cradled in this energetic security blanket ...feeling so calm, so peaceful, so at ease ...totally safe and protected ...Setting your intention to revisit the past-life that was the original cause of your current weight issue or other physical difficulties ...Re-experiencing it in a way that you are able to observe or know the details at a soul level without feeling the emotions and without your physical body having any degree of discomfort.

Feel or sense the arms of Spirit holding you in this blanket of love and light ...Now imagine or experience yourself being gently rocked by these loving arms ...Hear the voice of Spirit singing a lullaby to you ...As you are being rocked back and forth ...you feel or experience yourself becoming younger and younger ...feeling more and more like the younger you ...Numbers begin to appear in your mind's eye and you go deeper and deeper into relaxation with each number ...1 ...2 ...3 ...4 ...5 ...6 ...7 ...8 ...9 ...10 ...11 ...12 ...13 ...14 ...15 ...resting peacefully ...Now remembering something from your early childhood ...a pleasant memory ...one that you had forgotten ...perhaps something that only you knew about, a secret memory of something that made you happy ...If none comes to mind, create your own happy memory ...and this memory makes you smile.

The gentle, soothing rocking allows you to drift back past this time ...even further back ...back ...back to the time when you were just a baby ...too young even to talk ...a time when your connection to Spirit was very strong ...and you knew that your true essence was that of a spiritual being ...Go back to that time now ...and feel the connection you had with Spirit when you were a baby ...Open up your senses ...smell, touch, taste, hearing, seeing ...Inhale all the aspects of Spirit through your senses ...Let yourself be filled with Spirit from your head to your toes and throughout your aura ...You feel the soft whisper of

Spirit's breath upon your cheeks ... You are tranquil ... and totally at peace.

As you luxuriate in the rocking ... you experience yourself being lifted into the Light with Spirit's arms safely around you ... and you find yourself going up ... up ... up ... as you go deeper and deeper into relaxation.

On the count of 3 you will be there ... 1 ... 2 ... 3 ... In the Light now ... Again feel that total connection with Spirit ... knowing the nature of your true self ... and all that you are ... From here you are able to look down into the physical realm and see all your lifetimes stretching out as far back as you can see and also in front of you ... not in a linear fashion ... but somehow all interacting with each other at the same time ... understanding that changing one of them changes them all ... just as a moving, shimmering hologram adjusts all it aspects as changes are made to it.

Knowing now, at a soul level, that by releasing the negative energy of the original cause of your weight issue or physical difficulties ... this challenge that originated in one of these lives you see below ... you change them all ... and you transform the present as well ... empowering you so that you are easily able to attain and maintain your ideal weight and size or heal the cause of your physical problem.

Before you visit this past-life ... you activate all the benefits of your happy life by touching your hand to your heart ... Re-experience that feeling in all the cells of your body ... filling your body and mind with the sense of well-being, love, and joy ... providing you with the spiritual armor that will now replace physical armor of any kind that you have surrounded yourself with.

Now, as you are preparing to venture to the past-life that holds the key to understanding the physical issues you are having in your current life ... invoke the assistance of your Higher Self ... and your Higher Self joins you ... You know that you can ask for its help and guidance any time you desire or have a need ...

It is time ... From this vantage point you will be able to acquire an understanding at a soul level without reliving the physical and emotional circumstances that surround that life ... easily able to make the changes that will transform the pattern created then to a more positive one which will filter through all your lives from the past to the current and into the future ... Again, set your intention to explore the life that was the original cause of your weight challenge or physical condition in this one.

Look down from the Light at all the lives of your past, present, and future ...

Viewing all these lives from the protection of the Light of Spirit, one life lights up...The image expands...becoming bigger and brighter until you are able to clearly become aware of all of its details...Focus first on a neutral or positive experience so you are informed of who you were and the important circumstances of that life...Remember, your Higher Self is here to support you...When you are ready, you are shown the nature of the original cause of your weight or physical issues...This is revealed in a way that provides you with the information necessary to take whatever spiritual actions are needed to correct it...Allow those details to be brought to your consciousness...When that is complete, ask your Higher Self to help you know what you need to do...and then, with your Higher Self assisting you, do whatever needs to be done now...When that is complete, commit to changing anything necessary in your current life to release this pattern, whether it is your actions, thoughts, or speech...promising yourself to do whatever is required to free yourself of any physical manifestation that has not benefited you...replacing it now with spiritual armor that works only for your highest benefit. When your work is done...the image of this life begins to shrink and takes its place in the stream of lives...past, present, and future...Looking down at these lives, notice how they have all changed somehow...appearing brighter and more inviting...You feel a sense of peace knowing that you have done what you came here to do.

Before leaving the Light, ask that these changes be made easily and gently and that your physical body and your aura be filled with golden-white healing light...that the circulation of the body be so equalized as to remove pressure from all parts of the body and that the oneness of Spirit flows in.

It is time to return...Thank your Higher Self and bid goodbye for now...and you once again feel the arms of Spirit cradling you...soothingly returning you to current time...Your energies aligned and balanced...and you are protected by your spiritual armor...as you slowly open your eyes.

Regressions Addressing Physical Past-Life Issues

The information received in a past–life regression is not always monumental but even so can still be of benefit. An example of this was provided during one of my own regressions led by another hypnotherapist at the A.R.E. Health Spa in Virginia Beach, Virginia. As she was directing me to move from one past–life to another, I became aware of the need to retrieve a piece of information from the life I was leaving and told the hypnotherapist to delay moving to another life. I returned to a time living on a Polynesian island as a male, who was very much in tune with all aspects of nature. He informed me that I should take papaya enzymes to assist in the digestive process—something I would never have thought to do. Although this seems like a small bit of knowledge, these digestive enzymes continue to be of benefit to me today. In the physical regressions that are reported here, what the participants learned had far greater significance in their lives.

MARILYN'S PAIN IN THE SIDE

In the past several years Marilyn has had some very serious health issues which resulted in four major surgeries. These four, however, seemed minor after she was forced to undergo the removal of part of her colon, her appendix, a mass the size of a softball, a partial hysterectomy, and a colostomy (an incision made in the colon to create an artificial opening that is attached to the surface of the abdomen, providing a new path for waste products to leave the body and empty into an attached bag), all in one operation. According to Marilyn, the connection between the colon and the outside of the abdomen could not or was not made, as is normally done. This necessitated the gluing of the bag to the open hole in her side. A reversal of the colostomy was planned to take place a short time later after she had healed. This was not to be, at least in the time frame she had envisioned, because of numerous infections and an episode in which she almost died after eating corn. It took seven months before the surgeon was finally able to reverse the colostomy. When we did the regression, the reversal had recently taken place and Marilyn was on the mend, but she did want to understand the cause of these serious illnesses and do what was necessary to heal it.

Marilyn has done much hypnosis work over the years to help her change behavioral habits so she immediately slipped into a deep trance. As we began the process, an early child-hood memory came to mind of her grandfather putting oranges in his pocket for his grandchildren to take. This made her smile, and the oranges were to have some relevance in her past-life. Then, out of nowhere, a loud noise, whose source neither of us could identify, jerked Marilyn awake. It was not the noise that caused her to return to consciousness, but the past-life which she began re-experiencing as soon as she closed her eyes. It made her feel "weird." She told me she was a girl of about ten who had just been thrown into the water from a boat filled with many people.

When we continued, I took her back to a time earlier in that life, prior to this disturbing scene. It was 1791 in Argentina. She lived in a large house with her parents. There was an or-ange tree beside the house, and she had a mare that she rode. A servant was cleaning. Her father was making wine, and her mother was hanging laundry. They both looked familiar to her, but she was not able to identify who they are in her current life. This young girl believed that the house was hers, but it soon became apparent to me that her parents were also servants. Then, once again, she was startled by an internal noise that caused her to become dizzy and shot her back again to instant consciousness. [I want to note here that several unusual things happened during this regression. This is not meant to scare you; it merely indicates the depth of trance Marilyn had achieved. She did not even hear the dogs barking and the noise of the neighbor's lawnmower as he cut the grass while we worked.]

As Marilyn carefully returned to that life experience, she found herself again on the small boat which was filled with people whom she did not know. Her parents sent her unac-companied on this long trip, but she did not understand why and questioned whether or not she had been bad for them to send her away. Some of the people sat her on the edge of the boat and wanted her to swim by herself to the shore. They pushed her back and forth to the edge of the boat, telling her to swim, but she was afraid of the water. This terrified little girl could not see the shore and kept telling them she wanted to be with her mother and father. She thought they were being mean to her and believed she must have been bad. Eventually they pushed her into the water, and the boat moved away. Although she tried to stay on top of the water, her fear kept taking her deeper and deeper until she lost consciousness.

When she came to, she was on a sandy beach. A young man with pretty blue eyes was holding out his hands saying that it was so good to see her again, but she did not remember ever having seen him before. This man, Joseph, had rescued her from the water. Then his wife, Alice, joined them. He told the girl that he had not seen her since she was a baby, and they hugged. It felt nice, but she missed her mom and dad.

This is when the healing process began as we followed the feeling in her heart when she thought of her parents and let the truth reveal itself. Joseph and Alice were, in fact, her real parents. They had been poor and had either sent her away to live with the other couple in the big house or she had been taken from them. Her real parents were no longer poor, and she was sent back to them. As she walked hand and hand across the sand with her parents, she noticed the water on one side and orange trees (again) on the other. Joseph kept saying, "You are home now."

The next significant event, and the key one in regard to her physical condition, began in school when she was about fifteen. A boy sat next to her who had eyes like Joseph's. His name was Frederick. He kept toying with her, playing with her even though the teacher told them to be quiet. Then he asked if he could copy her work, and she refused. Frederick started poking her in the side and it hurt her. She kept telling him to stop and so did the teacher until he finally did. Later the students were outside playing and holding hands. Frederick was next to her and kept poking her, seemingly playing with her.

He poked her so hard that it hurt. When her mother came to get her, Marilyn discovered that Frederick was her older brother.

When they went home, there was a small birthday cake on the table with her name on it. The name was Sandra. As the family and other invited people sat at the table singing happy birthday, Frederick once again began poking her and would not stop. This was enough information to begin the transformative work. We investigated the place in her side where he hurt her with his poking. Marilyn saw this spot as black and blue as if she had a real bruise on her side. We replayed the scene with her asking him questions. Frederick informed her that he didn't want her there. He had lived alone with their parents while she was gone, and it was clear that he was jealous because she was getting so much attention. In essence, he was trying to **eliminate her** with his poking. After she forgave him, the birthday scene changed as he moved away and stopped poking her. We did additional energy work on the side that had been poked with help from the Spiritual Forces and released some energy of the anger she was holding. When we were done, her side felt better.

Marilyn still needed to understand why the people she thought were her parents really weren't. A spiritual teacher from the Light was enlisted to provide her with information about how and why this happened. She learned that her parents had done what they thought was best for her, and perhaps they had little choice and were somehow forced to do this by the owners of the house. Knowing this, she was able to forgive them also.

As is generally the case, important people in that Argentinean life also played significant and even metaphorical roles in her life as Marilyn. Alice, her mother then, lived several doors down from Marilyn and was her best friend—also named Alice—for years. The father, Joseph, was her late ex-husband who activated this imprint when he hit her in that very spot with a cast-iron frying pan. Frederick was again literally by her side when he lived right next door to her during the time of the awakening of the energetic wound, the wound which would eventually manifest in the physical. Interestingly, his name is Mark, as if he were marking the spot, the issue, for Marilyn to heal in this lifetime. The woman whom she thought was her mother then is Mark's wife. Her foster father reincarnated as her father this time around. This seems a little complicated, but it is a good example of how a small group of souls work together lifetime after lifetime in different roles to transform their negative patterns so that they might learn from each other and grow spiritually.

There were other correlations between that life and this one—the oranges and even the mare she was so fond of. Perhaps one of those in that lifetime which seemed familiar to her was her grandfather who gave her oranges as a treat. Marilyn was also amused by the fact that while she was growing up, her nickname was Mare!

Marilyn continues to heal and the process is now accelerating. This part of the healing was completed, but after we were done, we both sensed she still had more forgiveness work to do with her late ex-husband. She has decided to use the 40-Day Forgiveness Prayer. The hole in her side is now completely healed after fourteen months. Perhaps when she completes the 40-Day Prayer, the pain in her hip, on the side where she was poked and hit, will stop also.

STACEY—FOOD CANNOT MAKE YOU FEEL BETTER

This was Stacey's second regression. The first is reported later in the book in Chapter 6 on relationships. In this session she chose to discover the source of her weight issue so that she might change an unhealthy pattern that causes her to be heavier than she desires.

As we began, Stacey quickly found herself back in ancient Italy as a female in her twenties. Some of her first words were,

"I am huge, and my family calls me disgusting and gross. They call me horrible names." Her family shut her in a room by herself and came only to bring her food that was not intended to nourish her but to be a punishment that was an outlet for their anger. Somehow making her big made them feel better.

While they used food as a means of torture, this girl used it to make herself feel better. For some reason they thought she could take abuse. (In this part in the regression I had to ask her subconscious to translate her words as she was thinking them in Italian, a language she does not currently know.) This young woman was the youngest of many children, and her parents did not want her. They did not have much income and blamed her for their money problems; all of them, even her brothers and sisters, blamed her. The oldest sister was "the worst." Stacey recognized this sister as her maternal grandmother, the one for whom Stacey had been her guardian in the last part of her life. You can see here that in current times these two were playing out a reversal of roles in a way that allowed for a higher learning.

Imprisoned in this room, she felt sad and alone. We used the technique of looking at this situation from above, and she was easily able to understand that it was not her fault that she was born. By learning this, Stacey recognized on a deeper level that food cannot make you feel better. With probing, she acknowledged that she was holding anger in her stomach, just below the heart area and all the way down to the intestines. The color of this energy was black. (Black or gray energy often indicates a dark energy of some kind and is sometimes not our own. Also energetic blockage of the intestines could easily cause an accumulation of weight in the physical body.) We identified it as belonging to her older sister's/grandmother's energy and did a clearing to remove it. Stacey also recognized that she was holding her own anger, red in color in her heart. (Red energy held in the body or aura frequently represents anger.) Her energy was sent into the Light for purification so that she will be able to reclaim it in current time.

She was, then, able to understand at a soul level that her family needed this outlet to make them feel better, although she did not condone the way in which they chose to do it. Stacey completed the work by doing the necessary forgiveness—forgiving the members of her family and herself.

As a result of the regression, Stacey said that she no longer needs the weight for protection and plans to make appropriate changes in the amount and type of food that she eats.

JACQUELYN'S GENERATIONAL HEALTH PATTERN

Jacquelyn is an ordained minister and lineage holder of the First Church of the Angels established by Dorie and Andre D'Angelo. Since the founders have passed, she has been continuing their Angel work. She is a certified yoga teacher, Breath Facilitator, Reiki Master, Japanese flower arranger/exhibitor, and a sacred dancer. Jacquelyn, an A.R.E. member, has led what were formerly called Venture Inward Angel Healing groups for years.

During the past several years Jacquelyn has had serious health issues which began with gallbladder problems that were corrected by surgery and has suffered several other illnesses since. Just before she came to see me, she twisted her ankle. These health issues, combined with a generational pattern of getting sick and staying sick, were her motivation for this past-life regression.

As further background information, Jacquelyn is part of a group of volunteers who have learned traditional Tibetan Tara dances so that this culture might be preserved. (The Dance of the 21 Praises of Tara is based on Tibetan texts and has been blessed by His Holiness the Dalai Lama.) The dance helps to empower all beings and especially brings a sense of acceptance and love of being in a female form. It is believed that all who witness the dances are blessed by the experience. In 2001 she was part of a group of seventy-six women from twenty-three countries who danced in India and Nepal. While performing this dance in public for the Tibetan and other communities there, these performers which included Tibetan nuns gained acceptance and approval to once again dance the prayers. These dances were viewed not only by those in the communities and pilgrims but also by important Tibetan spiritual teachers such as the Karmapa, the head of one of the four major Tibetan Buddhist lineages. As you read about her regression, dancing prayers in public, especially as a woman, has great significance in relation to her health challenges.

We began by focusing on the ankle and some of her other health problems. Jacquelyn quickly recognized that the gallbladder had a different cause from this group and instead was part of the generational pattern. Therefore, we chose to address the gallbladder only after identifying the cause of the ankle injury. Having done this type of work before, Jacquelyn was easily able to access more than one lifetime at a time. In regressing to the creation of the ankle injury imprint, she remembered being a temple dancer and also recalled having been a dancer in many other lives. However, the life related to her hurting her ankle was one in France in the 1400's. By concentrating on that one she immediately began reliving that life and the experience of being tortured. Both of her ankles were broken by a fanatical church group because she was dancing prayers and was a free spirit. They broke her bones as punishment for dancing. It was not acceptable to them, even though no one was required to watch.

Looking at this life from a higher perspective, Jacquelyn learned that to heal the pattern of wounding her ankles she needed first to detach from judgment and then to create the wisdom that it is okay to dance the prayers in public. It was not necessary for her to forgive any of those who tortured her as she had never blamed them. Instead, she had turned on herself thinking that she had done something wrong. Therefore, she needed to forgive herself, which she did. "It is okay to make mistakes," she said. Then she flashed on a later life in colonial times when she was training as an understudy in classical dance. Something happened to the main star prior to a performance, and she filled in. While dancing she reached an ecstatic state—becoming one with the Divine. Her dancing has always provided the opportunity to merge with the Divine and send the energy out. That is how she embodies God or the Divine Light.

In order to heal the pattern of hurting her ankles, she must become more fully embodied in the physical. The difficulties Jacquelyn has been experiencing originated when she entered into a body and disconnected from the God source. Something happened to her when she came into the Earth in this lifetime that caused her to enter into her body only down to just above the knees. In order for that to heal, her spirit must fully merge into the physical and not be afraid of being hurt. It is also important for her to become more aware of her movements. She understood that not being fully in the body is causing her to get hurt, and she recognized this pattern as a distortion and released it. That finally allowed her spirit to enter completely. She said it felt good to connect her feet with the spirit of Mother Earth. Instantly she became aware of another energetic distortion that caused her to create illness so that she might rest. As soon as the recognition of the impulse came to her consciousness, she committed to finding a way to do so without becoming sick or hurting herself. Next, she agreed that it is okay to take care of herself and understood that being healthy will assist her in caring for others. The idea that she created illness to rest was a big surprise to her. She never imagined that she held an unconscious motivating factor for getting hurt or being ill.

Jacquelyn next recalled having lived when Christ did and training in the Essene community. Christ became a powerful teacher for her. This session helped to reestablish her connection with Christ, and she saw Christ wrapping her ankles on the spiritual level. He said to her, "You can heal yourself." Jacquelyn said, "We hear that all the time." However, she had not yet fully embraced it, and experiencing this vision of Christ was an important message for her not to doubt her abilities to heal herself. **We all have the power to reverse the process of injuries and pain** and she embraced that knowledge.

I, then, guided her to change the focus, and we moved to the gallbladder. First, she saw a vision of her mother and recognized the victim consciousness her mother had portrayed during her life. The pattern was created by Jacquelyn's great-grand-mother, even though her great-grandmother did not have physical difficulties while she was alive. Looking at this from the astral plane, Jacquelyn was able to see the maternal lineage, which was Hungarian gypsy. The women were disempowered and not able to speak about how they were treated or about such things as arranged marriages. They were not courageous enough to stand up for themselves. The pattern went very deep. Her great-grandmother's marriage had been arranged, and her feelings about this created a female lineage thought form of victim consciousness. This was addressed as the regression proceeded.

The past-life in which the gallbladder illness originated was in China during the Tang Dynasty. Jacquelyn's first view of that life showed a man wearing robes inside a room where he was obsessively writing and studying. He was a high-level healer who was experiencing excruciating pains resulting from guilt. As a healer he had failed to cure a boy in the royal family, and the boy died. Nothing worked, and he felt terrible. His punishment was banishment, but the family still depended on him for his skills and knowledge. The rest of that life was spent in banishment, but that did not bother him. His whole focus was on trying to find a way to heal the physical condition that killed the boy. The emotion of guilt was held in the gallbladder, and that is what he died from. We sent the guilt into the Light, and Jacquelyn forgave herself for not being able to heal the boy nor find a cure. While doing this, she learned that her body thinks it has to suffer, so she spoke to it and told it that it does not have to suffer that any longer.

Before she incarnated in this life, she picked this very issue of guilt to resolve by using her creativity and energy to help others and at the same time to transform her negative beliefs that caused her to reject the idea of embodying in a female form. For her, recreating a physical body in harmony with her etheric blueprint and God's plan for this incarnation is vital. Transforming her negative patterning from having an ill body to one of perfect health is the vibrational pattern that she is working on. That is why she is facing it again and why she picked the family she did. The thought form was a pattern originally created by her and members of her family at a time when she was part of a spiritual group, and her mother in this life was her husband then. Together they have had a lot of lessons to work on related to their being on opposite ends of the spiritual spectrum. Jacquelyn believed that in their former lives together her mother had acted the role of hampering her expression of being spiritual. In this incarnation she feels there has been a total healing and resolution of this relationship, and although her mother has passed, there now exists a deep love and acceptance of each other.

While on the astral plane, Archangel Michael presented her with a shield and sword to cut through any blocks and to protect her from creating new ones. These spiritual tools were enlisted to reverse the thought form, which was then healed from the time of its origin all the way forward through the generations until it was finally destroyed. Now Jacquelyn can spiral the energy out whenever she thinks of the pattern or feels the need to get rest. She is now free to express her needs and let others know when it is time to care for herself. Creating illness is no longer necessary in her life.

Jacquelyn's next physical concern was her back, and when guided, she immediately found herself as a man in jail. He was

handcuffed because he was a rabble-rouser and part of a freedom movement in France in the 1800's. When he was arrested,
he was abandoned by his friends and girlfriend. He felt betrayed by them, and this was a repeat of the victim pattern
which was being held by Jacquelyn in her back. The victim
consciousness in him thought he needed to be assisted by other
humans because he did not believe in the Divine. The next step
to the process was for Jacquelyn to forgive them. He had loved
his compatriots but held it against them because they had de-
serted him when he was jailed. Now she sees that he was sustained by Spirit and that she is always sustained by Spirit. She
now realizes that her back can support her because she knows
that it is and will always be supported by Spirit. [This is a good
example of the body sending us a message that points to the
problem because the back supports our physical being.] Angels put angel wings on her to provide her with a symbol of her
connection with the Divine.

As she thought about her body and health issues, Jacquelyn
dissolved the thread that tied to mass consciousness about being ill and about being female. She had always experienced
difficulty accepting the concept of being female. Embodying in
a female form felt disempowering because she had been a male
in many previous lives. The originating cause of this thought
was a life in Greece. As a girl, her birth was a big disappointment to her family. The Romans came as conquerors when she
was a young girl and placed her in a house of prostitution. She
was made a slave but not a prostitute because of her age, although she later became the mistress of a married senator. The
lesson of that lifetime was to learn to love, but in spite of her
having learned to love her lover unconditionally, she did not
learn to love herself. The work that needed to be done was to
acknowledge the power of the female and also the fact that we
all need both energies for balance. She then embraced the female energies, the physical form of the female, and the power
of the female. In the future she will be able to combine male

energy which is action oriented with female creativity so that she can be of even greater service. She liked that. The work was complete, and as she was coming back to consciousness, she saw the Dalai Lama's presence. This was comforting because Jacquelyn feels a strong connection with him as he is one of her spiritual teachers. When she met His Holiness the Dalai Lama, he hit her very hard on the head, and although it was not painful, it opened her up and changed her life as she began studying the spiritual teachings of the Tibetans.

After the session, Jacquelyn shared many benefits she received by doing this regression work. They included not only removal of stuck energies she had created in prior lives but also reconnection with the angels and Tibetan spirituality, a realization of the reasons for being incarnated now, and a reminder of her strong connection with the God Force and Christ. She also gained an understanding of the family generational dynamics and how radiant health can be hers, and everyone's, at any time. This past-life work brought Jacquelyn back to her true self and its wisdom. Since these sessions, she has been able to access more fully the Universal life force in her own life and for the benefit of others. She is inspired to dance the Sacred, honoring her essence in the female body. Those, who watch her, will undoubtedly be moved by her devotion to and love of Spirit that will envelope them as she dances, and through that experience, they will also feel a connection to the God source. She is happily more inspired as she moves forward to dance the Sacred honoring her essence in the female body and sharing dance as a form of creativity with others. Jacquelyn discovered dancing not only helped her spirit more fully embody but also expanded her divine mission on Earth.

Another benefit was discovering the pattern that supported her belief that the only way to get rest was to be sick. This was a revelation since she had been taught that being ill was a way to seek attention. However, in her case, being ill gave the permission she needed to rest. In discussing this later with a friend, the friend commented that Jacquelyn had once commented that she got rest only when she was sick. According to Jacquelyn, this regression has brought her more clarity and awareness.

Later, she sent me an e-mail saying that from this session she had gained insight into how the cause of an illness, such as her gallbladder problem, could be overlaid with not only guilt from a past incarnation of guilt but also her maternal lineage pattern of repression of not speaking out. She told me of a dream of seeing both her mother and grandmother. Her grandmother was standing behind her mother and looked healthy but acted like a protector for both of them. Her mother was seated and seemed weak, so Jacquelyn embraced her and lifted her up. This may have been symbolic of the healing of this pattern through all three generations. Because Jacquelyn had previously done so much spiritual work to benefit herself and others, it contributed to her being able to accomplish so much in just one regression. Her other regressions, which you will read in other chapters, were just as powerful.

DAWN—GLASS THROUGH THE BACK

One year before this regression Dawn had an emergency hysterectomy and six months after that underwent another emergency surgery. This time it was for a perforated bowel which necessitated a temporary colostomy bag. It took three months for the infection to clear and for sufficient healing to take place to permit the colostomy reversal to be performed. When we had the session, she was still recovering from this last procedure. She has had two previous injuries that significantly impacted her life. The first was a back injury ten years ago, and more recently she experienced carpel tunnel syndrome in her hands and wrists which continues to bother her.

Dawn is a relatively young and active woman and these illnesses keep her from leading the life she desires. This has frustrated her. The frustration is compounded because she tends to overdo what she is capable of doing while recovering and does not allow her body to heal properly. She set her intention for the regression to get to the root cause of these illnesses and to make the necessary corrections.

As we began the regression, Dawn saw a small film strip spinning around her. She didn't know how it got there, but it was new. In consulting with her Higher Self she learned that it was an index, not of all of her lives, but of various events from those lives. However, when she looked for the event that caused her current physical difficulties, it was not on the index. As it was just a reference and not going to be of benefit in this particular quest, she put it back on a shelf in the library of the Akashic Records. This may very well have been a blockage of some type, even though Dawn was not able to identify it as such at the time.

What followed was very sketchy, but as you read what occurred, you will understand why. Returning to that prior life, Dawn entered into the body of a very young girl, wandering alone in a garden that seemed very green to her. Unexpectedly, she felt a sharp pain in her abdomen — but not in the location of either of her surgeries. In order to understand what had happened, it was necessary for her to view it from an observation deck above the scene. During questioning she learned that she was in the house of people whom she and her parents were visiting. It was their garden in which she had been wandering.

From this vantage point as she looked around the house, she noticed big pieces of broken glass and realized that she had been pushed into the window. At first it was unclear who pushed her. By turning around she saw that kids were playing and that they had accidentally pushed her. When they did, the window broke. The children were standing at the window, staring in shock because the glass had gone straight through her. This very young, small girl then wandered out into the garden bleeding and finally sat down as the kids were screaming. Her

parents seemed to be nowhere around. As she sat there, she
began getting warm. Her vision faded until she could not see
anyone any longer. Then the pain went away; it just stopped. It
was apparent that she was no longer in the body, although the
little girl was not aware of it. I took her back to the time just
before she left the body. This was to ascertain if she had made
any pre-death vows or agreements or had any highly charged
thoughts around the event. She hadn't.

She just let the body go, and her spirit went into the Light
where it felt warm and comforting. Dawn handed the glass in
her abdomen to God and the pain went away. The energy of
the glass piece that had been held in her body from that lifetime was released.

It was clear by this point that Dawn had just been a toddler,
probably no older than two, when she was impaled by the shard
of glass and therefore, did not have much emotion or energy
tied up in this death. However, her cellular memory held the
energy of the trauma and of the glass itself and she did need to
forgive the ones who shoved her into the window, which she
did. [Dawn did not recognize any of these children as being in
her life this time.] That was all the forgiveness necessary. The
little girl wondered why the others had pushed her. A dialogue
ensued between the young child and Dawn to help her understand what had happened. Finally, the toddler realized that it
was an accident, and the other children were just playing.
Dawn was able to invite the healed girl back into her life.

After having identified the initial cause of her physical challenges, we asked what Dawn's body needed. The answer was
rest. That is all that is needed now, because she is in the process of healing. She understood and agreed to give her body
the rest it requires. The body needed to know that before it
could relax, which it then did. As we concluded, Dawn was
able to visualize her body being totally healed, and this will aid
the process as she can now allow herself to rest.

In the regressions you have just read, you learned how prior life causes can result in current life ailments. Learning the nature of the originating event was the opening these people needed to make necessary corrections as they re-scripted or changed the dynamic of their past-life scenarios. They can now take these new understandings and ways of responding into their current lives and into the future to reap the full benefit of their work. Forgiveness, as you read, was a key part of their healing process and enabled them to release negative energies and emotions held in their bodies, sometimes through many lifetimes. We have the ability to do the same.

Chapter 3

Mindwalking

We are the designers of our own reality through our thoughts. That reality can either take us to a new level of soul development, or it can entrench us even more deeply in our negative ways of thinking. Edgar Cayce encouraged us to take responsibility for our own creations, mental and physical, when he said that mind is the builder. Now quantum physics is proving that our mind does indeed shape the thing that it perceives and that positive thoughts are one hundred times more powerful than negative ones. Our individual experience of the external world is, indeed, dependent upon how we look at it through our mind. Imagine the power of that knowledge! This means that we have the ability to change our thoughts to transform our obstacles and to reshape the lives we lead.

Many of our thoughts are fear based, and this hinders us in our approach to life. Limitations of family upbringing, school, peers, and our own perceptions construct the filters through which we view and judge all of life's events. We may believe that if only someone will do or say something or if something happens, our lives will suddenly be better, not recognizing that change must come from within. It is possible to consciously alter the direction of our thoughts so that they no longer think us. Once we begin to study our patterns of thinking, we allow the emergence of other ways of interpreting a situation that can make our view of life a happier one. The way to transform our habitually limited thoughts is to first recognize them, go to their original source(s), and then convert them to thoughts that are more beneficial. We can gather clues to aid us in our further discovery of cause through past-life regression by first paying attention to the words and phrases we use daily that are not serving us. Also, noting the event or thought that triggered a negative response, the emotional state it evokes, any senses involved, and any physical reactions experienced are additional pieces of information that are helpful to take into a past-life regression to make it more productive.

Thoughts ARE Things

Our thoughts and mental focus have far greater power and consequences than we typically think. Cayce often mentioned that "thoughts are things." (105-2) Hugh Lynn Cayce, Edgar's son, would pick up a chair at conferences when he spoke about "thoughts are things" and tell the audience, "Your thoughts are as real as this chair." Edgar and Hugh Lynn were telling us something quite profound, perhaps a deeper meaning than we first understand when we read those words. They were talking about what our thoughts create on the energetic level. What the "thing" was they said we created with our thoughts was made crystal clear by a clairvoyant and intuitive who, with intention, concentrated his thought and energy on a spot next to his head. When he felt it was focused enough, he asked that a picture be taken. The photograph, which is included in the book *The Orb Project*, shows a bright violet orb of light with a circular band of white in it next to his head, right where he had focused his energy. This was a clear demonstration of the true meaning of "thoughts are things," and he did it in just a few minutes' time.

This is not a new concept, although it is for many of us. Alexandra David-Neel, French explorer of sorts, spent most of her life (1868-1969) on a religious and philosophical quest. Her travels and studies took her to Tibet, which at that time was a country closed to foreigners. During her time there she observed what she called phantoms or magic forma- tions and which the Tibetans called *tulpas*. Through intense concentra- tion she witnessed thought forms generated taking on the shape of humans, deities, and anything else that was being visualized. With enough energy, the *tulpas* not only materialized but also existed inde- pendently from the originator, not always with good intention.

Thought Forms

Our own thoughts take on life when we think them over and over again. The more we think the same thought, the more energy it accu- mulates, and it begins to coalesce and take actual form, although that form may not be able to be seen by most of us. The energy attaches to us, causing us to respond to people and events in concert with the thought. Our response, especially if established in a prior life, may not benefit us in our current one. These thought forms can follow us through lifetimes and often contain elements of emotions such as an- ger, fear, or sadness. An example of this type of thought might be, "I am unworthy of being loved." Negative thoughts such as this are the ones most frequently addressed through past-life regression therapy. Through this methodology we learn how it was created and what we have to do to disperse it. Then we will no longer respond automatically in ways that are inappropriate or destructive. We do have the right and ability to reshape our thoughts and responses in ways that are pur- poseful and directed for our highest benefit.

Vows and Agreements

Anytime we proclaim a vow, oath, or promise, especially if there is an emotional charge involved such as those made at the moment of death, the proclamation is recorded in our body-mind. These agree- ments affect our lives—past, present, and future—until they are cleared. Simply saying: "I will always . . . " or "I will never . . . " in one life is enough to create an ongoing commitment that we carry with us life after life, even though it may no longer be useful to us. These vows and agreements are very powerful thought forms.

Some examples are as follows:

As we lay dying of starvation we may have vowed, "I will never be hungry again," and in this life we are unable to control our appetite or to lose weight.

We took a vow of poverty as a religious person in a prior life. It may be affecting our ability to allow financial abundance into our life. The thought we may be holding is, "If I commit to my spiritual growth, then I cannot have wealth or possessions."

A former vow of obedience may unconsciously cause us to wait for an authority figure to make our decisions for us.

We took a vow of silence when learning secret teachings or when joining an organization with secret rites, such as the Freemasons. We develop forgetfulness to fulfill this vow.

A woman promised her fiancé to wait and never marry another when he leaves on a sailing adventure or goes to war, and he never returns. She may find herself unavailable in this life for any kind of lasting relationship.

A father made a promise to his children that he would never leave them yet died unexpectedly. As a father again in this life, he may linger on in a coma for years after a near-fatal accident.

Vows, oaths, and promises originating in another time can cause us to react automatically in the moment, not by conscious choice but by this pattern which no longer serves us.

The Brain Builds What We Think

Science helps us understand how our thoughts actually do create changes in the brain. In layman's terms, when we think a thought for the first time a new neural pathway in the brain is formed consisting of a string of neurons (nerve cells that transmit electrical, chemical, and hormonal information) connected together. Although the pathway is weak at first, every time we think or hear this thought it gets stronger as more neurons are added; it gets more and more entrenched in our personality, our emotions, our thoughts, and our reality. It becomes more robust and is activated more quickly each time the thought is repeated. The pathway starts connecting to corollary pathways forming a wider net which affects a greater range of our responses when activated. On the other hand, if we stop using a neural pathway because we no longer think that thought, it gets weak and fades away.

These pathways can become almost hardwired so that the response happens quickly and automatically often without our being aware of what we are doing. Nonetheless, it is possible for us to "shut off the power" to undesirable mental pathways, even those created eons ago, and replace them with new, more positive ones. These, in turn, will become automatic through repetition. So, with desire and determination we can assert control over our brain instead of having it control us.

Mindwalking—The Process

Mindwalking is a very different way to access past-life memories from the regressions presented in this book. This concept began several years ago after I had an out-of-body experience while in the dream state. In that experience, which was quite real, I was invited to mindwalk in someone's brain to change a misperception. I did this by entering into the person's actual brain cavity, identifying the part of the brain that carried the pattern of the erroneous thought, and then physically changing the brain!

This was something I had either done before or somehow knew how to do. The guidance that I received was that mindwalking is very important and that I should continue to work with it so that I could show others how to do it. It has evolved since that time. Now I want to share this remarkable process with you.

Mindwalking Preparation

Select a recurring thought form that limits you in some way. The following suggestions and examples are designed to help you identify that thought as you fill in the blanks:

- Think of something you heard about yourself when you were a child—something negative or unflattering that on some level you accepted as the truth.
  Example: "Eat, you're too skinny," or "Look at you. Look at how fat you are."

- Or something negative that you say to yourself about yourself.
  Example: How could I be so stupid?"

- Bring to mind a recurring negative pattern in your life when reading the following sentences and fill in the blanks:

  - I am/am not _____ (a negative trait).
    Example: "I am not lovable; therefore nobody loves me."

  - My parents/teacher/loved one told me that I am/am not
    _____.
    Example: "You are lazy and will never be successful."

  - I never or I will never
    _____.
    Example: "I will never let anyone get close to me so I won't be hurt again."

  - I will always or I always
    _____.
    Example: "I will always be afraid to say what I really think."

Select one of the above that you want to eliminate in the mindwalking experience. Then, create a new positive thought to replace it with.

_____ .

Note: You can do the mindwalking experience as many times as you would like, working through your list, even adding to it if more comes to mind, until all negative thought forms have been replaced.

Mindwalking Process

After making your selection of a thought, you are ready to embark on a walk through your mind! Here are some important things for you to know before you start.

In this journey you will be working in what Carlos Castaneda, who wrote of the teachings of Don Juan, and Michael Harner, anthropologist, founder and president of the Foundation for Shamanic Studies, called non-ordinary reality (NOR) in which you have the potential to actually transform your ordinary reality on all levels—spiritual, mental, emotional, and physical. In this state you will be able to easily access past-life events. Non-ordinary reality is the state of conscious that shamans enter into when they interact with, see, touch, hear, feel, and change ordinary reality. You can do this also, without having to be trained as a shaman. Setting a positive intention for yourself is the key.

To assist you in reaching this state of non-ordinary reality, it would be beneficial for you to listen to a drumbeat or altered-state music. Shamanic journey drumming of single or multiple drums is best for this purpose and will assist you in entering into the necessary state of consciousness.

The script references Archangel Michael, the Lord of the Way. He will protect you as you do your mindwalking, making sure that you are ready for the changes to come. He will also stand guard to prevent any outside energies from interfering while you are in the brain cavity.

Your third eye will be your energetic point of entry into your mind and into the brain itself. When you have entered into your brain cavity, you will think the thought you have chosen to change while at the same time feeling the emotion of it. This will initiate the process to discover the past-life source of the negative and limiting thought you have selected. Once you have identified the neural pathway carrying the thought, you will actually walk down it. As you walk, you will go back in time until you reach a past-life. This may be one of a series of related lives that built that thought, so you must see if the pathway continues even further back. You want to go to the birth of the thought. By clearing it, you clear all of the linked lives. Therefore, if the path continues on, you will keep walking until you reach the end. That will be the lifetime you are looking for. If the path ends at the first past-life you encounter, you have reached your destination. The original life will give you the information you need about how the thought was generated and what spiritual work is necessary to release it. After you have done your work, the energy is turned off to the pathway and its tributaries. It will shrivel up. With the replacement thought in mind, you will then create a new pathway to carry it. Before you return, you will ask that the energy of the elixir of the Tree of Life flow through you to finish the healing on all levels. The mindwalking is then complete, and you will return to consciousness.

Mindwalking—The Regression

Make sure you are comfortably seated. Begin with alternate nostril breathing as suggested by Cayce:

Alternate-Nostril Breathing

Left nostril is held closed, air is drawn in through right nostril. — Air is exhaled through mouth.

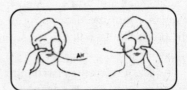

Right nostril is held closed, air is drawn in through left nostril — Left nostril is then closed, air is exhaled through the open right nostril

Close your left nostril, and draw air in through the right nostril. Exhale through the mouth. Do this three times.

Then, close your right nostril; draw air in through the left nostril; close the left nostril; and exhale through the right nostril. Do this three times.

Close your eyes ... Breathe in deeply ... and exhale slowly ... Take a couple of deep breaths ... and relax ... As you continue to inhale and exhale, slowly and deeply, find the spark of Divine Light that is within you ... that spark that is within all of us ... It may be in your heart, solar plexus, second chakra area, or somewhere else ... Wherever it is ... discover it now ... and as you do, you make a conscious connection with God's energy ... and the light of that connection expands to fill your whole body.

Now allow the energy of this light to travel to your third eye in the middle of the forehead just above the eyebrows ... Hold this light there with your higher consciousness ... and set the intention to go to the past-life source of the negative thought you selected, to heal what needs to be healed, and to replace it with a new, positive one ... Continue breathing slowly and easily as each breath takes you even more deeply into a peaceful and profound sense of relaxation ... a sense of settling into your being ... Experience the light gathering energy at the third eye, becoming stronger, more intense, more focused ... until it is so concentrated that it is like a laser beam.

As you are holding this light of your Divine connection, merge your consciousness with it ... Now call to mind your intention to shut off the energy feeding the neural pathway of the negative thought and to create a new one to transmit the positive replacement ... You are ready to begin your walk back through time ... As you focus on this intention, experience the light at your third eye, the one you have merged with, begin moving inward in the direction of the center of your head ... The process has begun ... You keep moving with the light ever inward as you pursue your quest ... Continue traveling deeper and deeper within ... All around you it seems cloudy at first, as if you are making your way through fog ... but your intention draws you further inward as you come ever closer to your destination, to the inner workings of your brain ... Notice the fog starting to dissipate ... and now it clears ... Find yourself at a doorway ... Take time to observe all the details of the door, as it holds information for you ... and when you have finished looking at the door, knock on it ... The door opens ... and you see or experience Archangel Michael, Lord of the Way, standing there in front of the entrance to your brain ... Ask his permission to enter ... He grants it and steps aside, inviting you to walk through the open door ... Walk through it now ... Archangel Michael points to a path for you to follow ... He will stand guard here and wait for your return, but you can enlist his help at any time by calling his name.

Walk in the direction that Archangel Michael has shown you ... as you continue to go deeper within ... Now find yourself in the space that houses your brain ... The light of your Divine connection illuminates everything around you ... and reveals a vast multidimensional grid of neural pathways stretched out like a network of highways going in various directions and crossing over each other on different levels ... Some are small ... pathways for those thoughts that are infrequently accessed ... while others appear to be like major highways ... strengthened over time with the addition of more and more neural connections through the repetition of thoughts throughout your lives ... turned on automatically when they are triggered by events that ... to the mind ... are seemingly similar to those that created them ... Observe the pathways switching on and off in response to signal lights that turn green or red ... You notice that when the light is green, energy flows to that specific pathway, and it grows stronger and more complex ... and that no energy flows to those pathways where the signal is red ... This whole place is alive ... and you recognize that you have actually entered into the workings of your brain.

As you look out in front of you at all those neural pathways carrying your thoughts ... you instinctively know which ones are operating for your highest good ... They are straight, clear, bright, and have a high vibratory rate ... Just as easily, you identify those that do not benefit you ... They are dark and perhaps look like a tangled web, or are bumpy with blind curves ... They may be quite large, yet they have a very low, slow vibration.

You are now ready to initiate the mindwalking process ... to walk back in time on the neural pathway of the negative thought ... back to its creation ... knowing that you are safe and protected as you do ... Call to mind this thought ... the thought that you want to eliminate from your past, present, and future ... and experience how its vibration affects your body ... Hold this thought in your mind and its feeling in your body, and with your Divine Light start scanning all the neural pathways ... searching for a matching vibration ... Look around now and identify that pathway ... Instinctively you will know it by how it feels to you ... And you find it easily ... Walk over to it now ... This is very natural for you ... just like walking down the street ... Notice or experience in some way, that the switch for the **green** light has been stuck in the *on* position, permitting unchecked energy to flow to this pathway, allowing it to become stronger, more powerful, and more automatic ... See just how many neurons are clustered here ... how wide, and strong, and robust this thought is ... See it in all its details as you prepare to mindwalk the length of this neural pathway ... If you have any hesitation about walking down the path, call on Archangel Michael to protect you ... You can also surround yourself with an energetic protective bubble if you choose ... Now start walking the length of the pathway, the pathway through time, thinking this thought ... again observing how your body is affected by its vibration ... and how it impacts your emotional state.

Open all your senses ... Listen ... hear your mind begin to speak to you through your inner ear, like a wise teacher ... guiding you back in time as you continue to walk the pathway, further and further back ... Remembrances from a time past begin to surface in your consciousness ... Allow these to come, taking all the time you need, until you find yourself back in a past life ... Before stopping, look ahead on the pathway ... See if it ends here or if it extends even further back ... If it continues, this is only one life in the pattern, and there are one or more lifetimes even earlier than this one that contributed to the creation of this thought ... You want to go to the very first one ... If there are more further down the path, continue walking until the path ends ... If not, stop here ... When you have reached the last lifetime on the path, this is the originating one ... When you are there, stop, and with the aid of your mind become aware of all the details that are important for you to know, but do it as an impartial observer ... This provides you with the knowledge of the work that needs to be done to release this thought ... whether it be forgiveness, letting go of resentments, or just understanding ... Do that now ... Through your intention it happens very quickly ... This part of your work is complete, and you find yourself back on the neural pathway ... Observe that the **red** light is now *on,* and the neural pathway is starting to shut down completely ... Watch as the vibrations cease ... and the neurons shrivel up smaller and smaller and finally disappear ... and the smaller pathways connected to this one also begin to shrink and disappear ... When this is complete, request that this area be filled with golden-white healing light ... And it is so ... This troublesome or limiting thought path is now a dead-end

...It is no longer a hard-wired response.

You are now ready to create a pathway that vibrates with the energy of the positive thought you have chosen ... Bring that new thought to mind ... Notice how good it makes your body feel ... how you feel emotionally when you think this thought ... This is the mental switch that sends energy to the pathway ... As you think that thought ... and feel the feeling of it ... engage your imagination and all of your senses ... Visualize a green light turning on as neurons, the building blocks of the brain, begin connecting and multiplying, linking together to form chains to create a new powerful, vibrant pathway ... Watch them do that, and see or sense them begin transmitting electrical, chemical, and hormonal information along with this positive thought as it travels from one end of the neuron to the other ... and on to the next neuron in the chain ... Watch as the pathway gets wider ... deeper ... stronger ... more robust.

Breathe deeply into this thought ... Experience positive, balanced energy begin flowing through your body and mind ... as the pathway becomes even stronger ... knowing that now whenever there is a situation that previously would have triggered the negative pattern, this new thought will be your automatic response ... Whenever this new positive thought comes to mind ... you will unconsciously breathe deeply, strengthening this path even more as your inner mind hears and feels the breath ...

Before leaving your brain, invoke the vibration of the Tree of Life elixir to flow down through your chakras ... healing any frayed connections caused by the erroneous thought ... restoring your mind and body and moving up through your physical body to the Higher Self ... and then flowing from the spiritual back down ... speeding up the repair work you have already done ... Feel that moving through your body now ... This will continue automatically without any conscious effort on your part, for as long as it is needed.

It is now time to leave ... Your consciousness travels back now along with the light of the Divine, back to the entrance of your mind where Archangel Michael is waiting for you ... Thank him for his assistance ... Before you leave, look back at the neural highways ... Observe that you no longer see the dark area of lower vibrations that housed the negative thought ... Instead you see the humming, bright highway of your new, positive thought ... Your heart sings ... knowing that you have lifted a limitation that has been with you through lifetimes ... and you can now take the next step in your soul's development.

Move with the light back through the doorway ... and back to your third eye ... as you slowly return to waking consciousness ... Your body and mind make these changes easily and gently ... Your energies are balanced and come into alignment now ... Returning back to your body ... back to the room you are in ... feeling refreshed ... energized ... Open your eyes when you are ready ... Rub your hands together and gently soothe the energetic field around your face and head.

In the days that follow this experience become aware of the shift in your thinking. You can test it by thinking the old thought and seeing how you react; it may very well surprise you.

Mindwalking Regressions

In the mindwalking sessions I have conducted, the results have been very powerful, even more so than with a past-life regression. I feel that the reason is because this work is done in non-ordinary reality, the place where shamans work, as opposed to hypnotic trance. Here results, even physical results, can happen instantaneously. The reports that follow give you a peek into the brain of these participants and impart a sense of what our thoughts have created.

Mindwalking

JULIE AND HER TWO COMPETING THOUGHTS

When Julie arrived at her mindwalking session, she was having difficulty deciding between two thoughts that were pulling at her. "Pick me, pick me," they seemed to be saying. Even though she had been thinking about it for over a week, she was still undecided. I suggested we address both topics even though they were very distinct and unrelated thoughts. She agreed.

The first negative thought was one that she had heard her mother say many times. Even though Julie did not believe it on a conscious level, in her head she could still hear her mother saying, "We are not a lucky family. Lucky things don't happen to us. Good things happen only to other people." Julie chose to replace these words with, "I am a very lucky person and attract abundance in every area of my life."

The second was a little more complicated because it involved her husband and his family, in particular how he treated her in regard to them. Her thought form was, "They [her in-laws] do not value me. I am not part of their consciousness. I feel betrayed, abandoned, disrespected. I feel non-acceptance from them. It is not fair. My husband has double standards for them and for me. It is easy for him." Instead, she decided to create this thought form, "I want (husband's name) to enjoy his family. When I say this or when I think this, I feel whole and our relationship is strengthened and grows deeper."

When Julie approached the doorway at the beginning of the mindwalking process, she suddenly felt as if she were a Zulu warrior, very tall with a spear and shield in her hands mentally trotting in the gait of a warrior to the entrance to her mind. What she saw when she viewed her brain looked like a big map of the Underground Railway System in London. Where the lights were red, the pathways were dried and almost crumbling. Neural pathways with green lights appeared very vibrant to her.

We began with her mother's thought of their family being unlucky. The neural pathway was dark and foreboding—a black void that looked like a tangled web. Julie called it "the witches' path" and was reluctant to start walking on it, so we called for Archangel Michael's help. She sensed a hole in the heart. Although initially she saw symbols on an ancient carving that was pre-Egyptian, she continued walking the path back to the original cause of this thought form. It was created during the time of Jamie the Brave in Scotland. A man who owned the land on which her tribe lived accused her of being possessed by demons and being filled with whatever was causing sickness in the people of the tribe. At first it seemed that this was his thought because he was punishing her and turning the tribe against her. Through further exploration she discovered that he had acquired this thought from his mother, and she, in turn, had learned it from her mother, the being who is Julie's mother in this life. Julie forgave this man, turned off the energy to the thought, and sent it into the Light, asking that the area be filled with golden-white healing light. She replaced that former belief with the new positive thought and sent energy to it.

As you can see, this "We are not a lucky family" thought was handed down from generation to generation and gained energy with each transmission, still affecting the ancestral line hundreds of years later up until current time. Julie's believes that this thought was passed on to her in the womb when her mother had an experience in World War II in London that triggered it.

Then, Julie immediately began mindwalking the pathway of the second thought form relating to her husband and his family and quickly found herself in the Bering Straits. A man, who looked like a Viking, was making some of them, including Julie, leave the safety of the group. There was a lack of abundance and not enough for everyone. His father and all the women over five-years-old were being shunned and sent away. They could not come back until they found food. They were considered the least valuable members of the tribe. "Only the strong survive."

She was nineteen at the time. The man was her brother in that life and husband in this one. She had been holding the thought that she did not have value or worth for eons, and she had not forgiven this being, who was her brother, for not valuing her.

Julie looked at this from a higher spiritual perspective and discovered that her brother did not know any better. He was the leader, and no leader knows everything. He could not allow his weakness to show because it was his job to protect the tribe. As a woman, she had no worth, but he cared about her because she was his sister. His heart died as a result, but he had to show that he was strong. She said, "I understand why. He is only a man. He does not know." Julie, then, forgave him, releasing that thought into the Light and creating the new neural pathway she desired.

Even though these seemed to be two unrelated thoughts when the process began, through the lens of the past-life regression we can see that they are really different aspects of the same issue—self-worth played out as abandonment and being shunned. Because of the lack of self-worth, it was reflected as a sense of a lack of abundance in its many forms.

The next day Julie reported back, "I slept really well, the best in ages. Also I cannot even bring those negative thought forms into my consciousness anymore. When I try to do so, my heart feels like it has a shield around it that cannot be penetrated. This is not a feeling I have previously been aware of!" Somewhat later she sent me an e-mail saying," I wanted to tell you that even now I have trouble holding the old thought pattern; it's as if my mind just won't go there, not that I want it to. I've just been testing it. Also I've slept really well since we did this work. It's been a couple of weeks now, and it hasn't changed."

STEPHANIE—THE KEEPER OF HEART INTELLIGENCE

In this mindwalking process Stephanie chose to eliminate a thought form that was with her from early childhood. It was "I am not smart. I will never be smart, and I will always be less intelligent than others." As Stephanie was growing up, her mother frequently told her she would never be as smart as her brother. Teachers reinforced the belief by also informing her that she was not smart. In spite of this negative reinforcement Stephanie had been successful in her life, even though on an unconscious level she had bought into what others had thought about her brain power.

When she walked into her brain, she traveled on what looked like freeways stacked on top of each other, and there was a huge number of them going everywhere. To initiate the process, Stephanie brought to mind the thought form about her intelligence so that she might identify the neural pathway that carried it. She found it and started walking it into the past to identify when it was originated. Her first stop took her to a life she shared with her husband Paul. He was her father in their life together in England in the 1700's. Stephanie and I had explored this life in a previous regression and done the necessary healing work.

She sensed that the pattern did not originate here so she continued on, still thinking the thought. That life faded away, and she saw a life as a Cherokee healer in which she was not allowed to work as a healer because of the jealously of the chief (her step-father in this life) and his son (her ex-husband). I had also previously regressed her to this life, and this one did not seem to hold the answer either.

Back and back even further she walked, asking where this thought had originated. As that life faded, she walked into a pyramid in Egypt. Her role was as a priestess and the keeper of heart intelligence. She learned here that heart intelligence is not the same as what we consider to be the intellect of a person. Being smart is not limited to being intellectually gifted.

From this experience Stephanie realized that she is, indeed, intelligent but not in a way commonly understood. This was extremely powerful for her. She shut off the energy to the neural pathway that had affected many lives and no longer felt that she was "not smart." Then she created the replacement neural pathway with the new thought, "I am successful, powerful, and highly intelligent in all that I desire," and she believed it. A successful walk through the mind!

STEPHANIE AND THE KEEPERS OF THE TABLET
After her first mindwalking experience Stephanie had planned

to journal what she had learned. Although she had good intentions, something was holding her back. Finally, she was guided to request a second session to understand "heart intelligence" at a deeper level.

We began with the same negative thought used in the first mindwalk, "I am not smart," unsure of what we would discover when she entered the brain. The neural network of all her thoughts once again reminded her of the Los Angeles freeway system. The negative neural pathway was still there, but it was no longer being fed any energy. Instead, it was merely serving as a marker for her until she returned to do this additional work.

This time she flew in a jet instead of walking down the path and went to a life in Rome many years after the original Egyptian one. We asked why this life when the other had been earlier. The answer was quite remarkable. In Egypt she had been a high priestess who carried the heart intelligence. She was part of a circle of women who were highly trained. They were "The Keepers of the Tablet." The tablet was the main structure for keeping the world together through its underlying energy. This heart intelligence energy lifted the stones for the pyramids, and it was very much sought after because of its strength. It defied gravity, and things happened using it that no one could explain.

During her Roman life, most people believed only what they could explain. This was around the time of Christ who brought in the energy of love. The Keepers of the Tablet reincarnated then to bring in the technology of the heart. As this technology could not be explained by the brain, not only were they considered stupid and labeled "not smart enough" but also dangerous. The women, including Stephanie, were imprisoned in a dungeon underneath the Coliseum. The heart intelligence energy allowed them to transport themselves out of situations. However, this time they chose to stay, and the technology was lost.

As for its influence and significance for this life, she learned that a couple of women who were in the original group will come into her life in the near future. They will remake the connection and reestablish the learning so that they might give it to others. (The energy of this actually made Stephanie feel extremely hot.) Her daughter was one of these women and will be the last to join the reunited group because of her skepticism.

When I asked her the question of who were in that life, she named quite a collection of people from that life who are also in her current one. They included her mother, step-father, his nephew and wife, and an ex-husband—and—they were the ones who put her and the other women in the dungeon! The roles they played in that life were of a senator and his wife, a handmaiden of theirs, a warrior, and a Roman soldier.

She was told that more information about this would come to her in the future, so we moved toward completion of the process. The original negative neural pathway was destroyed, but there were many smaller, contributory pathways. These were also "deconstructed." The positive pathway was already operational, but another one needed to be created. That new thought was, "I will let the heart speak its truth and recognize its power." This immediately became an eight-lane pathway.

After returning from her brain, Stephanie told me that the women stood in a circle around a stone and raised it with heart intelligence. This energy was also used for healing at the highest level, and it may again be as some of these women reconnect in this life.

STEPHANIE—LIFTING THE WEIGHT

Stephanie wanted to work with me to address her weight which she knew was there as protective armor because of the things that had happened to her early in her life and the negative relationship patterns that persisted. When we attempted to do this as a past-life weight regression, Stephanie fell asleep so she knew that she had more internal work to do before addressing it. When she was ready, she asked if we could tackle it through mindwalking. I asked her what the thought was that she wanted to replace. Although she came up with some answers, we both knew that they were not the core negative thought. It was very deeply buried within her subconscious. We postponed the session until she had uncovered it. Finally, she was ready. The thought, which rang very true for her, was "I have to be big to be seen and heard." It was time to begin.

As Stephanie proceeded to enter into the brain cavity, she sensed that the path was at the very bottom of her brain. Part of it wanted to stay hidden, and it felt scary for her. Archangel Michael had one arm across his chest and the other was pointing toward it as if to tell her that fear was not to stop her; she was to keep going. This negative pathway was, indeed, way at the bottom. It was deep, wide, and governed many things in her life. When she called the thought form to her mind in preparation for walking the path, she felt it in her heart and throat.

As she began walking the pathway back in time, Stephanie felt much tightness around the chest and pressure in the throat and sinuses. The first thing she saw was a French maid's uniform with a short skirt like those seen in the movies. But the pathway extended further back from that life so she kept on walking to the very end. The life at the end was in a city in China in 16 AD. In that life she was a sixteen-year-old male with a very slight build dressed in fine silk.

War was being waged everywhere. This young man was very peace loving, but because he was so small, what he had to say about peace could not be heard. His father was a warrior and very embarrassed by his son's size and slight build. (That father was Stephanie's mother in this life.) He did not want to have anything to do with his son because his son was so small and called him "the girl" all the time. The young man was very frustrated and angry because he knew he had many important words to say and had even written about how important peace and love were. He said, "They just keep killing each other, and it hurts my heart to see the death and destruction." His father gathered energy from the death and destruction and used it to seize more and more power. "The more power he gets, the more disappointed he is in me even though I have such important things to say," the young man said. Although he was the learned one, he was ignored, which was unfortunate because he had such a wonderful message to give. Nobody would listen.

She recognized some additional connections. The warring brother, the big brother, the one with whom the father was so involved was Stephanie's brother in current time. That helped her understand the special relationship that existed between her mother and brother. Stephanie's son was also in the picture. He was another brother and sought the father's approval so much that he sat in judgment of his brother who was small in size.

Then we moved to the moments just before the soul left the body. The thoughts at that time were, "I'll show them. Somehow, someway I will get my message across, sometime." He thought, "A vow of compassion and peace is a way of life, not anger and war." There was more to the message, and Stephanie knew that it would come later.

This was all the information necessary to gather in order to address the places in her body where Stephanie was holding onto the negative thought. She identified feelings of anger, hurt, and frustration in her heart and stomach.

The negative thought form that "I have to be big to be seen and heard" was what that slight man had wished for so that others could hear his message. He wished that he were big so that they could see him and hear what he had to say, that he would no longer be ignored and scorned. It is easy to see how this thought, especially as its energy was held in the stomach, would lead to a subconscious desire to hold onto weight.

The thought was her own thought and energy, so it was sent for purification before it came back to her. The thought "I'll show them" was also sent. However, it had some positive aspects and they were retained to help power the message of peace and understanding. The pure energy of love, compassion, and peace replaced it. The energy tied to her father/mother that related to this thought was held in the heart by the neural net. Its color was black. It was removed. We, then, moved to the part of this thought form that had been held in the stomach. What remained there after the previous work had been done was some of her brother's anger, and he reclaimed it.

At this point the neural pathway of the negative thought form shriveled up, and its connections to the neural net were severed. A new pathway was created with her replacement thought, "I am seen and I am heard even better now when I am slim and healthy and filled with energy, which I am." It felt good to her as this beautiful, positive thought form replaced the dark vibration of the old one. It was like gold.

This was another very powerful experience, and her relationship with food immediately changed. Her desire for food has diminished, and her intake has decreased. Stephanie knows on all levels that she no longer needs body weight as armor for protection.

RHONDA'S SUDDEN FEEBLENESS

Rhonda just turned sixty. After her birthday she suddenly began to think of herself as old and feeble even though she quite capably does volunteer work that requires strength and agility. The neural pathway that carried the thought "I am old and feeble" was huge, dark, and tangled, and the thought itself was being carried throughout her entire body!

The regression opened with Rhonda being lost in a swamp at the end of a pathway. She was stuck, this time literally. It felt as if she were in a drain or vortex that was sucking the life out of everything. That was just prior to her drowning in the swamp, as we discovered.

Going back prior to that death, she experienced herself as a ten- to twelve-year-old girl in the South in the 1800's wearing a long white dress. It was hot and humid. She was always getting into trouble because she wanted to do what the boys could do. She got lost running in the hills when a storm came up. She was afraid because she could not find her way back home, eventually getting stuck in the swamp and drowning.

As her spirit looked down at the body, she was sorry that she had not obeyed her parents. This girl was always resisting everything, at least in part because there was something physically wrong with her leg. It was shriveled although she could still run. She said, "I hurt it and couldn't fix it. It was my fault that I couldn't fix it." This made her feel broken and angry. The anger was held in her heart, and it was white hot. As Rhonda mentally poured water on the anger, she felt her heart start beating. She next put some needed love into her heart. The young girl forgave herself for the injury, for disobeying her parents, and for drowning.

At this point we asked about the origin of the thought form. As the girl was dying, she thought, "If I am old, it is not my fault. I am no longer responsible for my failing."

Rhonda shut off the energy to the neural pathway carrying this very limiting thought and then created a new one. The replacement pathway now sent the message throughout her body, "I am young, capable, strong, and full of life and energy."

The work was complete. The thought that she is old and feeble now makes Rhonda laugh, and she realizes how full of life she is. In following up with her the next week, she told me that the neural net attached to this thought had been so pervasive throughout her body that she actually experienced her physical body adjusting to the new pathways as the result of the work she had done.

VIRGINIA AND HER TWIN SOUL

In the pre-regression discussion Virginia mentioned that as she was filling out the mindwalking form, she thought to herself that this exercise was "really good in cultivating the gold nugget of what I am working on." Curiously, she told me, "I sentenced myself to this." That sentence has been to live the negative thought form she had now chosen to change — "I will always be less than everybody else."

The replacement thought was — "Who I am is a great and powerful Divine being emanating love and wisdom to all in my path. I always live up to my full potential and self-expression without comparison to others. I lift myself and others with my light."

She began with alternate nostril breathing. Virginia had created a safe place in previous sessions and was already in connection with her Higher Self. When she got to the door that was at the entrance to her brain, she described it as a big, brown wooden door with a brass knob and a little window opening she could look through. The window had a grate on it. That type of door is not made anymore. It was from another time. This description, reminiscent of a prison door from much earlier times, was very much in keeping with her thought of being sentenced.

Virginia easily saw first the network of neural pathways and then the individual pathway carrying her negative thought form. The green light was stuck on, but the pathway was murky. It was big, and she was very hesitant to walk it. She requested Archangel Michael's protection. Then, with his protection, she started mindwalking while thinking and feeling the thought, but she felt as if she were not all the way on the pathway. What almost immediately came up for her was a feeling of being rushed although she offered that she was not being rushed. Also she felt angry about being rushed. As she continued to hold the thought, she felt angry because it was not perfect. It shouldn't be like that. It was necessary for her to request additional spiritual assistance. We used the resistance to help the memory of the lifetime come to the surface. To her it felt as if she were walking slowly and was stuck, that she was immobilized and not able to move forward. Her bare feet were stuck in gooey black tar. She could not move, could not get out of there.

I suggested she go back just prior to the event of being trapped in the tar. When Virginia did that, she experienced calm. However, when she started moving forward, she felt as if she had been captured and something bad was going to happen. I had her lift up to the astral plane and view the pathway from there with her Higher Self. Then, instead of seeing herself, she saw a young man, an Amazon warrior, and he was outside. There may have been a few others with him, and he was trapped somehow by them. [She kept calling him "that person."] Virginia not only felt that person's anger about being trapped, but she was holding it in her heart and chest. When she recognized it, she believed that this anger was his, not hers and described it as a fury, a rage, for getting into this mess that he could not get out of, for being stuck. She agreed that it was possible this man could have been her in another life, but it did not seem that way to her. Even so, Virginia was positive that it was not her energy, but she could still feel it. We removed the anger which was a black energy, and after releasing it, her heart and chest were lighter. She felt happier, no longer holding on to that dark feeling.

Virginia tried to talk to the man, but he did not respond. She asked him if they were the same soul. She did not have a clear sense. The answer was not a straight yes or no; it was almost as if it were both.

We moved this man moved forward in time to when he was slaughtered. In the moments before his spirit left the body, he was not scared. Instead, his final thoughts were about anger and revenge. No wonder the anger Virginia had in her heart was black. Before he exited, he realized that he had listened to them (whoever they were), and they had lied. He thought he was stupid for doing that, and he was angry. He was not scared; he was just angry. "It was so stupid to listen and believe." When his spirit looked down at the body, there was still confusion as to whether or not he was Virginia in a prior life.

As Virginia witnessed his death and learned of his final thoughts, she felt very sad for this person. "It was a waste," she said. When his spirit went into the Light, hers went also. There they connected at a soul level so clarity might be gained about the nature of their relationship. Virginia discovered that he is her twin soul. She was not certain if she had been in that life with him, but she was perhaps somewhere in the background. When he died, Virginia took on his anger and pain and then had a sudden revelation that she has been doing this with men her whole life. Now that she recognized this pattern, she does not want to repeat it anymore.

The two talked at a Higher Self level. She felt a lot of love when she connected with him. It was very emotional, very healing, but very sad in a good way. She had been holding onto a dark part of his energy for a long time. He, on the other hand, was waiting for that part back. It was returned, and he was finally at peace. This freed him, and now he could be happy. Virginia, in turn, felt light as she has given him back his piece of being so he can be whole again. She had been unaware that she was holding it. Nevertheless, this negative energy bound them together. There seemed to be some guilt that she had held on to a piece of him even though she did not want him to feel the anger and pain. She asked his forgiveness, which he had already given, and then she forgave herself. This part of the process was complete.

The next step was turning off the energy to the thought form. At this point, energy that had been held in her body all this time began releasing. Her feet, knees, and ankles began tingling. This thought had had an energetic hold on her feet and legs. That is why she was feeling stuck. Her feet, legs, and ankles were held back, up until now. The words Virginia began using to describe the energy release were coming from her emotions and not from her mind. She thought they were more pure and unlearned.

Then, the pathway shut down and the vibrations ceased. Virginia stood at a doorway of what had formerly led into the dark pathway, but it was gone. The tributary pathways also shriveled and disappeared.

A new pathway was created to carry the positive thought form. Not only did Virginia feel loved when it was activated, but she could feel it going throughout her entire body. She could feel it everywhere. Then her body began moving with energy in a beautiful, fluid, and healing way. It was like a wave from her head to her toes freeing up everything and releasing what was stuck. Her chest felt very open.

After she finished the mindwalk through her brain, Virginia said that she could hardly believe what had happened. She would never have imagined what came during the process. The heavy energy had been very anchored in her mind and body. Her consciousness was now seeing all the different places where she had lived out this negative thought form, this prison sentence.

When she tried to describe her relationship with the warrior, she was still having difficulty. He was part of her but not all of her. He was so sweet and his energy was so stuck in her. In the Light they had merged in purity yet were separate somehow. She had been carrying his pain and darkness, thinking that she was helping him. Instead, not only was it hurting her, it was also hurting him. She was still amazed that she had been playing out this scenario with men all her life—but no longer.

We checked the old thought form to see if it had any juice, but it was no longer true for her. In closing, Virginia said that she was filled with gratitude. She had wanted this for her whole life!

JACQUELYN—HEALING THE PATTERN OF ILLNESS
Jacquelyn took the opportunity to address many limiting negative thought forms from her childhood during the session. Her shopping list consisted mostly of negative self-talk, some origi-

nally created by family and also a few that were leftover from her regression for physical ailments and included:

- *You are a wild little Indian. What's the matter with you?*
- *I'm such a hoople head. I'm accident prone.*
- *I am not successful/perfect.*
- *I will always be short of my goals.*
- *I will be ill.*
- *I am always getting hurt, always being ill.*
- *I judge myself on how I make mistakes.*

Her father, who is a Harvard Business School graduate, told her she has all the traits to be a millionaire success. These questions were ones he asked her frequently.

- *Why do you want to do service work? Why are you doing this for free? Why don't you want to be successful financially at what you do?*

As Jacquelyn prepared to begin her mindwalk, Archangel Michael handed her a shield and sword as tools. Looking at the inside of her brain, she said it seemed like something out of the science-fiction series "Star Trek." She could actually feel the pressure of these neural pathways. They were different colors and looked like fiber optics of various blues, whites, and pinks and seemed alive. She focused on the ones that had red cables and were thicker than the others, as she held one in her hands. The negative ones were gray and dark.

I repeated the thought forms, and everything felt very heavy to her and seemed darker. She also called on Archangel Michael for protection. Jacquelyn was actually feeling these thoughts in the belly, back, neck, shoulders, and a little bit in the hips, knees, and toes. They had invaded her whole body. They were a tangled mess, and the colors were definitely not as bright as the positive ones.

She saw herself as a woman in the Middle Ages who had the gift of prophecy. She was married to someone with status, perhaps a nobleman. Because of her husband's position, she was the wise woman using her gifts in secret to help the commoners and did not want nor need payment for what she did. Sneaking out of the castle to help others made her feel guilty. Her husband was in charge of everything, was not interested in the spiritual, and did not pay much attention to her. What was most important to him was that to the community she had the required appearance of a noblewoman. It was like leading a double life. Her husband had wanted an heir. When she gave birth to a girl, they were going to kill it. She had the midwife smuggle it out and pretended that the baby had died. There was two-fold guilt—the guilt related to denying her daughter's life and the guilt of denying her gifts.

Jacquelyn continued further down the path to a life that preceded the one in the Middle Ages. This time she was in Atlantis serving as a healer/priestess. She had an arranged marriage that she did not want, but it was part of the Prince's plan to create a master race of people who were intuitive and spiritual. Her scientist husband was an older man who was intelligent and kind. She felt like a breeder in this experiment. After their baby was born, it was taken away as a weapon in the program. She loved her baby and wanted to be left alone.

As Atlantis was being destroyed, she helped the people escaping on ships. Part of her very being wants to be of service and help people, yet she did not want to be part of this nonsupportive system. She kept her gifts and healing talents quiet because if others discovered them, they would use them in some way to arm people. Being secret was connected to her being torn in two directions.

The pattern went back further than Atlantis to when she first embodied on this planet. It was primitive. She was golden light that evolved into a flesh form, and she felt trapped in this heavy form. She was a healer, priestess out in nature, and everything was in harmony. The earth cycles were somewhat different from now. This was when she began to integrate the light body into the physical form. She was a receiver of mass consciousness forming thoughts from other beings in the community. She received and embodied these thoughts—she took in their negative thoughts.

It was necessary for her to disassociate herself from these thoughts by using the protection Archangel Michael gave her. She broke the ties and cords and cleared all the lifetimes on this neural pathway with the sword and shield she had been given. The method was to lift up the shield and to cut the neurons. Instantly, a red dragon came out, and she sealed off the severed neurons with the fire of the dragon. They are unable to come back. After she did that, many connected pathways began to shrink and quickly disappear.

Jacquelyn created a new pathway to carry the thoughts: "I am whole and complete. I do my divine mission with joy, beauty, success, and radiant health." It made her body feel lighter, and she felt happy. She experienced pressure and tingling on her eye as this was happening. These new thoughts were all separate but yet connected and radiating golden light. There was a physical sensation at the back of the head as the pathway was building. In the future when this new positive thought comes to mind, she will breathe into it to strengthen it. The dark area was gone, and the shopping list was replaced by these bright, shining new thoughts.

Mindwalking seemed to be particularly effective with these people you have read about as they have each done much of their own spiritual work through the years. They all had a willingness to look at the darker aspects of their emotional and mental selves and take corrective action. It was easy for them to journey into non-ordinary reality, to walk through their own brains, and to do spiritual surgery on their negative thought form conduits. Consider taking a Sunday walk through your own brain and remodel your pathways.

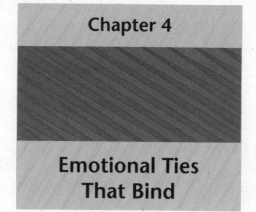

Chapter 4

Emotional Ties That Bind

Emotions as described by Cayce are those urges that come from the physical, superficial body and have been intensified through our experiences not only on the Earth but also during our sojourns in consciousness made between lives to the other planets in our solar system. These urges, even fear and anger, have their proper place when they are in balance. It is when they rule us that they are problematic and can hinder our soul development. Indulgences of the emotions can become habitual. If we continue to feed this negative energy, we become more easily influenced by them.

Haunting memories bring forth the emotions of past traumas and transgressions. Sometimes feelings well up inside and overwhelm, and the reasons this happens may not even be evident. Warring emotions may flip us from one extreme to another. It is almost as if they have a life of their own, and there is no way to control them. That is because situations in our present lives rekindle emotional wounds experienced many lifetimes ago, and we respond accordingly. They continue to re-play in our minds and our dreams until we have taken action to correct our behavior patterns and to forgive ourselves and others involved. The moment we do this, the interaction begins to change. By addressing these emotions at their source and using our ideal as a guide in reacting from our current situation, and not a past–life one, we can live a more physically and mentally balanced life.

Anger

Anger can benefit us when we recognize the message it is sending and act accordingly. It may, for example, be telling us that someone is not respecting our boundaries and is trying to control us. Cayce said that "one without some fire, some determination, some exercising of self's will is worth little . . . (4405–1)."

In that same reading the person was told that "one unable to control self, or to control temper, is worse than one that has none . . . (4405–1)." Cayce called anger a disease of the mind if it cannot be controlled. We are now beginning to understand that anger can also produce diseases of the body. If anger is not held in check, we can lose those we love, our jobs, and even our lives because of it. That is one of the reasons why it is very beneficial to investigate the root cause and dig it out.

Fears and Phobias

Fear is part of our warning system and is necessary for our well-being. Unwarranted or exaggerated fears, on the other hand, can cause us to shrink inside ourselves and be less than we are. It blocks the channel of spiritual energy flowing to us. The source of these unfounded fears and even phobias can often be found in the past. A woman asked Cayce why she was afraid of the dark, and he told her that it was due to a prior experience in a dungeon. Another woman questioned about being fearful as a child of animals, spiders, and sharp knives and learned that it resulted from a life in France when the person was bound and tied to the torture rack. Knives were also used, and this most likely was during the Inquisition. A phobia, such as agoraphobia (the fear of go-ing outside), could easily have been created in a prior time after leaving a home in the woods, thinking everything was safe and then being attacked. These fears that have no relationship to our current situation hinder us and are waiting to be released.

Words as Emotional Triggers

The emotions that come with the interchange of communication between two humans are often quite different for each person. The automatic reaction we have to certain words is less about what is being said and more about how the words relate to something in our individual past. Our *hot buttons* are often triggered unknowingly by someone who has no such intention. We carry the emotions within the imprint of these words in our energetic being. Hearing them activates the stored emotions automatically. Until we recognize our response and make efforts to change it, we will act right on cue every time we hear particular emotion-laden words. It does not matter what the other person says in explanation; we will be in denial of his/her intention. Calculate the ramifications of this across our vast range of experiences, and the impact is enormous. The good news is that even a minor adjustment will be felt throughout our vibratory pattern. We can transform ourselves bit by bit, first in little chunks, then in big ones.

Energy Cords

Energy cords are invisible energetic projections of communication connecting one of our chakras, or energy centers, to the chakras of others. Invisible cords of energy are formed between the people we interact with each day, during conversations, through thinking of another, or through desire for a person or for something that belongs to another person. Strong psychic cords often exist between relationship partners, parents and their children, and between siblings. Most casual cords fade away a few days after being formed, but stronger cords, such as those formed through a love relationship, may last for months or even years.

These informational-energy cords can cause the receiver of the communication to act in a way consistent with the thought of the other person. They can also drain energy from one to another. Non-beneficial energy cords can pull us away from being centered, leave us out of balance and affect our daily decisions.

Karmic cords can last through lifetimes. These cords can link us not only to others in a past-life but also to our own previous personalities. Emotional situations can reawaken the memory of past-life situations. Unconsciously we respond to what happened in the past versus what is currently happening and drain our energy into past-lives and into other people. It is beneficial to remove those cords during a past-life regression.

Regression to Heal an Emotional Pattern

This script, intended to heal a negative emotional pattern and wounding, has been adapted from the one in Chapter 1 which led you to experience a happy past-life. You will again receive the assistance of your Higher Self as you go to the source of an emotional problem. This problem may have been caused by you or by someone or something else. Because this trance work deals with emotions, you will observe the former life from the level of the astral plane looking through a telescope on the observation deck there. This will allow you to do what is necessary without reliving the emotions. You can also take a time out and go to your safe place if you feel the need.

Emotional Regression Script

While you are comfortably seated or lying down . . . take a moment to breathe deeply and slowly . . . and as you exhale, you find that your eyes automatically close . . . and you just settle in . . . as your body unwinds . . . Slowly and gently breathing in and breathing out . . . Allow yourself to be in this place of easy relaxation for awhile . . . sinking deeper and deeper . . . down into that in-between place . . . that place of letting go . . . no longer awake . . . yet not asleep . . . a peaceful place . . . *pause for several minutes.*

Bring to mind your safe place . . . and you find or feel yourself instantly there . . . Ask your Higher Self to join you . . . and you experience and acknowledge its presence . . . In preparation, remember a recurring feeling or fear you just cannot

explain or an emotional outbreak that seemed disproportionate to the circumstances ... or an emotional issue or pattern that reappears in your life, perhaps
wearing different faces ... When you are ready to continue, set your intention to
go back to the past-life that was the original cause ... seeing it at a soul level in
a way that you can understand what created this emotional pattern ... and know
what is necessary to transform it ...

Now ask your Higher Self to guide you back in time ... In response, your
Higher Self touches your third eye ... and instantaneously you and your Higher
Self are standing on the path back in time underneath the archway of trees ...
This is the path that will lead you to the lifetime that originated the pattern ...
Engage all your senses to take in this beauty ... As you prepare to start walking
down the path, once again bring to mind your intention to discover the original
cause of the emotional wounding that created this pattern ... knowing that you
are totally safe and protected during this process.

With your Higher Self by your side on this journey of healing, take the first
step on the path of remembrance ... As you walk, count backwards from 100,
either out loud or silently to yourself ... placing one foot in front of another ...
Each step taking you further and further back in time ... walking further and
further back with each number ... feeling more relaxed, more peaceful as you
continue to walk this path ... coming closer and closer to that time ... Continue
to walk and count until you see or experience an opening of some kind in front
of you ... It might be a door or portal ... This is the entrance to the astral plane
... However it appears to you, when you sense the opening, discontinue counting and walk through it with your Higher Self beside you ... You find yourself in
the astral plane ... and you and your Higher Self are in this place of no-time
standing on an observation deck with a large telescope there for your use ...
Through this telescope you can observe all your lives—past, present, and future
... lined up in front of you ... and can easily identify the one you seek.

When you are ready to continue, bring to mind the negative emotional pattern you wish to change ... and from the vantage point of the astral plane look
into the telescope at your lives ... holding that emotion and pattern in your
mind as you scan them for the one that holds the original cause ... Now feel
your attention being drawn to one particular life ... Focus the telescope there
and adjust the zoom lens so that the image becomes clear and you can observe
all the details ... Continue to fine-tune the focus until, on the count of three, you

able to see or sense in some way the circumstances and people involved in the creation of this pattern ...1...2...3...able to impartially observe it from this distance with no emotions attached.

Allow this life to come fully into your consciousness now ...If you move the telescope slightly, you are able to move from one significant event to another ...comprehending all the details and people involved ...Take as much time as you need to identify each of the players and the circumstances ...and also how they continue to affect your life now ...Request that your Higher Self help you understand at a deeper level the relevance of the events from this past lifetime in relationship to the emotional difficulty in your current life.

Then ask what is necessary to heal the emotional wound ...and what you must do at a soul level to transform this pattern ...Commit to doing that in the present and in the future ...If forgiveness is required of anyone else or of yourself, freely give it now ...knowing that Cayce said, "that which is forgiven is remembered no more." (404-14) ...The next step is to release these negative emotions and related pattern from your body and mind ...Ask that they be sent into the Light ...and you sense them being removed into the Light ...As you look through the telescope, observe that happening and see the life that is in front of you change in response ...Have your Higher Self assist you to understand any additional learnings from that life at the deeper level of the soul.

Before this process is completed, there is one more step in healing that life ...Using the telescope, look inside your body in that lifetime and see if there are any gray or dark patches anywhere in the body or mind ...If there are, call on the Light and ask that these areas be healed and brought back to their original, perfect pattern ...and it happens as you request ...Continue to look at that past-life body and see if there are any cords of light, especially dark ones, that are connected to it and also attached to your current body ...You identify them easily because they light up now ...Cut all of them, and send that energy into the Light ...Ask that spiritual salve be applied to the connection points on your former and current bodies ...Next look to see if there are any inappropriate cords coming to you from other people in that life ...You will recognize them easily ...Cut them and request that spiritual salve also be applied to their connecting points ...Next request that any energies belonging to others from that past-life that are attached to you now, be returned to them, as appropriate ...Finally, request that any of your energies from that life that are held by anyone else come back to you ... Become aware of how good you are feeling now ... Bring to mind that old emotion and notice how it no longer affects you in the same way ... Your work is done, and it is time for you to return.

With your Higher Self by your side, leave the observation deck and easily find the opening in time ... Go back through it ... Walk back through the archway of trees ... and back into your safe place ... If you choose, take a moment here to visualize how you will react in the future under similar circumstances ... Dialogue with your Higher Self about the experience ... Thank it for its help, and say goodbye for now .... Feeling better than before ... Feeling peace and harmony within.

Slowly count from 1 to 5 as you breathe deeply and exhale slowly ... Your energies aligned and your emotions balanced ... Remembering everything you choose to remember ... When you reach the number 5, slowly open your eyes.

Emotional Patterns/Woundings Regressions

The emotions felt by those in the stories you are about to read range from overwhelming sadness to numbness. During the sessions a few of these people experienced physical sensations as they began to clear the negative emotions held in their bodies all this time. The sensations passed quickly as the emotional release progressed. For some, this re-experiencing of the past was sufficient to address and change the emotional imprint. For others, it was the peeling away of one of the layers of the problem, and more work will be required when they are ready.

JOY'S CONNECTED LIVES

When Joy and I began discussing her intention for the regression, she initially zeroed in on her career. Earlier in her work life she wanted to do something that she truly loved and brought her delight, but she never thought she could follow her bliss in a creative way. Reinforced after having a family, Joy held the belief that she must work for money, not for fun, to contribute to the family's financial well-being. Keeping her nose to the grindstone is the way life is, or so she thought. In fact she used joy as a spiritual ideal for a year in order to accept that **joy can be a valid reason to pursue a particular career**. This helped to shift her consciousness, and recently she began working in a successful business. The nature of the work is something that called to her when she was younger, but she is doing it in a new way other than she had originally envisioned. This is exciting. Her fear has always been that this pursuit was somewhat frivolous, and making or not making money at doing it was a clear indicator of its worth. This new venture has more structure than her previous concept so that it will produce not only satisfaction but also financial rewards.

I delved deeper as this did not seem to be her most important concern. After further probing, Joy began asking herself why she did not put value on her own guidance and therefore, did not follow it. She had been acting as if her husband's opinion was superior to hers. She felt intimidated by him and deferred to his thinking because she believed, on some level, that his thoughts were better than hers, that the two of them were not equal, and that she was beneath him. This pattern was what she chose to investigate. The emotion of it was being held in her throat, and Joy said that she could not talk and knew there was something to say that she could not say.

From the observation deck of the astral plane during the regression, she viewed an adult man holding the hand of a very small girl. Joy knew that she had been that girl. The two of them were Pilgrims, and she felt, even as young as she was, that she had no control over her life. The man Philip was her father in that life, and her husband in this one. The small girl was Priscilla, his daughter.

Her father was doing a lot of talking about how she should act and what she should and should not say. At the same time she was consciously thinking about what he was saying because she wanted to please him.

This small child was different from the others in the community. She "saw" things. She saw "the way it really is." When she was two, she had seen an angel. This made her happy, and while she was alone, she sang about her experience. As she was singing, she suddenly found herself being shaken by her father while her mother stood by watching. He told her that this was not allowed because God does not speak through people. He speaks only through the Church. She was too young to understand differently and promised, "I won't do it [speak about what she saw]."

At this point Joy became nauseated. We did some energy clearing and voided the promise she made about not speaking about the extraordinary things she saw so that she would no longer be bound by it. Her nausea immediately disappeared.

In looking at the life from the soul level, she saw that her father had been protecting her from the community. While the girl was forgiving him, he went down on bended knees. Now she knows that she no longer needs to hide her abilities. This is important because some of those abilities have carried over in her current life.

From this vantage point Joy saw the small girl grown up as a result of the release of the vow and the forgiveness of her father, and she now accepted herself for who she was. Many of her soul parts had fragmented and gone into hiding for protection during this time. They spontaneously returned to merge back into her being.

When we rechecked the emotion in her throat she had experienced at the beginning of the session, she instantly felt fear. The fear immediately transported her back into another life in which she was wearing a dress and buckskin shoes and had black hair. She was working around a blacksmith's anvil in the woods. This life was all about hard work. A man, husband now and her father or close relation then, was pounding something on the anvil with a hammer. Her sense was that she felt she was below him in status. He was saying that this is what the family had to do to survive. There was no chance to do anything else. This was pure drudgery.

We sent the two limiting thoughts — (1) that work had to be

drudgery and (2) that she is somehow less than this man who is now her husband—for transformation to release them from her energy system. To complete the process we did the spiritual work to remove some gray energy in her stomach, which had probably caused the nausea. Joy severed the cords that connected her at her throat and stomach to the little girl in the first past-life and that still drained her energy. Then she cut all the other cords that existed between her and others in both of these prior lives—cords that caused her to respond to current situations from the perspective of unconscious patterns created then.

After the regression it was clear that her two initial questions which had seemed unrelated at first, were, in fact, intertwined and reflected in her current relationship with her husband and with her concept of meaningful work. Her Higher Self had taken over (with her permission) and led her from one past-life into another so that this energetic pattern between Joy and her husband, created in one life and added to in another, could be changed to one that will be more beneficial to them both in the future. This regression was very emotional for her, and she was happy to learn that she did not have to accept that they were actual past-lives in order for this to have been of benefit. [She was undecided.] Although Joy had already begun to find ways to make money doing what she really wanted to do before the session, the missing ingredient was her belief that she could do it. Now she has that belief and the strength that comes with it to go after her dream.

DAWN'S CHOCOLATE HEART

As Dawn attempted to focus on a particular emotional issue she wanted to address with the regression, she kept drawing a blank. In our discussion she began speaking about her frustration with her younger sister who seems to be unfeeling. Dawn has never been close to her even though there is not a big age difference between them. She is not able to control her sister's relationship with their mother, and it disturbs her because she cannot. She wants to because her sister's lack of family involvement bothers their mother.

At this point Dawn began crying, so we used this part of the session as the stepping stone to launch the regression and explore this blank that was keeping her from recognizing its underlying emotion(s). Immediately she was surrounded by darkness, and there was a dark brown/black material all around her. As the scene became lighter, she found herself as a woman in her twenties who was confined to a bed in a small, dark bedroom with wooden walls. The material was a curtain around her. The setting was somewhere in the United States in the 1920's or 1930's. She knew there were other people in the house because she could hear them but could not see them. The woman had been confined to her bed for some time due to a fever but was too sick to identify the nature of her illness. She originally became sick at the age of ten or eleven and was now sick again. Whether these illnesses were related was unclear.

She was very weak and had no strength. This was not her home; she did not know where she was and felt a sense of overwhelming loneliness. There were no noises to indicate that anyone else was about, but as the scene played out, doctors and nurses began rushing around in her room. There was much confusion. Some people were staring at her, and she was unable to concentrate or focus. Her family was not there, and she felt scared.

Then she experienced a darkness inside of her at first and then coldness as she was dying. After her soul left the body, she connected with the Light. Here she felt warm. From that vantage point Dawn looked for the energy cords connecting that past-life to this one. There was a red cord connected to her back. As Dawn believed that this was her own energy, it was sent into the Light for purification after it was severed. It will be returned to her in purified form so that she can reclaim it in current time. It is important to note that Dawn has had back problems for ten years.

Next we addressed the relationship with her sister. From this viewpoint Dawn was able to understand that this is just how her sister is. This knowing will make it easier for Dawn to interact with her in the future although she still feels a frustrated love for her sister.

The last step in the multidimensional healing process was to fill her blank heart, which she did by placing her hand over the heart and imagining it being filled with milk chocolate. At first it wouldn't fill all the way and the chocolate was just an outline, so Dawn spray-painted it on her heart. This seemed very comforting to her. Afterwards, she said that she actually smelled chocolate while doing this and that she had also smelled someone baking with chocolate during the session.

Dawn was scheduled for additional surgery a couple of weeks after this regression. We planned another session following the surgery to address the physical issues she has been experiencing and which were highlighted in this regression. [You read the results in Chapter 2.] Somehow these seemingly disparate emotional and physical issues were related, and Dawn was able to use this process for healing.

PATRICE—
HELPING OTHERS SEE THEIR LIGHT WITHIN

Nobody loves her, yet she desperately wants to be loved. That was the emotional pattern Patrice wanted to heal during her journey to another time. All of her life she has felt totally lost and rejected. As you will see, this is an excellent example of how it is not always a major event that creates trauma but an ongoing repetition of a pattern that creates the wounding.

When she viewed the scene from the prior time in which this pattern was originated, she saw three people—two adults and a child—holding hands skipping around in a circle. They were outside their hut on the cobblestones, and the surrounding area was yellow and hilly. A crop was growing that had the color of wheat. This was Germany in 1624, and Patrice was the child.

Moving forward in time, the family was in a hut seated at a table with heavy wooden chairs preparing to eat a meal. The food was being served by the mother. The child (Patrice) did not want hers. She found it distasteful, did not want it, and dismissively pushed it away. Her father yelled at her saying, "Your mother cooked this good food, and you are being a spoiled brat." She did not care because she did not want this peasant food. From the viewpoint of the child (who was not yet five), she was sent away from the table because she was naughty. The little girl got up and walked away crying, pouting, and sad. The house was small and dark, and she sat down on the dirt floor with her head down and her arms around her knees to console herself. Her sadness increased as she heard her parents talking, hearing them say she was a bad girl and just does not listen. This event, small in itself, was the beginning of the wounding that created the feeling of rejection. It contributed to her eventually having a sad heart.

The only place in which the girl seemed to be happy was in the nearby forest where she was surrounded by trees. She liked to look at the play of the leaves as they moved and the way the sun came through them. This small girl was happy here by herself and happy to be communing with nature where she felt free and whole.

As we continued to pursue the events that created her pattern, Patrice next saw herself as an eight-year-old outside in a mountainous scene that was reminiscent of the movie *Heidi*. The significance of this scene was that her father was once again unhappy with her. He was scolding her because she tripped and spilt the chicken feed she was carrying. Her father helped her up but was angry and told her that she was a bad girl. This reinforced her perception of his rejection of her and her sense that he was mean. She was intimidated because he was so much bigger than her and loud. In comparison, she felt as tiny as a bug and just wanted to crawl away to get away from him. He made her feel so small.

As Patrice looked into his cold, angry, blue eyes, she was horrified to discover that her father was her childhood sweetheart in her current life. In looking from a higher perspective at what had occurred, she recognized that his anger over her spilling the chicken feed was because it was precious. The family did not have much, and she had wasted it. On a soul level he knew he was wrong in how he treated her and felt bad that he had yelled at her.

As part of the transformative healing process, we replayed the scene with the girl apologizing and telling her father she had tripped. He then patted her on the head and told her it was okay. The little girl had difficulty forgiving herself because she blamed herself for always being clumsy. With further investigation she discovered that she shuffled her feet because they were deformed. This caused her clumsiness. Having gained that understanding, she finally forgave herself. As a result, her father felt compassion for her and hugged her. He still wanted her, and she felt warm and cherished and part of the family. It was now okay. "I am sorry, Daddy," she told him.

Her mother, however, was still angry, still unhappy, with her. Patrice said that her mother looked down her nose at her in disgust and dismissively said, "Oh, that child!" Patrice recognized this woman as her mother in this current life and their relationship was very much the same. The mother was mean and seemed to be eaten up inside with unhappiness. Through a dialogue between their Higher Selves, Patrice came to realize that her mother blamed herself and at the same time hated her daughter because the daughter was not perfect; she was deformed. Patrice forgave her at the Higher Self level. Her mother softened, puts her hands on her daughter's shoulder, drew her close, patted her on the head and said, "Okay, sweetheart. It's okay now. It's okay." Pat felt blessed and happy that this woman who was her mother in both lives could now find some happiness within.

Both parents were angry because the child wasn't born perfect. Patrice looked at this from a higher perspective and learned that she was born with deformed feet to help her mother come to understand and accept who she, the mother, truly was and to be at peace. Patrice did this so her mother could see that she really is a good person inside and saw a light within her mother now where there had been only darkness before. She can shine. Patrice now recognizes that this life challenge wasn't about her or about being rejected. She was really loved, but her parents did not outwardly express it. As a result, she felt that she was just a stupid little girl but now knows that she actually came into that life with a deformity to help her mother.

The next step was making a heart connection with her father. When that happened, they became equals and accepted each other. Now he could let go of the meanness and know in his heart that he loved her, no matter what. It softened him, softened his heart.

Patrice had difficulty making a heart connection with her mother because she was experiencing flashbacks of her mother's "evil" self. I explained that the pattern they had established will continue through time if this relationship is not transformed; they would have to come back and do it again. It was important for Patrice to forgive in order to release the hold this negativity has on her. When she understood what this meant, she did make a heart connection with her mother. Their hearts were happy at last, and her mother told her to forgive herself. Even though she was able to forgive her mother, she found it more difficult to accept herself because she was not perfect in that life. In consultation with her Higher Self she was told that she was sent to heal and that she was sent from God. That was what she needed to know. Now she is okay because she understands that what she thought was a lack of perfection was, in fact, a good thing. It was the vehicle to help other people. Before entering that life, she agreed to do this so that she might be the catalyst to benefit others.

As the healing process continued, Patrice saw a fiery red and orange cord attached to her on the right side linking her back to a fire outside. She cut the cord. It looked like a flesh burn to her, and it immediately started healing. When it was complete, the skin became smooth like ivory.

Then she discovered a negative energy attached to her from that lifetime in Germany. When she tried to release it, the energy seemed so angry and unhappy that it took Patrice's breath away. Spiritual assistance was required to remove it, but when it was done, everything was peaceful, and the people in her German incarnation were content to live their lives.

The feeling of nobody loving her remained in her chest in the heart chakra, however. It felt like a deep heartburn. After we identified it as her own energy, it was sent for purification. As that happened, her chest lifted up and expanded. It was intense, so we asked that the "heat" be turned down in her physical body as this energy was being removed. The golden-white healing light that filled the void left after this energy was lifted began filling all the holes in her heart which were created by all the hurt she had experienced. The healing light felt refreshing, but her heart also needed to be caressed, which Patrice did on the imaginative level. During the healing process Patrice felt tears dripping down her face, although she was not shedding real tears. The release of pent-up emotion and the energetic tears continued until the healing was complete and the thought that nobody loves her began floating away.

We moved on to the feeling of being totally lost and rejected that was buried so deeply in her chest that it felt as if her chest were caved in. Although the color of it initially fooled her into thinking that it was positive, after further investigation it almost seemed evil, so we again enlisted the aid of the Spiritual Forces. After the energy was removed, she could breathe again, but it revealed a hurt right in the center of her heart. She described the feeling as being ragged and raw, like an open sore with ulcers and puss. As it was her own energy, we requested that the Light purify it and that when that was done, it be brought back to her. Then she was able to breathe more easily, and the area became a nice pink color and looked more normal. It healed over. At this point the thought that nobody loves her was replaced by the thought that she wants to be loved.

However, she still found it hard to love herself and was in tears at this point. She felt that parts of her were not right. She does not like herself, her body. Her body was ugly to her. To her it was fat and ugly, and she said that everybody thought she was fat and ugly. When we winnowed down who "everybody" was, it was, in fact, her first husband, who was abusive. At the time they were married, Patrice was skinny, but he told her that she was fat and she believed him. This was his energy, so it was returned to him. She reluctantly chose to embrace her body as it is necessary to live this life. It seemed like a lot for her to work on, but it did make her laugh as the energy shifted. She asked the healing light to go through her body and transform it. To close the loop we rechecked the thought that nobody loves her, and she said that she is lovable now.

Then I revisited her feeling of being totally lost and rejected. The question made her jerk sideways, and the movement originated from inside the abdomen. We zeroed in on that spot and found that poisons from medicine taken were being held in her liver. This took her back to another lifetime in which she was being given herbal medicine to drink by a medical healer to make her well and drive out the evil spirits. Her liver was blowing up. The people wanted to kill her to get rid of her because they thought she was bad and evil. They hid this from her. They wanted her to go away, and this was an attempt to get rid of the evil within her under the guise that they were trying to help her. Pat cut the cord to that life in a way that was easy and beneficial to her body. The liver began leaking and all the poisons began to flow out. The liver was transformed as it returned to normal size. It was healthy again.

Lastly, we tackled her thought of being lost and rejected, Patrice recognized that she is lonely in her present life but does not have any idea about where she is going, reinforcing her belief that she has no purpose. The tears started to flow again because of her intense feeling that she just wants to go home. She was so tired of this life, being here in a body. I guided her to connect with God's energy, and when she did, she learned that her **purpose is to bring light and understanding to others**. She wants to go "home," but she is not finished yet. This made her laugh a resigned laugh. She said she will complete her assignment, acknowledging that she always does what she says she will do. Sometimes it seems like a heavy burden. Her Higher Self said that when she felt the weight of the burden or felt alone, all she has to do is call on it for help and make that connection. As we closed the session, she handed the feeling of "being a burden" over to God and experienced lots of love and felt energized.

Patrice told me that prior to this session when she "starts to lose it," she can't pray; she can't read; she can't do anything but be miserable. She can't even feel. She is totally numb. The Higher Self will assist her if she asks for its help [because of free will we must ask], so she made a commitment to herself that either at the beginning or end of every day she will connect with it to develop a closer working relationship. In the future whenever she feels that life is becoming too much for her, she will remember the spiritual guidance that is available to her and automatically connect with her Higher Self.

As we concluded, she was filled completely with golden-white healing light. Although she felt better than when we had started, Patrice knows that she has more work to do in strengthening her connection with God's energy. Her Higher Self will support her in the work she has chosen to do in this lifetime. When she came back to waking consciousness, her Higher Self was still holding her hand. Patrice was laughing and happy as we ended. She knows that her Higher Self is always there for her, and she asked me to write that down to help her remember—which I did.

JULIO—A PERFECT EXAMPLE OF FORGIVENESS

Some years ago Julio caught his neighbor Anthony breaking into his daughter's bedroom while she was asleep. This young man subsequently went to jail for assault and battery and carjacking. He is currently back in prison serving time for a felony. Julio knew that Anthony had suffered through a horrendous childhood, so he felt compassion for him in spite of what he had done, visiting him in jail and writing him letters. He thought his spiritual work was done with Anthony and that all the ill feelings had dispersed. It surprised him when Anthony's name surfaced during a regression we had, and it touched something deep within Julio in regard to his children. We decided to do a past-life regression that focused on the emotional aspects of Julio and Anthony's relationship so that the healing might be completed. When the session was over, Julio saw this incident in a completely different light—one without negative feelings. Instead he now sees it with loving gratitude and is thankful for the lessons he learned through it.

On his trip back in time Julio easily returned to a Mayan lifetime in Central America in the year 8. This was a lifetime that we had explored in a previous regression although the dynamic between Julio and Anthony was not covered then. This was a life in which Julio had abused his powers as a shaman, and he knew that from the prior session. This time Julio discovered that Anthony and the woman who is now his daughter had a relationship. They were in love.

What the shaman did to these two people in love was one of the instances in which he used his power for his personal advantage. Julio was a bully and manipulated the situation for his own benefit, making Anthony feel helpless. He saw this woman as a potential conquest for his own pleasure. Because of his position, she and Anthony were forced to follow his dictates.

Once the circumstances of that life and the nature of the relationships became known to him, Julio began his introspective work. He immediately recognized that Anthony is a mirror for him in this life. Julio was actually seeing himself *in* Anthony and feeling how he felt — how helpless he felt because of Julio's power. To understand this at an even deeper level Julio said that he needed to look into a [spiritual] mirror in his mind, which he did. Then he understood the harm he had done and how this was being reflected back to him when Anthony broke into his daughter's bedroom. Julio knew that he must apologize to Anthony and also forgive himself. He did this at the Higher Self level, following Cayce's guidance which he remembered during the regression: "that which is forgiven is remembered no more (404-14)."

He released the residual negative emotions and patterns related to Anthony and that Mayan lifetime from his body and mind and sent them into the Light. Looking at that scene after this was done, Julio observed that the life had changed and their hearts were at peace. He felt that this was cleansing.

The last piece of work, surprisingly, was to reclaim the energy of empathy that was stuck in that lifetime. He chose to bring it back into the present as empathetic understanding. All the healing work was then completed. Now when he thinks about Anthony, he sees him with new understanding. In closing, Julio gained two final insights. He can see clearly now, and his heart is lighter.

In the post-regression wrap-up, Julio told me that he had prepared for the session by meditating and requesting that what unfolded be in the highest good for all involved. No wonder he was so easily able to see his actions reflected back to him through another! He recognized that he was meeting himself. This work helped balance the scales of understanding, and he can see clearly now. Julio anticipated that these lessons would be waiting for him in his next meditation to help him become aware of the next step in his own soul development. He re-

membered Cayce saying that we are continuously meeting ourselves and recognized that revisiting this prior incarnation is a
good example. Julio said, "I met myself" through the opportunity of knowing Anthony in this life.

In our past-lives we have all committed acts and said things that
would be shocking and unthinkable to us now. In our soul's work, we
must face our dark side or else the process is incomplete and our biggest lessons have been left undone. This kind of information, however,
will only be revealed to us when we are prepared to process it. Our
Higher Selves will be the monitors during these regressions and will
allow us to remember only when it is time.

Emotional soul woundings resulting from our own actions or from
what we have suffered can be very deep and compounded over many
lifetimes. Yet, on a spiritual level they can be overcome through understanding, forgiveness, and love. We are loved by Spirit, no matter what
we think we have done or what has been done to us. By accepting this
love we can be motivated by our soul to come more into awareness of
our relationship to Source so that we are no longer ruled by our physical emotions.

Chapter 5

The Patterns of Our Soul

Our real identity does not reside in our bodies, in our personality, or in the person we think we are, but in our eternal souls, our individuality. According to Cayce, we are all "corpuscles in the body of God" (3481-2) and portions of the thoughts of God that have been given the opportunity for expression so that we might become companions as co-creators to God. Free will was given to us so that we might do this in our own unique way. Through the exercise of free will, choices can be made that are not in alignment with our divine nature and purpose. These choices take us off course and create a barrier to remembering what we are about. Once we have taken a fork in the road that leads us away from our destination, we continue down that path lifetime after lifetime compounding the error of our decision until we make a different choice. We are never so lost that we cannot find our way back, and help is always there if we ask. Our purpose is to find that erroneous decision point and then move in another direction that allows us to come more into alignment with Spirit and fulfill our destiny of becoming co-creators.

Each life on the Earth brings with it the opportunity to use all of its experiences for the development of our soul. The act of venturing out into the world is a very brave one. Even though this earthly experience is custom designed for us, we are anxious and apprehensive at the same time. After all, there have been many prior opportunities to learn. In some lives we did, and others were a setback, but nothing is truly lost. Each is a stepping stone for a greater accomplishment. No trial in overcoming our negativities is ever designed to be more than we can bear. P.M.H. Atwater, who had three near–death experiences of her own, found herself "inside" the Akashic Records during one of them. She came back with two important understandings. The first was that we each have the opportunity to make changes, corrections, in our lives at any point. It is never too late. The second was that the power of forgiveness is real, but "eternal damnation is not."[4]

We can ask for spiritual assistance to remember the reason we came into the Earth this time around. Through this understanding the underlying distorted patterns that permeate our lives can be identified and positive change can take place. By learning the origin of a negative pattern, in whatever life it was born, the karmic seed can be plucked and the cycle broken so that it will not blossom again in another life. When this happens, we feel more at peace or whole and in attunement with the divine plan that we agreed to—the plan put in place prior to our entering this physical body.

Soul's Purpose

Our purpose in coming into each lifetime is much more than righting our wrongs; it is to expand our universe; each of us doing it individually yet in concert with all other souls. We know our mission when we enter into a body. It resonates within us and propels us to fly. Our minds tell us we are mortals, but our hearts know that we are not. The voice of our heart guides us to greater glory when we listen to it.

---

[4]P.M.H. Atwater, *We Live Forever: The Real Truth About Death* (Virginia Beach, VA: A.R.E. Press, 2004), 55.

As spiritual beings in a physical body, we each have an individual duty and function to perform in this world. We have all we need to carry this out, and all the resources are provided; nothing is missing. We each have the unique talents and intelligence necessary to accomplish the purpose which we were born to do.

Although we may not consciously recognize or acknowledge that we do have a specific purpose, our subconscious knows what we are here for. It reaches out to us, sending messages through our dreams, intuitions, and innermost longings. This call manifests in our drives and abilities, shapes our careers and relationships, and influences the quality and directions of our lives. If we are not living in accord with this purpose, it may feel as if there are missing pieces; we are always looking for something more. We sense that there is something here for us to do or be, but it eludes us.

Dramatic events or problems that cause us to rethink our focus indicate that we are still searching for that purpose. These feelings, these events are prodding us to awaken and come more into alignment with our true purpose. Sometimes it seems as if our life is directed by accident or coincidence, but a key concept in the Edgar Cayce readings is that there is indeed a purpose in all life. All experiences come to us for good reason. That purpose is inseparably linked to our true nature as spiritual beings. Cayce went so far as to suggest that it is within the ordinary aspects of life that something extraordinary can happen.

Creating and Using a Spiritual Ideal

Cayce said that the most important thing we can do is to set a spiritual ideal. This sets up the conditions for how we navigate through life and the standards we use to judge it. The ideal is a motivating force, and when we add the energy of thought and emotion to it, whether it is a spiritual ideal such as love or a physical ideal like money, the universal law of attraction pulls it to us energetically.

The ideal is not just a mental concept. It must be actively put into practice in our lives. Application of a **spiritual** ideal helps us meet and overcome our challenges originating in this and former lives. Spiritual support groups are wonderful ways to assist us in putting our ideal into practice in all ways. Groups such as the A.R.E. Search for God study groups which meet across the United States and in many other countries around the world provide the environment to further our own spiritual walks.

Spiritual Errors

Spiritual errors are caused by wrong thinking. The primary error arises when we believe we are separated from God. Looking at our lives through this lens clouds our vision and distorts our understanding of external events. Other errors branch off from this one and result when we set our primary goal as something that satisfies only the physical. One example is holding the thought of accumulating money as an end in itself. Another might be becoming a powerful politician to use the position for personal gain even if it is not in the best interests of the constituents. Whatever this overriding goal, the ideal is so potent that it becomes our standard by which we measure success. In these two examples the connection with the spiritual is either ignored or is used as a façade to cover up the real intention.

Interrelated to the erroneous belief that we are separated from our Source is the thought that we are victims. It is a role we have chosen somewhere in time, and we will continue to repeat it until we understand that there really is no such thing as a victim. This may be difficult to grasp when we watch the news and learn of some of the horrendous things that have happened to people until we understand that this is a spiritual pattern some have selected to play out in the physical. The role can be discarded by changing how we think about ourselves and our circumstances. Then we can confront situations in which we are uncomfortable or feel out of control to bring about necessary change and to fortify us for even greater challenges. When we have learned enough, we can choose differently.

Mary Roach, who is a well-known psychic living in Virginia Beach, commented on the archetype of the victim during her participation in a panel discussion of four psychics at the 1997 annual New Year's Conference at A.R.E. Headquarters. The psychics' topic was "Intuitive Visions of the 21st Century." Mary told the audience that she saw the patterns that the soul has been engaged in during the Piscean Age (the last 2000 years approximately) were finally breaking. In her work she said she was seeing "the patterns hit walls with people. If they always had a pattern of running away and did this for six different lifetimes, they are now being challenged, probably extremely, so that they have to stop running away." Mary believes that the victim pattern is not only changing; it is ending. One of her predictions for this new millennium that began in 2001 was that "in the Aquarian Age, once people have broken the patterns, there is a huge trend from lessons to creativity—to be creative with God."

It is time to clean up the residue of our erroneous choices of the past that keeps us stuck. As we move further into this new era, we can use what we learned from our many incarnations to launch us into a higher dimension of evolution.

Misuse of our Powers

Not all errors are unconscious. Some are made using free will. Among the most troublesome is perverting the intention of our spiritual gifts by using them to satisfy the ego and the desire for power and control. This is again the case of indulging in physical urges of many kinds at the expense of the soul. These instances are more prevalent than we would like to imagine and even more troublesome when they are committed by those who hold positions of trust. Unfortunately, it seems as if more reports are being aired daily of a religious person or spiritual practitioner of some kind misusing that trust. Misuse of psychic abilities can be subtle. During one of my trainings I heard about several people, who lived in a remote town, deliberately manipulating others with their thoughts. They were on the alert for the unsuspecting to do just that. This most certainly has negative karmic consequences that must be atoned for at some time.

Using the Spiritual Script

In this chapter's regression, which is an adaptation of the basic script, you will first journey back to a life in which you made some type of spiritual mistake or misused your spiritual powers. After you are there and discover the details of your error, you and your Higher Self will walk over a rainbow bridge to another lifetime. This will be the life in which you experienced your highest spiritual connection. Here you will reawaken that remembrance in your consciousness and take it back with you to the first life to make the necessary corrections. When you return to the present, you will be able to recall that deep connection with Spirit any time you choose.

Rainbow Bridge to a Rich Potential Script

As you are seated comfortably or lying down ... close your eyes and allow your breath to relax you ... Breathing relaxation into your toes, your feet, your legs ... breathing out tension and tightness ... continue to breathe relaxation into your hips and lower torso ... breathing out stress and strain ... breathing relaxation into your upper body, shoulders, arms, hands and fingers ... breathing out the need to control ... breathing in softness and peace into your neck and head ... as you let go of anything you no longer need or want ... Completely relaxing now ... *pause for several minutes.*

Bring to mind your safe place ... that special space you created just for yourself where you are totally safe and protected ... When you do, you find yourself instantly there ... Look around, identify a comfortable spot, sit down, and enjoy this place for a moment ... Ask your Higher Self to join you ... Acknowledge its presence.

When you are ready to continue, set your intention to remember in some way, the details of a prior life in which you made a spiritual mistake that is negatively affecting you in this life ... or one in which you misused your spiritual powers ... an error that you have chosen to correct this time around ... Ask your Higher Self to guide you as you go back in time, first to the life in which the spiritual error was made so that you might understand what needs to be done ... and then to the life in which you had your highest spiritual connection ... You will use the knowledge you gain from that connection to correct the error you made.

Focus on your third eye and place yourself on the path leading back in time ... the one underneath the archway of trees ... with your Higher Self beside you ... Engage all your senses as you prepare to start walking down the path ... Concentrate on your intention to return first to the life in which the spiritual mistake was made ... then to go to a life in which you were highly spiritually connected, where you will retrieve this knowledge and take it back to the first life you visited to correct the error ... understanding that after transforming the mistake you will be able to use your spiritual gifts wisely ... You will also bring that high spiritual connection back into both your current life and into your future to support you in living your soul's purpose ... It will be easy to travel from one life to another by crossing a rainbow bridge through time.

Now, with your Higher Self by your side, take the first step on the path of remembrance ... and start counting backwards from 100 to 0, either out loud or silently to yourself ... As you place one foot in front of another ... each step on this path beneath the archway of trees takes you back and back in time ... walking further and further back with each number ... feeling more relaxed, more peaceful as you continue to walk this path ... having a sense of anticipation as you come closer and closer to that time ... See or experience an opening of some kind in front of you and discontinue counting when you do ... This opening may be a door, a warp in time and space, or something else that you recognize as a portal into the past ... Then walk with your Higher Self through the opening into another place and time ... fully protected, knowing that you can call on your Higher Self for help or go to your safe place, if necessary.

When you have walked through the opening, orient and ground yourself ... First, notice where you are in relation to your body ... Are you looking out of your eyes or are you looking at yourself from outside? ... Are you above, behind, or to the side of your body? ... If you are not completely in your body, direct your consciousness into your body, and look out of your eyes ... Feel your feet standing on the surface ... Send a grounding cord from your root chakra at the base of your spine down to the center of Mother Earth and connect there.

Once you are in your body and grounded ... become aware of what you are wearing, how old you are, what your sex is, and anything else about yourself that is important ... Then take time to look at your surroundings ... Enlist all your senses so that you might fully experience this life ... Notice whether you are inside or out ... if you are there alone with your Higher Self or if there are other people with you ... What is this place like? ... What time of year? ... Are there buildings, and, if so, what are they like? Set out with your Higher Self and explore ... Perhaps you even hear someone speak your name.

When you are ready, ask your Higher Self to take you either forward or backward in time in that life when you made the spiritual mistake or misused your powers ... Allow all the details to come into your awareness so that you understand fully the nature of the error ... Do this at a soul level so that you do not need to re-experience this physically or mentally ... Now it is time to take the next step in the process of realignment and spiritual healing.

Find or make your way outside ... When you are there, scan the sky around you ... and notice a rainbow with its bands of color ... red, orange, yellow, green, blue, indigo, and violet ... At the end of the rainbow is the life in which you had your highest spiritual connection ... This life has rich potential for creating the new you and the new life you desire ... You and your Higher Self walk over to the rainbow ... When you reach it, you discover that it is a bridge ... and you both begin walking over the bridge back to the past-life you are seeking ... Continue walking, feeling more and more in touch with that time ... and when you and your Higher Self reach the end of the bridge, you are fully back in that life ... Become aware of all the details of the role you played in that life—perhaps as a priest or priestess, a farmer, mother, or father ... whatever it was, this is the life of your highest spiritual connection ... Next, remember what that connection was like ... how you felt being so closely aligned with Spirit ... how easy it was to live a spirit-led life ... and recognize that this connection was never broken ... It is still intact ... You also become aware of the correct use of spiritual knowledge ... that it is to be used for the highest benefit of yourself and others ... Take it all in with each of your senses ... Feel, hear, smell, touch, and even taste every aspect of this understanding which will benefit you in the quest for spiritual healing and soul development ... Take as much time as you need, and then meld that sense of connection and alignment, that remembrance, into your very being and into your consciousness so that you might carry it with you into your previous past-life and into your present ...

Now you are ready. With your Higher Self by your side, walk back over the rainbow bridge into the former lifetime ... knowing that you possess the spiritual tools necessary to do what needs to be done ... to forgive yourself and others, to repair, release, realign with Spirit, and transform this spiritual mistake

...so that it can become a learning experience of rich potential for your soul's journey and is a stepping stone to a greater awareness...Do that now...Take as long as is necessary...

Ask that you be filled with golden-white healing light and be shown the new life that you will lead now that you have chosen to live in conscious connection with Spirit, using your spiritual gifts wisely...It is done...It is time to return...

With your Higher Self by your side, you easily find the opening in time...and walk back through it...back through the archway of trees...and back into your safe place...If you choose, take a moment here to dialogue with your Higher Self about the experience...Thank it for its help, and say goodbye.

Slowly count from 1 to 5 as you breathe deeply and exhale...feeling your energies aligned and balanced...happy and at peace...remembering everything you choose to bring back with you...being able to recall that spiritual life any time you choose just by closing your eyes and feeling the connection... When you reach the number 5, slowly open your eyes to the rich potential that is awaiting you.

Spiritual Patterns Regressions

The three regressions detailed here include a wide span of spiritual topics. Icléa's tells of the misuse of her gifts and their unfortunate consequences for her in this life. Teresa's reinforced a decision made earlier in her life to create peace, and she was given a view of the future of this planet. Joe's regression is interesting for a number of reasons. It raises the possibility of parallel lives (a topic often explored in science fiction). Even more importantly, it shows that when a person is not ready to know certain information, the Higher Self will prevent it from being remembered. For those who are afraid of what they might discover about themselves during a regression, this is important for them to understand. Only remembrances that they are ready to process will be presented to them.

ICLÉA—THE PRICE OF BLACK MAGIC

Icléa, whose past-life dream you read about in the first chapter, is originally from Brazil where she was raised in the Spiritist religion. Her mother is a medium, and Icléa is a spiritual teacher and healer. Through the opportunity presented by a past-life regression, Icléa wanted to clear and heal a karmic pattern that was played out by her husbands in this life. She has had four husbands. The first two she divorced and they died sometime later. Her third husband died while she was married to him, and her current husband, the fourth, has Alzheimer's and is in the process of crossing over.

Icléa has been trained in self-hypnosis so it was easy for her to quickly go into a deep trance. At first she experienced nothingness. Exploring the nothingness, she discovered herself all alone in the desert and lost. This was before the time of Christ when she lived in Mesopotamia. I directed her back prior to her being lost to discover what had led up to it, back to her being alone in prison. The remembrance was painful so it was necessary for her to observe it from the level of Spirit. From this vantage point Icléa saw herself as a twenty-year-old female imprisoned for having killed the woman who belonged to her lover. Not only did she kill the woman, but she did it using black magic because she wanted the man for herself. As we progressed forward in time, some people had taken her from the prison out to the middle of the desert on horseback. Then they left her there without food and water. We had arrived back at the place where the regression began.

In the moments before death, her last thoughts were, "I will not give death [cause death]; I will give life. I will not starve, and I will not thirst." Her lips were dry. Her spirit passed out of that body, and I gave her the suggestion to go into the Light and also that she was no longer thirsty. Her words indicated that she was not with God. We discovered she was off crying somewhere, feeling sorry for what she had done. It was clear that her soul was earthbound at this point because she said "they" did not want her. When I suggested she look up and go into the Light, it was too bright for her. We corrected this, and the loving arms of her sister reached out for her. I checked to verify that this had indeed been a former life of Icléa's and was not the remembrance of an earthbound entity attached to her before taking the next step. "She is Icléa, and I am her. We are one." It was indeed one of Icléa's former incarnations.

Icléa's spirit needed to understand that it would be welcomed by God, so we requested a spiritual teacher to assist her. A Native American answered the call. Icléa asked him how to correct the pattern she had initiated in that life. He told her that she was doing it in this life by helping others and by having helped two of her husbands. Two of them, however, she had not. "They were bad husbands." To correct this pattern at a spiritual level, she was instructed to **pass** all her past **knowledge** from that life **on to others for good**. Icléa had already made that commitment and this message reinforced its importance. Sometimes she wants to quit, especially when she is in physical pain, but she says she can't.

I then directed her to the source of her physical pain, which was in the back. This was a congenital problem caused at birth due to a difficult birthing process. Icléa had been too big for her mother who was not supposed to have any children and suffered very much as a result of Icléa's birth. Icléa thought it was her fault for her mother's suffering. When she asked her spiritual teacher about any agreement between them, he told her that her mother had agreed to have Icléa even though she would be unable to have more children, which she desired.

Icléa recognized that this arrangement was her mother's choice and they had both agreed to it. She finally forgave herself but said, "They are telling me that the reason for her having only me was karmic from a previous life." In that life her mother had many slaves, and her husband had children with the slaves. She took their babies and sold them so that they would go far away. To repay the karmic debt, she only had Icléa, and Icléa went far away [to the U.S.]. In this lifetime her mother had only black women as maids. These women had babies, and her mother was godmother to all their babies and gave them assistance, clothes, and food.

Icléa did not understand why she had to suffer for her mother's karma, so she asked her teacher why. The answer was that Icléa sacrificed for her mother's atonement. Knowing that, she was then able to forgive herself for causing her mother pain because of the difficult birth. However, she still had pain in her back and left leg. As we pursued the cause, Icléa discovered that she has to go through this pain to atone for something she herself had done in another past-life. In that one Icléa beat her sister on the back with a stick because her sister had stolen her gold coin. She expressed regret for her actions and asked her sister for forgiveness, but her sister did not want to grant it. Icléa spoke to this sister at the Higher Self level asking for forgiveness and it was given. This was when Icléa was finally able to forgive herself fully. She said that she had wished to have a sister in this life, but she did not. [The karma of both the mother and daughter is played out for them with this current life agreement.] The only other thing she was instructed to do regarding her back was to follow doctor's orders. She agreed to do so.

The last step in the process of healing was to revisit the pattern of her husbands' deaths. During their marriage she was mistreated by the first one. The second one stole from her. The third she loved very much. The fourth one was good to her but was hard for her to understand. Icléa learned she must forgive three of the four of them for whatever they had done to her in this life, and she had already started this process. In order for the pattern to be completely cleared, there is more work for Icléa to do regarding the first and second husbands. As she was having difficulty completely forgiving the first two, she again asked for help from her Native American teacher. He said that she should pray for their spirits every day, which she agreed to do. When I asked if there was anything else necessary to clear the pattern, she said that it was done, and it felt good.

As the regression came to an end, Icléa connected with the

Light, feeling God's energy, and was filled with a bluish, purple light. It was calming, and she was a peace.

TERESA'S VISION OF THE FUTURE

Teresa was in a place in her life where she chose to understand more fully her life's purpose and to re-experience her highest previous spiritual connection. That was the intention we set for the regression.

As we began, she saw the presence of Christ. Next, she saw His Holiness the Dalai Lama, and he laughingly said, "Yes, yes, yes." He was there to assist her. Teresa sensed her Higher Self as a male presence. It appeared to her as a being of light. She felt a lot of emotions of love and expectation. I suggested that she let go of the feeling of expectation to open herself to all possibilities and not to limit them as she began her exploration of her Akashic records.

When she received her personal record book from the keeper (an obscure-looking man to her), she looked at her name on the cover. The soul name appeared as a white, bright vibration. The book was light leather, and her soul name was in gold letters, which she eventually recognized as stars.

After opening the book, Teresa was back in time in a sandy desert, barefooted. The ocean was nearby. She was part of a group of musicians playing music of sorts with Tibetan instruments: gongs, chimes, and horns. They were practicing for each other and were intensely focused on the unusual, although harmonious, music they were playing. Teresa told me, "I've heard it before." It felt very good to her and made her happy. She was very aware of her connection with Spirit.

Going back to a significant event earlier in that life, she saw herself as a child, a young boy, in a brightly colored temple where he had come to live. He felt sadness even though he was treated as being very special. The sadness was acknowledged and released. That made her feel better, and she recognized the sadness was about the boy's connection with his mother. Teresa said, "Everyone loves me and wants me here so much." The boy was helped to recognize that the **love connection** with the mother was **still there even though** they were **physically separated**. The boy's purpose for living in the temple was for the teaching, the discipline, and the opportunity to serve the "clergy."

The boy moved forward to the next important event. At that time he was an old man who held a cabinet position. He was wearing special gear and using an unusual pen made of intricately carved dark wood about twelve inches long. The writing he was doing pertained to the future of the whole Tibetan culture. There were other people in the room, and he was recording the discussion taking place although he was not participating in it.

When I asked Teresa about the significance of this, the answer was that what was happening then is important now in our time. However, she understood that even though she was participating in this discussion by recording it, she was not to feel that she was better than anyone else [This must have been an important position.]. "Ultimately we complete our lives, and then we go on again. **We must accomplish as much as we can in our lives and continue creating peace. It is important to live the belief that peace within is possible and can be spread around us.**" Her ultimate goal was/is to be totally at peace, and it was achieved in that life. I guided her to once again experience that feeling of total peace as the man was dying. The blissful feeling went out from his body into the death state and then moved into her current body. It is within her now.

I made the suggestion that she open her Akashic book of records to a page in the near future to view herself living her life's purpose, a future that was now available to her as a result of having reestablished her spiritual connection from the past. The book of records showed her outside with other people, who were dressed nicely. They had all come together for a discussion of the future of the planet. There were no buildings nor were there any children, birds, or life outside. Everything was very basic. Although Teresa was not a key player in this group, she was assisting. The meeting was "a big deal," and it was being held approximately **ninety years in the future**. This was a view of her **next life**, not this one!

In this future life she will again be female, and her job will be as an assistant to a male. This felt good to her. The group was exploring how to sustain life on the planet at the time and how to stay and maintain it. There will be a choice to leave this planet in a spaceship or to remain behind with a small group if they decide to stay.

I asked her how the thread of being totally at peace from the Tibetan life weaves from the past through to her life as Teresa and also to her life in this future time. Teresa answered that early on in this life she took vows to be a peaceful person even though she has some fire within and does not always want to be a peaceful person. She recognizes now that the fire can be used in a peaceful way. To keep that high spiritual connection and feel that inner peace, Teresa was told by Spirit to walk the walk and talk the talk. This made her laugh because we have all heard that wisdom many times. She believes that she has already made the commitment to be a peaceful person in all aspects of her life. In order for her to take this quality into her future life, she needs to be a very loving human being and **to teach people through love**. She *is* currently a teacher of sorts. Teresa recognizes that her lessons are sometimes subtle and that at other times they are created by her even though they might not be what she wants to handle at the time. In the way that she lives and the way she is, she must always do it in a loving manner because that is how people will be learning from her.

When we asked if there was anything more she needed to do before we finished, the guidance she received was, "**You are not alone. The help you need is always there. Do not ever feel you are alone.**" This made her feel very good. Then she saw the Dalai Lama who told her, "You just ask for what you need, and be that loving person." She understood what he meant was that whatever she needs to be that loving person, she should **ask for it**, and it will be given.

Teresa is an optometric technician and uses touch to calm people during their appointments. She consciously tries to be a loving, peaceful person, especially for them, and projects that when she speaks. Interestingly, even though she had anticipated going to a lifetime in Atlantis before we started, her highest spiritual connection was in Tibet. Teresa is now feeling a draw to work with children and does tutoring part-time. The biggest lesson these children will learn from her may very well be to experience inner and outer peace.

JOE'S PARALLEL LIVES

Joe is a retired senior who is on a lifelong spiritual quest. His place is filled with stacks of spiritual books on various topics that he is reading and investigating. He was very curious about revisiting a past-life that would assist him somehow in his spiritual development. We chose to explore a lifetime in which Joe had committed a spiritual error, consciously or inadvertently, then go to the one in which he had his highest spiritual connection so that the error might be corrected for all time. At least that was the intention. This was Joe's first regression, and it is a wonderful example of the Higher Self allowing a person access to prior information only when he or she is ready. As you read about these various lives, it is important to know that Joe was born in 1945. The experiences are those of Joe in parallel lives which overlap in time. I have used as many of his words as possible so that you can get the flavor of the different individuals.

In the first life he visited Joe was a middle-aged male dressed in a Hawaiian shirt and white pants with a sunburned face and living on one of the Hawaiian Islands. There were beautiful and expensive houses of various colors on the seashore. He had come into some money to fulfill his dreams, and his Higher Self took him to a meeting in the 1960's with an architect who was going to design a house for him that was so magical it would respond to the energy of the weather—the sun and wind—to open and close the windows appropriately and to regulate a pool that opened up from the ground. The walls, windows, and ceiling all opened and closed using the weather's energy. I asked Joe about the use of the magical powers as this was a spiritual quest. He told me that it was the magic of transmutation of the brick, glass, sunlight, and air to perfect them into a cohesive mechanical, manipulatable house. Joe had made an agreement of some kind to use the powers of energy for transformation. He said, "If the wish can be willed, the means can be found."

The technology that Joe described was not available in the 1960's and may not be available even today, but this experience seemed so real to Joe that he was not sure it wasn't his current life. This episode was one of several parallel lives he re-experienced in this regression. Joe did not indicate that these "magical powers" to transform energy were used inappropriately so we moved on.

We journeyed back further, holding the intent of the regression. Next he found himself as a young man writing a book in Exeter, New Hampshire in the 1940's. This man was very lonely, introspective, and looking for answers. By writing this book he was trying to do something creative and capture the magic of New England by talking about its towns, people, and its "hidden undercrust." Through that he hoped to find self-realization.

I sensed that it was important to follow the thread of his having used and tried to control magic, so I again instructed Joe to return to the original lifetime in which he made a spiritual error. At this point it was necessary for him to request spiritual assistance for himself, and he asked for the help of "the mystical, spiritual being of the other world," the god Pan from Greek mythology. That allowed him to go to another life, this one in Ipswich, Massachusetts in the 1930's during the Great Depression.

Thomas F. Duffy was teaching history in a high school there and was not affected very much by the Depression. He was thirty-nine- or forty-years-old with no family. He had taken so much time to pursue his own career that he had no time for family. Thomas joined a Rosicrucian group, but it was secret because the town was so conservative. As part of this organization he tried to commune with spirits and get revelations from above in order to guide his future. His intention was more selfish and less sacrificing; it was more ego-based.

He ran for Congress in 1942 and tried to catch the wave created by President Franklin Roosevelt's (FDR's) administration. He made a lot of noise, made some fine speeches, and got people interested in his ideas. Although he was not elected, he received a lot of praise and attention from his peers, other teachers, and students. His purpose in running was to go to Congress to help FDR change the world, to win the war. However, Thomas also wanted power: to be a player in the grand scheme of things, to be part of the "great crusade" to take Hitler down, and to destroy the forces of Fascism.

This seemed like an opening to explore our initial question so I asked if he had been in a crusade of any kind before. This was when his conscious mind, and probably his Higher Self, kicked in. Joe said he would like to think so, but probably not. There was only one grand crusade that was worth joining, according to him, and that was the one conducted by the Knights Templar in the Middle East to regain the Holy Land taken by the Muslims. He described this military order as the "most exclusive, profoundly spiritual group," and he did feel a spiritual connection to it resonate in his heart. To him their efforts were a beautiful, courageous crusade against the infidels. The connection appeared as a golden hue for him, so I instructed him to walk into the middle of it. As Joe contemplated this, he told me that there were initiations one must go through first and these initiations go in stages. He expressed reluctance to enter because he had to give everything up, including all of his property to the organization, and he was not at all enthusiastic about this idea. The Franciscans, on the other hand, were much easier for him to identify with and giving up everything did not seem to be as problematic because he said they were the purest of Christianity—the very essence of Christianity. Even though I suggested that he take a look without giving up his possessions, he still resisted, once again saying that he did not want to give them up in order to become part of a bigger order. He does not like to give anything up. He said that he likes to possess things, to his detriment perhaps, and, yes, he made the choice not to give them up a long time ago. He had a great deal of money and would not part with it for anybody. He just wanted more. At this point it was clear that it was not Joe saying this, but one of his former incarnations.

I took a different tack and instructed him to go back to a time when he first chose to hold on to his possessions and not give them up for anybody. Thomas began telling me about his life and how he had made money in stocks using insider information about industries in Massachusetts. He wanted more possessions. As his life progressed, he lost most of his possessions after making some bad investments. Thomas was forced to start over. He felt that this was not good and that he had made a mistake by not seeing it coming. Thomas began making even more compromises by no longer trusting businesses, stocks, or much of anything else in relationship to money. There was a change of heart, and Thomas decided money was not a good "cause." It was a fleeting thing, not good at all. Instead he went inside of himself and believed this was good as the kingdom of God is within.

That state of mind did not last after he inherited money from his father. The money allowed him to drink and party a lot. He retired from teaching and had a good time, although he was still involved in good causes. At the time of his death, Thomas was in his late fifties and alone. He had always been alone and never married. He did not believe in permanency. Excessive drinking had damaged his health. Thomas felt disappointment but did not seem to be aware that this was his last day. The thoughts he had just before his spirit exited the body were that if he had to do it again, he would be a Franciscan teacher and take a vow of poverty "because you can't take anything with you. You come into this world with nothing and leave with nothing. The best way to be in this world is with nothing." After lifting out of the body and reviewing that life, Joe was able to see that it was an unhappy, self-absorbed, but partially successful life. It had meaning to an extent, but no real spirituality. He had ambition but no self-control and was caught up in materialism which has no true worth. The thought that he does not need anything, that material possessions have no value, is probably not beneficial in this extreme in his current life although Joe believes that all material things are dead things, ashes. After we discussed this, he agreed that some material things are beneficial in that they enhance the spiritual side of life. There are things that have value, so he made a division between the selfish part of the material that was limiting him which he released, and that which was beneficial which he kept. He learned and taught a great deal as Thomas Duffy, but he misapplied it. Too much learning gave him a strong ego. And too much interest in power misdirected his energies, and having money by accident gave him too much luxury and too many good times. When he once again connected with God's energy as his spirit moved up into the Light, it was very awesome and the only thing worth pursuing, he said.

The next stop was intended to be the lifetime in which he had his highest spiritual connection. Joe said that it was his current life in the 1960's when he was in the eighth grade and served as an altar boy at the local Catholic Church. This was the time when he was a true believer, but lost it later.

I gently tried to guide him to a lifetime prior to this as he was resistant at first. Finally, he went to 1923 to a place where the people were wearing gray and the men had on strange suits and ties that were reminiscent of Calvin Coolidge. The women had on so much clothing so that they seemed to be suffocating. He was a twenty-year-old man named Robert McManus living in Buffalo, New York and just starting out in life trying to find his vocation. Though Robert had some college education, he had not yet found his true interest but thought he would like to work in a corporation that had a future, hopefully in New York on Wall Street. Although he wanted one, he did not have a family because he believed he lacked sufficient funds to support it. He was a Unitarian and believed in the Spirit, in a higher consciousness, and in the fact that there are no real answers. Part of his belief system was that God is too complex for man to describe. One can only feel the spirit of God or the Universal Mind. Robert reported that most people find Unitarians strange, but that Buffalo is a very tolerant city with much diversity of opinion and many different sects. It has a good cross-section of people, ideas, industry, and political persuasions. It is a good mix, a good place.

Robert eventually purchased a bookstore in Albany, New York. He was very happy selling books, drinking coffee, and engaging in conversations with his customers. Everyone in the town knew him. He also smoked, and it affected his lungs. When he was in his fifties, Robert died of lung cancer. As he was about to leave that body, he vowed not to smoke if he ever got the chance to live again. Then he wondered to whom he was going to leave all the books. He also wished he had found more answers; he never did solidify his spiritual connection. The one vow he made was to never smoke and drink again. When Joe's spirit was once again in the Light, he realized the truths of the spiritual quest are all inside of us; we just have to find them. This felt liberating.

When I asked Joe's Higher Self why it had picked the lifetimes of Thomas and Robert for him to see, I was told that they most closely parallel his present state and show a progression of thinking which will lead him to ultimate self-realization Also, Joe *did not want to go back to a life* prior to the late nineteenth century if he lived in the United States. He believed for some reason that he was going to learn only from the end of the nineteenth and the twentieth centuries and anything earlier would be unproductive. As a result, he placed obstacles in the way of accessing them. These lives were chosen because he was moving in a parallel direction. Then he told me something very important. He said that there was a divided self; he was in conflict between his past and future because of past experiences that he was afraid to relive. He knew that there was a lot of repression and it was too much to lift.

This is a very important point. Regression work is not a toy and must be treated with respect. I am not a trained psychologist and must operate within the limits of my professional abilities. It also reinforces the fact that the Higher Self will allow us to "remember" only what we are ready to deal with. We should never push past the roadblocks that are placed in the way for our protection. Joe's Higher Self was very clear that these memories were all that he could allow himself to bring to consciousness at this time. This was even more apparent when he looked down at his life from the astral plane and saw a volcano erupting. It was very deep. There were dark clouds over it with some light at the top, so I removed him even further from this scene until he saw sunshine, fresh air, mountains. He finally felt safe there. His Higher Self told Joe that he needs to learn to be at peace, not to worry, to take life as it comes, to be in the moment, to be here now, and not to fight the forces within him but to flow with them because he may not be cognizant of the harmony he needs to attune with.

To answer the question of why these lives were so recent, his Higher Self said that it was only as much as Joe could handle. The message for him to be gained from revisiting these incarnations was that things that were tried then did not come to happy conclusions, instead things need to be tried with the highest spiritual quest and that peace could come by not being in so much of a hurry. The fact that these lifetimes overlapped in time raised questions, but the answer was that "**time does not really exist. Time — past, present, and future — are all the same. It is only the corners of the mind that cloud it.**"

His Higher Self wanted Joe to gain as a result of these experiences and to fear not — to fear no man or woman. For his own spiritual growth Joe needs to let go of worry about money; he should let things happen naturally and not to force them; he should not hurry things because that is when mistakes are made. Let things come naturally by themselves. That is the truest and best way for him to proceed. He also needs to think outside of the box and be less self-contained. Instead he was advised to be more open and let in the spirits of God's kingdom and not to put up barriers to other influences, thoughts, reasoning, and friends' ideas that were not the same as his own. Other guidance included the suggestion that he not be intolerant of other people and instead listen to others carefully and connect with them. Most importantly, do not be so worried, and **do not feel like a victim**.

I asked about the Crusades and was informed that he has a romantic connection with it. In his love of history this is the time he is most fixated on. It was a time of greatness and extraordinary deeds, a time of true religion which was uncorrupted in its beginning. It was a time when a renaissance of learning occurred when East met West. It was a time of awesome deeds and bravery. Surprisingly, there were health issues that were obstructing Joe from retrieving any information about his participation in the Crusades. Instead he received advice to resist the will of others who would lead him astray. He was told just to throw them aside to the dirt and go with the gold. He was advised to ignore intrusions and not let them affect his stream of consciousness and spiritual quest. His Higher

Self told him to relax and have more fun, while at the same time stay true to his vision. "That which is visualized must be conceived. If the wish is willed, the means will be found. The will must be strengthened to fulfill the wish. The means themselves are not important; they will be given." His Higher Self agreed that it would be beneficial to send someone to guide Joe and facilitate his increase in consciousness. Joe requested this, and the Universe will respond.

It was time to conclude the regression, although Joe was enjoying where he was so much that he was reluctant to return. When he did come back to waking consciousness, he said that this session was of very much benefit to him and that he would be more capable of putting aside distractions. Then when I spoke to him a few days later, Joe said that he was really relaxed, uplifted, and mellow. In fact, other people at the senior center he attends noticed the change and asked, "What's different about you?"

The overlapping timeframes of the lives of Joe—the man in Hawaii, the young writer, Thomas Duffy, and Robert McManus—would seem to indicate that Joe was accessing parallel incarnations of his soul. If time were linear, these could not have been Joe's past-lives. This experience, however, could be his Higher Self showing him that his soul is exploring different possibilities of existence simultaneously. Perhaps they are lives in this universe in different bodies or even incarnations in parallel universes. This is possible because, as we know, there is no time. Through their emergence in his past-life recall, these parallel or overlapping existences present enigmas for him to solve and are also an opportunity for him to integrate their truths into his life.

Our spiritual lessons are at the core of why we are here. Whether those lessons take us on a search that leads to past-lives or parallel lives, they all meet at the same place—where we are right now and where our soul wants us to be. This type of exploration can take us to new dimensions of understanding in that quest. Overcoming patterns, limitations, and choices of the past are all part of our soul growth. Our spiritual development must first begin right there at the spiritual. It is then that the mind, or the mental, can build it into our physical existence. We don't have to wait for a crisis to reassess where we are. We can chose differently NOW.

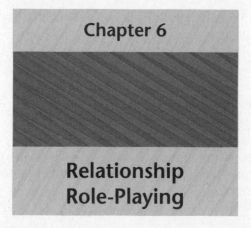

Chapter 6

Relationship Role-Playing

"Know that no meeting with other individuals is chance. Rather should it be—and is—as an opportunity not only for self-expression but for the expression of that for which the real self stands." 1248-1

Relationship challenges offer tremendous insights into our inner self and are vehicles of opportunity for soul growth. How we respond to others and to situations determines to some degree how other people and the universe respond to us. In the journey of life we can use our relationship opportunities as spiritual gateways to learn, grow, heal, and live more joyful lives filled with the love and support of others.

Soul Groups

Imagine that you are part of a theater ensemble of about fifteen people who have worked together for many years. The group meets after a play's closing to assess its successes and failures and to review individual performances. When that is done, a new script is chosen, the lead actor selected, and the secondary parts assigned. You each like to switch roles because it challenges you, adds to your individual capabilities and talents, and also allows for strengthening those aspects which are weaker. Sometimes you get stuck playing the same role over and over wanting to "get it right" or helping another of the actors improve. Other times you accept a role that stretches you beyond what you think you are capable of doing, but the ensemble members are there to support you. This is not unlike a soul group—a few like-minded souls at the same level of spiritual development who work together through time to achieve their common goals.

Michael Newton, PhD has done some groundbreaking hypnosis work in which he takes his clients back to the time between lives. His subjects have reported returning to a small group of souls, their soul group, when they leave their earthly bodies. The primary group consists of usually between ten to twenty souls, while secondary groups may include up to a thousand souls. Family and important friends in our lives are often members of our soul group who show up together life after life. An example of a secondary group might be the many people the A.R.E. has attracted who are interested in ancient Egypt and could have been part of a larger soul group that lived during the time of the building of the pyramids and of Ra Ta, an earlier incarnation of Edgar Cayce.

Members of a soul group have been together through time as we know it. When we return to the spirit world, they are there to greet us and assist in the healing process, if necessary. These souls lend their support and provide insights as we review the life we have just left and make decisions about the next one. With the help of our guides during the pre-birth planning process, we determine the circumstances of our next adventure in the physical realm. It may be necessary for us to replay a role we have enacted many times before or switch parts with someone else to balance the karma and gain greater understanding of the impact of our words and actions. The cast of characters is set by entering into agreements and contracts with various members of our soul group or others in adjacent soul groups. These contracts define the nature of the relationships as well as the situations and opportunities that will be presented. Some of these arrangements may be difficult for the members to agree to as they love each other, but it is their love that prompts them to do what is necessary for the resolution of karma and for the learning necessary in the fulfillment of the destiny of each in the group.

Family Circumstances

The role we assume when we incarnate, therefore, is predetermined by us before our spirit enters the body and we announce ourselves with our first cry. The conditions into which we are born—sex, race, religion, country, type of family, etc.—are part of the script we picked for a divine purpose. For some, a loving family is what is needed to support our life lessons, while for others, the family is the lesson. Once we are here, we may question how we could have decided to be part of a family that is so very different from us or why we would have chosen to come into a situation that is extremely difficult. Many decide to be born into dysfunctional families of greater or lesser degree with an ancestral line that may include alcoholism, drug abuse, physical, sexual, mental, and/or emotional abuse. Others purposefully come into a situation in which they know that they will not receive the nurturing and comfort expected from parents or caretakers, perhaps one in which they do not even have an awareness that love and a feeling of security exist. It is possible, however, that because of free will choices of other participants, such as the mother or father, the conditions are no longer those we chose to experience. At this point we may decide to exit and try again or to stay and adjust to what is.

Members of our earthly family and their baggage set the stage for our life's scenario and trigger the lessons we have chosen to learn. Although blood ties might very well indicate membership within the same soul group, our earthly relationships may not always be amicable. Brothers may be very close, or they may be at loggerheads with each other, competing for rewards and attention. Sisters can have the best of relationships, or they can be at such odds that they refuse to speak to each other for years.

From our physical perspective it seems inconceivable that we would have selected the circumstances of our existence if they are unpleasant, but our soul seeks opportunities to complete its journey of returning *home* by creating conditions that have the potential for moving us closer to that goal. If we keep repeating our negative patterns, especially in regard to our relationships, and do not make appropriate changes, the grip of karma continues to enslave us. The cycle can be broken by learning to respond in ways that are loving and kind and move us into a state of grace. Once the lesson is learned, it no longer needs to be repeated although we might need to tackle another aspect of it at a deeper level in the future. When these barriers to establishing loving relationships with others have been breached, love is, then, free to enter. With this knowledge, although perhaps not with full understanding, comes the help to shift us from thinking of ourselves as helpless victims to taking accountability for what we create in our lives, especially in regard to relationships.

Loving Relationships

Other important people in our lives, in addition to family, may also have been with us in prior ones. Loved ones, friends, and acquaintances make our lives richer and support us in our journey. They make us laugh and cry and sometimes share our greatest adventures. The facets of their personalities can reflect back to us our true essence, and they can also be a projection of aspects of ourselves we are usually unaware of, casting a light on our shadow side. They provide mirrors to those patterns that, at least on a soul level, we desire to transform. It may not be easy for us to recognize that what they are reflecting back to us is us, but it is desirable to see ourselves in them if we want to take an easier road for learning our relationship lessons. Those whom we love and who love us can provide a graceful way for us to choose more wisely, transform negative patterns, and come into wholeness, if we would only look in their mirror.

Negative or Difficult Relationships

Unhealthy relationships, on the other hand, present more obvious and difficult learning experiences. These are the ones that offer the greatest opportunities for soul growth as they very often embody our soul lessons and reinforce those first presented by our family or childhood situations. Negative relationships help us face our less than positive traits and limiting beliefs. They provide a vehicle for us to discover choices more in keeping with our best interests as we find a better way of interacting with others. In all of this, we are not victims. We are not being punished. Those very people who are the most antagonistic in our lives may have contracted with us to bring to the surface engrained habits or karma that we have come to clean out. Their "job" is to keep throwing out the bait, pushing and prodding with their words and actions over and over again until we recognize that responding in the same way is no longer acceptable and we say *enough!* It is, then, that we have the greatest opportunity for uncovering the root cause of this pattern in our lives. Once we do that, the real work begins because after recognizing it and understanding why it is happening, we must learn a new way or be forced to live with it. The reward comes when we consciously, step by step, transform this deeply ingrained negative imprint. When that is done, there may be a positive shift in our old relationship, or we may find that a different kind of person is now energetically drawn to us, the kind who loves us and enriches our lives.

Healing Relationships through Past-Life Regression

Our fellow travelers can help us identify our strengths and weaknesses if we look for the message they convey through the nature of our relationship with them. They may even assist by angering or frightening us with their words and actions. How we respond when this happens determines whether we have learned the lesson or if the cycle needs to be repeated so that we might have the opportunity to choose differently. Past-life regression therapy is a wonderful tool to gain insights into the nature of the prior relationship with those in our lives, to understand what we need to do to make course corrections, and to aid in the healing. Although not necessary, the process can be enhanced by identifying the nature of the relationships we have had throughout our lives. If there is a negative, recurring pattern, especially in love relationships—such as continually being abandoned, abused, used, or choosing someone who is unavailable—this is something that would benefit further exploration. If there are those from whom we have closed ourselves off, either a person or group of people, revisiting the originating reasons could transform the nature of the relationship and release the knots of energy that keep us stuck. The potential available through regression is amplified by choosing to heal unresolved issues with others in addition to understanding the nature of the difficulty and then using the power of forgiveness to catalyze what could be characterized as an alchemical change.

People who have experienced this type of regression therapy often report that their relationship situations have changed completely. Perhaps the others have changed, but more likely it is the individual who has practiced forgiveness, and what he/she now sees being reflected back from others is actually him/her, the transformed person. He/she also notices that people representative of the negative recurring pattern are no longer attracted to him/her and are replaced by more positive and loving people. You can use the *past-life regression to heal a difficult relationship* so that your own interrelationships can blossom.

Past-Life Regression to Heal a Relationship

When you are ready to begin, close your eyes ...With your dominant hand very slowly draw the numbers 0 though 9 in the air ... At the same time trace those same numbers with your eyes without moving your head ...Then, relax, lower your hand, close your eyes, and sink into a deep state of stillness and peace ... Stay here for as long as you chose.

When you are ready to continue, invite the protective white light of Spirit to enter in through your crown chakra. As it moves through your body and mind, it soothes and relaxes you as you let go of any stress and tension. Imagine it flowing through your scalp and forehead ... down your face and the back of your head ...all around your neck ...into your shoulders ...arms ...hands and fingers ...through your chest and torso ... your hips ... down your legs ... and down through your feet and toes ... Breathe deeply and exhale slowly ... Feel the white light caressing and infusing your being, protecting you and preparing you to enter the Place of Forgiveness and Reconciliation.

Now ask your Higher Self to join you ... and as you do, you see your Higher Self waiting for you in front of a gate surrounded by trees ...This is the entrance to the Contemplation Grounds ... At the very center of these grounds is the sacred fire in the Place of Forgiveness and Reconciliation ... where you will heal your relationship with a person with whom you have or have had difficulties ... or even with yourself.

You greet your Higher Self ... Open the gate and walk together through the opening into the Contemplation Grounds ... They are nestled in a natural wooded setting ... You can hear the birds singing ... and smell the wonderful fragrance of the flowers and the pine trees ... It is quiet, secluded, and totally safe and protected here ... Feel the healing energy of this special place ... this place that has hosted many others who have come here before you to trans-form difficult relationships ... Just being in this place gives you a sense of deep peace and calm ... and a knowing that you are on the right path.

You see a bench beneath the trees ... Go to it, and you and your Higher Self take a moment to sit there in preparation for the healing work that is about to begin ... Take time to dialogue with your Higher Self and ask questions or ask for any guidance you desire ... Now you are ready to continue ... You and your Higher Self get up from the bench and continue walking down the path ... following the guideposts that point the way to the Place of Forgiveness and Reconciliation ... It is in a clearing at the center of the Grounds ... You reach there now ... This place is inviting, and you feel surrounded by unconditional love.

Here, at the very heart of the clearing, you see the eternal flame of the sacred fire burning in the fire pit ... It is contained in a special receptacle set in a hollow in the ground surrounded by a ring of copper ... You and your Higher Self sit on the ground at a comfortable distance from the fire ... As the first step in the work you are about to do ... set your intention to revisit the initial life that caused this difficult relationship pattern to be formed ... This enlists the aid of Spirit ... Be still in that connection.

Now slowly become aware of the person with whom you are having, or have had, a difficult or unhealthy relationship (or a version of yourself) entering the clearing and sitting down on the opposite side of the fire ... The reconciliation is about to begin.

Look deep into this person's eyes through the flames of the fire. As you con-tinue to look deeper and deeper, you notice this person beginning to change ... Perhaps she or he is becoming younger or older, the color of hair, eyes, or skin morphing into someone else in appearance ... The clothing is no longer the same ...Continue focusing on the eyes through the flames of the fire ...letting the eyes draw you into a different setting, into another place and time ...in some way re-experiencing this life in which the dynamic of your relationship was created ...Moving forward or backward through the events of that life until you have an understanding of what caused the pattern ...Ask your Higher Self to help you recognize how this pattern has also affected other relationships in your life ...From a soul level, understand now what work you must do to release the pattern and change the nature of your relationship to one that is more positive ...When you have that understanding and know what is required of you, throw your hurt, blockages, anger, fear, and all other negative emotions into the sacred fire for purification and transformation ...Watch what happens as a result ...Now it is time for you to forgive him or her ...not forgiving the acts committed or words said, but forgiving this person at a soul level, so that you are no longer influenced negatively by him or her ...Speak directly to his or her Higher Self ...and when you have forgiven, send that person blessings ...See this person and your relationship in a different light as you continue to gaze into the eyes through the flames of the purifying fire ...This part is done ...The next step is to forgive yourself ...Do that now ...Become aware of how your own image has changed as it is reflected back to you by the fire ...Feel how that feels ...Commit to making any other adjustments to your words, your thinking, or actions based on what you learned while revisiting this past-life ...Experience the healing light of Spirit cleansing and healing both of you now ...The reconciliation is complete ...and the other person slowly begins to fade from sight.

Now it is time to return, having done the work you came here to do ...You and your Higher Self leave this sacred place of forgiveness and reconciliation and walk back through the open gate, closing it behind you ...Thank your Higher Self and say goodbye ...You are ready to return to the present, with your energies aligned and balanced ...You feel calm and at peace for having done this healing work ...knowing this relationship and the deeper pattern has been transformed ...You take a deep breath, exhale and prepare to come back ...counting down from 20 to 1 ...20 ...19 ...18 ...17 ...16 ...15 ...14 ...13 ...12 ...11 ...coming back ...10 ...9 ...8 ...7 ...6 ...5 ...Energy moving through your body now ...4 ...3 ...2 ...1 ...Take a deep breath ...Feeling good ...and when you are ready ...exhale and open your eyes.

Regressions—Repairing Relationship Patterns

When you read the following reports of relationship regressions, note the change in perspective and the growth of understanding gained by these individuals who journeyed back to their pasts. In many cases they were able to uncover their sometimes surprising connections, to forgive themselves and others, and to heal their energetic wounds. In the future their associations with their loved ones and with all those who come into their lives will be more positive, and they will have reaped the fruits of their efforts.

JULIO AND THE OTHER SIDE OF THE ROMAN COIN

Julio has done a number of past-life regressions in the past few years to gain insights into how to address various issues in his life. He recently participated in a group regression I conducted that was directed toward healing a relationship difficulty. He chose to work on a very painful incident that happened with his eldest son several years after Julio and his wife divorced. At the time of the incident his son was seventeen, and they had a confrontation that Julio remembers very vividly. During this conflict, his son, who normally hid his emotions, said, "It's too late," meaning that it was too late to have a close father-son relationship. It hit Julio at the heart level because he was trying very hard to create a family environment but recognized that damage had been done to both of his sons because of the divorce. However, he also knows that it is never too late for healing to occur.

During the regression Julio looked into the eyes of his son through the flames. As he did that, his son morphed into his father in a prior life—a bigger and hairier man wearing a Roman uniform. Julio recognized him because the eyes were the same. In that life their relationship was strained because he was disappointed with Julio as a son. The father was a warrior—strong, aggressive, a man's man. Even though Julio was a soldier, he just did not measure up to his father's idea of a man; he perceived Julio as a weakling. Julio was a soldier in name but not a warrior like his father.

As the scene played out, Julio recognized that he and his son's difficulties in this life are karmic. In some way he learned that he is experiencing the kind of pain he inflicted in that past-life. It was unclear at the time exactly what this referred to. However, Julio recognizes that he has gained from their father-son relationship in this life because his son has taught him the meaning of unconditional love.

Julio felt that the fire was very cleansing. He forgave himself for how he had treated or acted toward this person who was his father in that former time. Now when he thinks about the confrontation they had when his son was a teenager, Julio no longer sees it as a painful experience but rather an opportunity of **growth through forgiveness**.

He felt that this might not be the final resolution of this issue [Doing a regression as part of a group without the potential for interaction can limit the healing potential.]. Nonetheless, he released some of the pain and will no longer think of it in the same way. He has gained a deeper level of understanding—a very positive benefit resulting from first knowing how the dynamic of their relationship was created, doing the spiritual work necessary, and then finally seeing it as a stepping stone.

A short time after the regression, Julio recognized that this was the same life we had explored in a previous regression which probed for the initial cause of injuries he sustained while playing football when he was seventeen. Those injuries almost killed him. In the Roman life he remembered being left to die on the battlefield and feeling abandoned [perhaps by his father]. He came into this life to heal that feeling of abandonment. As we discussed this further, he came to realize that the issue of abandonment was at the core of his difficulty with his son. His son felt abandoned by Julio because of the divorce even though both he and his brother lived with Julio. He had never abandoned them. That is what the reversal meant. As

Cayce told in one of his readings, the soul inherits what it has built in its previous experiences and relationships with others. This happens so that we might learn a better way, and Julio is working very hard to live that better way with his sons. He sent me an e-mail after the regression writing, "I've benefitted greatly and on multiple levels. Thank you."

STACEY'S NEED TO DO IT ALL

The importance of first gaining clarity about your question or the information you are seeking was borne out in my interview with Stacey before her regression. Initially she wanted to focus on how her father related to other members of the family and how that, in turn, affected her. Her mother and father were divorced when she was nine. Although she lives near her father and is in contact with him, he has not played an active part of her life. He has been emotionally unavailable and seems more absorbed in himself and his girlfriend than in her and her family. After some probing she realized that what she really wanted to learn about and heal was her own relationship with her father. This was her real question and the one she decided to explore by revisiting the past-life that had created the disengaged nature of their association.

During her prior life recall, Stacey found herself as a very young girl in a situation in which her father was screaming and yelling and then left. Her mother was scared and stood behind her. The rest of the family lined up behind the mother. They had put the smallest one (Stacey) up front as protection for them.

Stacey's father did not really talk to her or the others. He was a farmer and was either working in the fields or was gone somewhere. It seemed to Stacey as if he were gone all the time, and she did not think he was a good man. It made her sad and, at the same time, glad that he was not around much — sad because of the nature of their relationship and glad because of his emotional outbreaks when he was at home.

When she was able to observe him at a soul-level, Stacey discovered that her father, the farmer, was very sad because he did not know how to connect with others, especially his family. He was angry with himself and blamed everyone else for his angry actions. This made him even meaner.

When I asked Stacey what her soul lessons were from this life and this relationship pattern (discovering these lessons is part of what make these regressions transformative), she said that it was not to take it personally. She must ask for help when she needs it, and she cannot protect everybody. In that life and in some respects in the current one, she was protecting her family from him even though she was a little girl. She has the same lessons to learn in this life.

This pattern has affected the quality of her relationships because she acts as if she does not need anybody else. "I can take care of it on my own, and I don't need anybody's help," Stacey said. She takes on more than she can handle. She pushes others away and takes control of the situation. She forgave herself and wants to change the pattern. In the future when she recognizes that she is trying to control a situation, she will try to **ask for help** and **let go of trying to control each and every aspect**.

Stacey learned that she was holding her anger in her back, neck, and right wrist as her way of blaming him for not being there for her. She threw it into the fire. At first when she forgave him at the Higher Self level, he closed up like a little child. That action made her want to protect him. Immediately she recognized this as a reflection of her unhealthy pattern. As soon as she acknowledged it, he became more open, and this felt better to her. He became more respectful and quieter. She felt herself become more childlike, softer, and more at peace.

The next day Stacey's father came to visit her and gave her tomatoes from his garden. He was calmer than normal—all this just twelve hours after her regression!

ANN'S NEEDY MEN

Ann is a counselor in her professional life. She has never had any trouble attracting men, often dating more than one at a time. However, these relationships have not been satisfactory because it seemed that all of these men had one common quality—they were needy. They wanted all her energy, time, attention, and required that nothing else to be important to her but them. She desired to change this pattern so that she could attract a man who would provide a more balanced approach to the relationship, allowing her to have her own space when she chose and, at the same time, bring joy and love into her life.

Doing this regression necessitated one of the more unusual arrangements for conducting it as Ann lives in another state. When I was in her area, I had worked face-to-face with her. This time, however, we did the regression over the phone, using a speaker phone. A close friend stood by her to relay information between the two of us if the need arose. It did not.

In our pre-regression discussion, Ann did not think that any of the men in her life, past or present, truly represented the pattern she wanted to access in a past-life. Instead, she decided to work with herself as the other person at the Place of Forgiveness and Reconciliation. While looking into her own eyes across the fire, she saw her face begin to change. With little effort she was back in a rough-looking house, perhaps a log cabin, as a female in her twenties.

The significant event Ann re-experienced in that life, the one in which this negative pattern with men was initiated, involved her father then. [Ann did not recognize him as anyone she knew in her current life.] In the event she revisited, her father slapped her in the face. As he hit her, he told her that she was bad, naughty because she had disobeyed him. This punishment resulted from her walking through the woods after he told her not to leave the house. It was a very innocent trip; she had merely spent time by a stream there and then went immediately back home. He punished her for disobeying him and did not believe her when she told him where she had been. This was not the first time he had hit her.

This incident, and probably the energy built up from the accumulation of similar incidences, caused her to create a thought form that men are not trustworthy. They are not wise; they do not believe what women say, and they think women should be punished. When Ann looked at the scene from above the body, she observed that her father's issues were about control and his belief about what women must do, while her issue was about appropriate boundaries. Her energy, held in the thought form, was purified, and she reclaimed it. This changed the dynamics of their relationship, and in the replaying of this event, her father's whole attitude changed as she watched him. He was smiling, put his hands down, and believed what she had told him. Ann experienced an easy, flowing energy, but she had one more step—that was to forgive herself for not doing what she knew to do—and she did this.

When she moved forward to the end of her life, she was at peace. She saw herself in a cabin lying on the floor with a small white cap on her head and looking very peaceful. There was a big brown bear outside the door, but it was not scary. To her, it represented the maleness that can now be incorporated into her life in a healthy way. If necessary, in the future she can now take a step back in a relationship without feeling anger.

Viewing how these changes will now play out in her life, Ann saw herself feeling very peaceful in a church on the East Coast to where she will be moving soon. A man was striding up the aisle toward her. He was holding both hands out to her in welcome. The sense was, "Hello, old friend." Their relationship was peaceful and joyful. The setting then changed to the A.R.E. parking lot in Virginia Beach. Ann was scanning all the buildings looking for clues as to why she was seeing this. She sensed that soon there would be a task or mission involving the A.R.E. that she and this man would be working on together.

We also did an energetic clearing of this pattern of attract-

ing needy men. At this point Ann began experiencing an emotional feeling of irritation in her heart area and third chakra.
After identifying the tension as a dark energy of some kind, it
was removed. Next, she felt a queasy, unsafe feeling in the third
chakra. This was residual energy stuck there from this past-
life. After the energy was purified in the Light, she reclaimed it
in present time and saw a single red rose with a long stem in its
place. The rose was a very positive symbol for her.

As we closed the regression, Ann was feeling good — strong
and healthy, expecting a good day. Interestingly, she felt taller.
She then shared that she had been feeling irritated before the
session began. Often our spirit is working on the issue even
before we begin to tackle it on a conscious level. The energy
and information is at the surface of our awareness when we
start our healing process. Ann was ready, and she is confident
that her relationship with men in the future will be more **balanced and mutually satisfying** than in the past.

STEPHANIE'S ARMOR

Although Stephanie was very anxious to continue the extensive and intensive work she had been doing on her relationship
patterns, something was blocking her. On the first regression
attempt she sorted through the list of important people in her
life and could not settle on anyone, thinking she had already
done the work necessary with them. Although normally able to
go into a deep trance state almost instantly, when she closed
her eyes this time, she could do nothing more than drift around.
On the second attempt she fell asleep. Before trying for the
third time, we talked about her list of potential candidates in
more detail. The name of her former husband who had been
mentally and physically abusive to her kept surfacing even
though she thought she had completed her forgiveness work
with him. When she finally said, "He made me feel like nothing," we knew that this relationship should be the focus of the
regression.

Stephanie was then easily able to access their past-life together in a Native American village. The first thing she said was, "I'm very cold. It is very cold." She was a very frightened and cold fourteen- or fifteen-year-old female who had just been given to the son of the chief of another tribe to be his wife. This man, her abusive ex-husband in this life, was very angry and also very cruel.

After they had a child, he killed it in a fit of anger. She tried to run away, but he hunted her down and beat her. She tried to hide from him as much as possible. The members of his tribe would have nothing to do with her because she was an outsider and her husband hated her and did not want her. Not surprisingly, she was extremely frightened and angry although it took some delving for her to discover this anger. Eventually he left her out in the cold, and she froze to death.

Just as her spirit was about to leave that body, her thought was, "I am sorry you hated me. I guess I hated me, too." As she looked back at that life after her death, Stephanie could see how very wounded he was and that this situation was not her fault. She was surprised to discover that she had been a very beautiful woman and that perhaps was why the others in his tribe hated her. Even though her husband was so cruel, her sweet spirit was never broken.

In exploring how this pattern impacted her life as Stephanie, she realized that it limited her in coming into her potential when she was younger. Another insight she gained—one that she had not anticipated when we began the session—was that this life with him, if perhaps not the original cause, contributed to her current weight issue. Her husband in that life beat her with his hands and fists when he was displeased and gave her food as a reward or withheld it as punishment. She never had enough food then, and her deathbed vow was that she would never go hungry again. Vows made at the time of death are extremely powerful, and we did the work necessary to release this one.

On a subconscious level, Stephanie still held a part of a multifaceted belief that she had to please men in order to be loved although she had done a lot of previous work around that very issue. This aspect of the belief was that if she did not do everything for them, she would be hit or beaten again. In the present life, these two souls had replayed that same pattern to provide them both the opportunity for individual transformation. Stephanie recognized that this pattern made her fearful of men.

In reviewing this life and its lessons, the message she received was, **"I have to be true to me, to my feelings. I have to like me. I have to be all that I can be. Nobody else can affect that** anymore."

Before the regression ended, she forgave him and herself for their parts in this dynamic. She put all of her anger, fear, blockages, and other negative emotions regarding their relationship into the fire. Then she experienced the layers of armor being cut away and thrown into the fire also. As she left the scene, she saw them both dancing around the fire.

Although there was more work yet to be done, this piece was necessary to allow the next step of releasing the armor on the physical level to occur. She took that next step when we did a mindwalking session.

LORRAINE'S RELATIONSHIP WITH MEN

When Lorraine arrived for her regression, she told me she wanted to understand why she could not get married again. She was always quite shy with men. She quit drinking seven years ago even though her "liquid courage" had enabled her to let her guard down. Perhaps, because she no longer had alcohol speak for her, she has not had a meaningful relationship since she stopped.

As background, her dad was very insulting toward her mother, and Lorraine vowed that she would never get herself into that same type of situation. She ran away from home and married at sixteen. Her underlying belief was that all men are condescending, insulting, and want to control women. She had spent several years in traditional psychotherapy addressing her father issues. In the past Lorraine attracted many men like her father, and they confirmed her belief.

Lorraine was somewhat apprehensive to open up to a past-life reenactment. She was fearful because she sensed that she had been burned at the stake and that this was related to her current deep-seated distrust of men. Nevertheless, the desire for a significant relationship with a man overrode her concern.

At the start of the regression Lorraine found herself walking down stairs descending into darkness and then discovered herself as a young Native American woman nineteen- or twenty-years-old. This woman was a lot smaller than Lorraine. When I instructed her to look down at her feet and she saw that she was wearing moccasins, she became anxious, immediately knowing that something bad was going to happen. I directed her to go back in time prior to the event, and she moved back to a year earlier.

Then she was in a village by the river somewhere in America, perhaps along the Mississippi. The tribe lived in permanent structures that looked like huts. Everyone was happy, and they helped each other. This was not a warring tribe. She and a young man planned to marry, and she liked him. He was more serious than she; she was fun-loving but shy.

Members of another tribe attacked the village. Everything they had was stolen. She was violently raped, and both her younger brother and sister witnessed this. She tried to protect the children but was pulled by her hair at knife point and taken away to the camp of this violent tribe. They tied her up to a stake, and because she was swearing at them, they thought she was more trouble than she was worth and abandoned her to the elements. She eventually died, still tied to the stake.

This had been her only experience with sex in that life, and it was very violent. Her thought prior to dying was that men are so violent and cruel. She vowed, "I am not going to be trusting. I am going to be protected. I am not going to be vulner-

able. This won't happen; I will not be physically vulnerable."
In current time she still had a general feeling that this is how
everything works and that in some way she should protect children. Lorraine is a teacher, and that career choice reflects the
need to watch over and safeguard the young because she was
unable to help her brother and sister in this Native American
life.

When her spirit left the body, she looked down at herself
tied to the post where she had starved. It was clear to her that
her people were peace-loving. They were very unsuspecting
and were not prepared for what happened, and personally, she
had not had any weapons to protect herself. In asking for guidance for what needed to be done to change the thoughts that
kept recreating this relationship pattern of the past, surprisingly the first thing she received was that she should quit smoking. [Smoking is frequently used to form a protective barrier to
keep people out. This is something Lorraine may be able to
tackle now.] She then did the necessary forgiveness work so
that she can now trust her intuition with men and lower her
guard because she can **trust her inner knowing** about their
nature.

Lorraine told me that her friends have advised her that she
was somewhat cutting and harsh and that people sensed hard-
ness in her. This puts people off and keeps them at a distance.
She acknowledged this and told me that she never let anyone
see her vulnerability. She said, "I still have a mouth," and realized that in a sense, up till now, she was still swearing at the
men from the other tribe who took her—recreating the same
pattern of "mouthing off" for protection that she exhibited in
the past-life. This led to her physical demise in that life and has
contributed to the demise of relationships in this one. Her
words, in essence, create a hard shell and point to a habit or
trait that deserves more attention. She learned during this healing process that she does not need such a sharp tongue as a
protection, and it, in fact, never did protect her.

Before finishing we cleared the energy of being hurt. To Lorraine it seemed like a big hammer slamming down on her heart and bruising her energy. Energy cords were removed from her heart area. Work was also done on her second chakra where she felt very vulnerable and on her root chakra.

The image of her being left to die tied at the stake would not leave her mind so I suggested that she view herself as an action heroine who could come to the rescue. She chose Rogue, a comic book character whose fear of her own power keeps her from having physical contact with others including her love interest—a reflection in some way of Lorraine's actual life. Rogue loosened her from the stake, and they both flew off together. The picture of her at the stake then disappeared.

I met with Lorraine a couple of months after her session and asked about any results she had noticed. Without going into detail, she shared that she did feel an "internal something" the week after the regression. Lorraine described it as "an internal coalescence" into a feeling of being more whole. Also, outwardly she is now less anxious and defensive around the opposite sex. She said there definitely was some sort of shift. This regression had been very real to her, and it seems to have provided an opening to a new beginning.

MARION'S LOVE OF ORDER

Marion is an on-going client who is using all her spiritual resources to change the pattern of "living with and taking care of crazy people" that has been with her throughout her entire life. Emotionally she cannot feel anything. She feels frozen and wonders what she is doing here.

Initially I regressed her to a neutral life so that she could ease into feeling emotions. Marion saw tall houses with different colors lined up on a street. She was a tall female living in France in the 1800's. Even though this supposedly was a neutral life, she experienced being tired and needing to rest. She was sad. It seemed that her whole life centered on taking care of the house, her husband, and their children.

The one thing that she really liked about this place was the tall houses. She enjoyed their structure, look, and orderliness. The comfort she felt in looking at them was held in her third chakra. She could feel the resonance there and through this remembrance learned that it is okay to feel the color and order which she so enjoyed.

Suddenly Marion felt this pleasant feeling leaving. Energetically her father in this life was taking it away. He likes messes and is a contributor to her relationship pattern. She became aware of a former agreement with him that she cannot have order in her life. This most certainly did not benefit her, so she broke it.

That transitioned her into a life in Germany in the 1700's in which she was in a cage. The man and woman who imprisoned her play the role of her current life parents. They were white, and she was a small brown male. As Marion looked at herself in the cage, she said that she looked awful. The people who kept her there were mean and it was scary. They believed it was their purpose to capture her because they did not like brown people.

Her final thoughts in that life were, "It is impossible to live like this. It is best to be gone. I need to be free. I don't need to be around people who take away my freedom." However, on a mental and emotional level that pattern is replaying in Marion's current life because the energetic tie remains waiting to be cut.

As the spirit of this imprisoned male transitioned into the Light, it looked down at that life to identify energy cords that were still connected to Marion—cords that drain energy when imprints from those past events and people are triggered. She chose to sever cords with her former husband, parents, and family members in their roles then. One cord which was attached at the heart connected to her and her sister. It was allowed to remain although it needed to be cleared. That was done.

At first Marion had difficulty forgiving her parents for their actions in that former life until I reminded her that she was doing this at a soul-level and not condoning what they had done. She forgave them not only for their actions and treatment of her in that life but also in this one. She discovered that she had been holding on to some of their energy and returned it. Marion recognized that this is another step in her process of healing on all levels and knows there is still more work to do to transform this network of negative patterns. The guidance she received during the session was that not only did she need to forgive all of these "crazy" people and keep doing what she has been doing, but that she always needs to do **proactive forgiving**. What that means will become clear to her in the days ahead because she is committed to making the needed changes.

Marion moved from the question of the cause of relationship patterns to asking why a door has not opened for her. The door she was looking for will lead to her doing something she wants to do with her life rather than what she is doing now, which is being a placeholder.

On the journey to a life related to the open door, Marion found herself as a fifty-year-old female riding on horseback around a big ranch. At this place people were helped spiritually and physically. People came here to stay to do their own inner work. The ranch had a big presentation hall. Many different kinds of spiritual work were practiced here, and various teachers and masters were there to guide others in their own traditions.

As she rode up to the ranch house, she commented that the house was big and nice. It was very orderly [again, she was drawn to those things that are orderly]. It felt good. Her husband, then, was one of her deceased husbands in this life.

At the retreat ranch she was the coordinator of everything — the huge kitchen, garden, flower gardens, and stables. She taught about nutrition and food. The teachings were well received, and she liked it. The garden was the favorite part for her, especially the organizing of it. It was a healthy life.

This was a place that Marion had seen in her mind for years, and she was drawn to it by the organization and orderliness of it. I then guided her into the near future. She saw this same ranch house, but it was by the ocean, which had not been in the visions before. The destiny she saw in the next few years is that she will have her own house which is round and has a warm fire inside. Speakers, teachers, and body workers will be available to those who come here. It felt right to her. When Marion started experiencing disbelief that it would ever happen, she had to sever energy cords from other family members who had their own agendas for her. Then she had to clear fear from her third chakra as she energetically opened the way for this to materialize in her life.

Marion is committed to do what is needed to bring this future to her. Now that there is a clear vision, she has more faith that it will happen.

Through a journey of discovery and reconciliation, Julio, Stacey, Ann, Stephanie, Lorraine, and Marion replaced trauma, hurt, guilt, and shame with peace and understanding. Some of the patterns they came into this experience to heal were revealed, and they did the spiritual work required to release themselves from the ties of the past that bind. In the future they will find that as they become more forgiving of themselves and others, the people who will now be attracted to them will be more compassionate and loving. These human connections will add to the richness of their existence and assist them in achieving their purpose in incarnating as they open to a higher potential for themselves and for humanity.

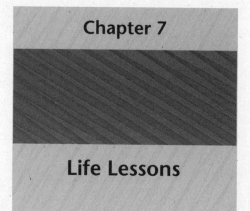

Chapter 7

Life Lessons

As we sift through the patterns of our lives and look closely enough, we discover a repetition that is almost like the beat of a heart. Life goes on, and we keep repeating our lessons in *oh* so many different variations until we recognize their threads running through the fabric of our existence, each one interweaving with the others to form a complex design. Some of the threads are created by love, kindness, and compassion, while others are built with anger, fear, and hatred. The Divine Plan would have us contemplate these later threads of disharmony to discern their origin. It is through recognition and understanding that we can begin to deconstruct them and craft them in a new way, transforming the pattern and therefore, the whole design to one that is more reflective of our true nature. When one thread changes, the whole cloth is affected; nothing remains the same. This is a journey of many lifetimes, a journey to wholeness.

When we die, we lay aside the physical body and the soul becomes our body in the spirit world. It is during this sojourn in the inter-life (the in-between state between lives, the *Bardo*) when we decide on the major life lessons we will work on in our next incarnation; we usually agree to three primary learnings to further our soul's growth. The choices of body, circumstances, and potential parents offered to us as part of this "educational plan" are determined to a large degree by our personal karma and our stage of development, with advanced souls being thought to have greater participation in the options presented to them. The selection is intended to provide us the cauldron necessary for purifying and freeing ourselves from our karmic influences as we accomplish these life-learning experiences. The people in our lives are also there for a purpose. They play their part in helping us to complete our soul's contract, as explained in Chapter 6 on relationships. By having greater clarity about our birth choices and the reason for them, it becomes easier to move from thinking that we are the victims of circumstances to acknowledging that we were instrumental in their selection. With that understanding, we can take responsibility for our lives and be more proactive in carrying out our mission.

Life Lesson at the Taj Mahal

Life lessons are ones that are so comprehensive and so significant that they reverberate throughout the physical, mental, emotional, and spiritual dimensions of our existence. Past-life and pre-birth vows and energy cords that connect one life to the next and attach one person to another are components of the task we have chosen and are part of the lessons.

One such example was reported in the July/August 2007 issue of A.R.E.'s *Venture Inward* magazine in an article I wrote titled "Love Manifested at the Taj Mahal." It detailed the unfolding of one of my own life lessons and the steps I took to complete it. The following is a shortened version. It includes all the relevant information necessary to show you how Spirit brought the pieces of my life together in such a way that I might resolve a persistent past-life pattern that was ready to be healed and release a vow that would have prevented me from completing my life's contract. This, perhaps, may provide insights for others.

The karmic blueprint began to surface when Frank, my husband of twenty-two years, died suddenly of a heart attack. During the days that followed his passing, I heard messages from him in my mind's ear. I was not surprised to "hear" from Frank. As a student of the Cayce readings and a hypnotherapist/past-life regressionist, I did not need to be convinced of the continuation of life after death. Communication from him reinforced my belief that we belonged to the same soul group and have been connected through the ages.

After his death I had an absolute knowing why, in past times, widows in India joined their husbands on the funeral pyre—a traditional Hindu custom called *sati* (now outlawed in India, but still practiced in some rural areas) which was often not the widow's choice. Initially, I thought that all widows had this same understanding but later learned that it was my experience, not theirs. Why the knowledge came to me after Frank's passing was not to be revealed until later.

Soon, thereafter, while attending the National Association of Transpersonal Hypnotherapists as a presenter, I met Dr. Sunny Satin. It was through him that I learned of the upcoming World Congress for Past-Life and Regression Therapies that was to be held in Delhi, India a little more than a year after Frank's death. I registered not only for the Congress but also for a past-life regression training course taught prior to the start. This would give me about a week and a half in India—an exciting thought because I had always felt for some unknown reason that going to India had to be earned.

In preparation for the trip I read a book about Indian customs and discovered that widows are not looked upon favorably. They are considered to be bad luck and a burden on society. There are movements to change how these husbandless women are treated, but I read that they still undergo humiliation and ostracism. This triggered something deep within me that made me very fearful. When it came time to leave for Delhi, I decided not let anyone know that I was a widow so as not to be shunned. Usually quite organized when taking a big trip, this time I just threw whatever clothing seemed appropriate into my luggage.

I was fortunate to have a private room at the Tivoli Gardens Hotel in Delhi where the events were occurring. I even had a private patio enclosed by high, wooden doors with a bench, table, and beautiful flower petals strewn on the stone floor. It was the wedding season so every evening there was dancing and fireworks at the hotel. The women were dressed in beautiful saris in all the colors of the rainbow.

I was the only American in the past-life regression class; all but one other was Indian. I told no one of being a widow. My clothes, as I discovered after unpacking, were almost all black. So, here I was in the midst of women in vibrantly colored clothing with beautiful designs, wearing widow's black.

After the class ended, the Congress began and several A.R.E. members arrived, some even from Virginia Beach. After the opening ceremony (where we were showered with flower petals as we entered the room) the first event was a bus trip to the Taj Mahal in Agra. Although I was extremely careful with the water and what I ate, the night before the trip I became ill. When I got on the bus the next morning, I was even more reclusive than I had been because I was not feeling well.

Time has a different essence in India than it does in the States, and everything proceeds at its own rate, not necessarily at the prescheduled time. The trip that was to take two hours took an agonizing (because of my physical condition) four-and-a-half. We arrived in Agra in time for lunch. I ate with the people from Virginia Beach and asked them not to mention to anyone that I was widow. I was becoming even more paranoid about being found out.

Finally, we were at the Taj Mahal, and I began to explore this magnificent place with a couple of A.R.E. members. The Taj (as it is called in India) is a place of the heart chakra—a place built as a testament to undying love. It is also heavy with the grief of losing a loved one. Meandering our way through the gardens, we walked toward the crypt which is at the far end. People were passing us in both directions. One of the American men crossed in front of me dressed like Frank often did in a blue, button-down oxford cloth shirt and a floppy Australian hat, and, poof, suddenly *there was Frank!!!* His manifestation didn't last long, but there he was at the Taj Mahal seemingly in the flesh and blood. I was stunned and could barely breathe as we continued on to the mausoleum. Suddenly, *there he was again!* He walked right past me, and then he was gone. By then I was in shock. Finally, I was inside the crypt, inside the heart of this place built as a monument to everlasting love—love through all time. Thankfully it was dark, so I was able to regain a little bit of my composure. As we exited and looked down at the Yamuna River, this sacred river seemed to take on some of my pain.

The journey back to Delhi seemed interminable as I needed solitude to process all of the emotions that had been building and were now raw as a result of just having seen Frank, not once, but twice. Their intensity continued to escalate. During the following days I found myself withdrawing further and further away from the other participants as I went deeper and deeper within. Nonetheless, changes were occurring, and I found myself juggling my clothes to bring in color and soften the black.

One of the final workshops I participated in was intended to find and release past-life experiences in the body. As we were led into a deep healing past-life regression, I found myself suddenly in a village in India in a former time. My husband (Frank in this life) had died. I was a widow, and the villagers were shunning me. Then I actually felt their hands on the right side of my head and shoulder pushing me onto his funeral pyre!!!! It was terrifying. Now I understood why I had the knowledge of *sati*. As this was happening, I realized that **their hands were on my head at the exact place where I have experienced TMJ (Temporomandibular Joint disorder) pain and headaches!** Whenever, consciously or unconsciously, I fall into the attitude of the victim in this life, I activate this past-life memory and the weakness in my right temple and jaw. I respond to tension and feeling out of control by gritting my teeth and internalizing it. This clearly was a pervasive mindset through many lives as I had previously relived the victim experience of being hunted down to be hung in Georgia by Frank and others, of having my head cut off on the execution block, and of being imprisoned in an underground cavern with a heavy metal door over it. No more. I choose not to repeat it.

Once having recognized not only the cause and the pattern, it was clear what I was in India to do: to heal the spiritual error of thinking that I was a victim. Additionally, I decided to release the vow made in one of our lifetimes together that I would never leave Frank, one that I identified after he died. It benefited neither of us. That night I asked for guidance. The answer was that I had to tell someone at the Congress that I was a widow. Okay, I could do that.

Of course, as I set that as my intention, the opportunity presented itself the next morning on the very last day of the Congress. At break-fast a gentle woman from Denmark joined me, and it was very natural to tell her of my husband's death. She was quite kind and expressed her concern and did not ask many questions. That was easy . . .

I was then guided to take the next step, the big one, and tell an Indian man that I was a widow. That evening on the way to the closing ceremonies I encountered Dr. Sunny Satin (an Indian man) and Walter Semkiw, MD from San Francisco. During our conversation it was very natural to tell them that I was in the process of moving back to Califor-nia from Virginia after the death of my husband. Amazingly I was nei-ther shunned nor thrown onto a fire. I survived!

The next day I had all to myself to finish the healing. When I awoke, I got up and without thinking, combed my hair to the opposite side of where I had combed it my whole life, seemingly a small thing but indi-cating a complete reversal in thinking. Then I sat on the bench in the patio for most of the morning as I talked out loud to Frank, pouring out my feelings. The words flowed like beautiful poetry quite unlike the way I normally speak. They seemed to match the lovely flower petals at my feet.

I left India the next evening knowing that I had completed what I had come there to do. After I returned home, I became very sick for almost a week as the body still had work to do. The physical is the densest energy so it had to take its own time to purge each cell of the old contract and patterns so that they would not be replicated by new cells. The memory of victimhood was being expunged from all the cells.

This whole process was not a mental exercise. Clearly, Frank's desire to help me and mine to release the vow and the emotional charge of this past-life's pattern enabled him to manifest in the material at the precise time he was needed. Each pointer along the way: the energy of *sati*, the messages, meeting Dr. Sunny Satin, the book about customs, Frank's appearance at The Taj, and even the illness and the black clothes were all instrumental in raising the interlocking threads of the past-life and the limiting thoughts and agreement from the subconscious to consciousness to release them. This *is* the nature of our work in the material world—the type of lessons we are here to learn. Now I finally understood why I had always thought I had to earn the right to go to India. It was not about somehow being rewarded; it was about my being ready to do the difficult work that was required. After I left India, I put my black clothes and the victim mentality to rest.

When we are in a physical body, it is the decision of our free will as to whether we do the work that must be done or merely continue to reinforce our negative ways. Circumstances—some small, some life-changing—are orchestrated by Spirit to bring us back full circle to our knowing who we are. Some of these circumstances are part of our life plan, and others are to guide us back because we have strayed off course. None of us can go through life without reacting to our unconscious triggers or without making mistakes. It is important to address them all, but the larger ones—the ones that we see emerging again and again in the unfolding of our lives—are the ones we most want to change. They are part of our learning process and part of why we are here on the earth plane. The mistakes we make and the difficult situations we find ourselves in often come from our own misguided responses, but they are instrumental in bringing us to a place in our soul development where we might question, evaluate, change, and choose differently. But if we choose not to learn from them this time around, we will have the opportunity to try again, with more difficulty, in another lifetime. Why not do it now?

A View from the Top

Past-life exploration is a powerful vehicle available to us to temporarily pull aside the veil of ignorance that clouds our vision during our sojourns on the Earth. As we walk the spiritual path, the veil begins to lift during this journey toward self-realization, and we begin to glimpse a new life full of hope and joy. Our self-image and way of being in the world fits tightly at first and resists our efforts to change, but with persistence they begin to become more expansive and our view shifts from our personality to our individuality, the eternal "we." It is the same as when we are climbing a hill in the forest. Our sight is foreshortened by the brush and trees that are in the way. As we climb higher and higher, the foliage begins to thin and the visibility becomes greater. We can see more clearly into the distance, and when we reach the top, our view becomes one of 360 degrees—full circle. It is the same when we are fully immersed in a physical body and can see only what is immediately behind and before us. A regression can allow us to see in all directions—past, present, and future.

In this chapter's regression you can access your personal Akashic record of the lifetime in which the need for one of your current soul lessons was created. This particular script is directed toward addictive patterns. These could include alcohol, drugs of any kind, food, gambling, compulsive shopping, hoarding, even collecting people. If you are experiencing one of these serious difficulties, proceed cautiously. It may not be advisable for you to use this particular regression without expert help. Perhaps none of these situations applies to you. You can still use the script by asking your subconscious to take you to the record that was the originating cause for a life lesson you are in the process of learning or to any other information you seek.

Life Lessons Past-Life Regression Script

Take a long, slow, deep breath ... and another ... Focus on your intention to go back to the past-life, to the original cause of a soul wounding that manifests itself as an addictive pattern of some type in your life ... to understand its deeper meaning and the changes necessary to transform the pattern at every level— spiritual, mental, emotional, and physical ... Being able to access the memory in a way that is very safe for you ... always able to visit your safe place if necessary.

Continue to take long, slow, deep breaths ... as you bring your attention to your chakra system ... the organs of your energy field ... and points of contact between Spirit and body ... Visualize or imagine this system interpenetrating your physical and subtle energy bodies ... Become aware of all of your chakras receiving energy from the universal energy field around you ... and providing vital life-force energy to your whole being ... as you continue to breathe deeply and slowly. Begin to sense a shift taking place in how you feel ... noticing all the subtleties of vibrations around your entire auric field ... your human energy field ... Feel your whole body becoming heavier as it releases all tension ... and your mind relaxes, as you go down and down ... deeper and deeper relaxed.

Now that you are deeply relaxed ... open your mind's eye ... As it opens, see, feel, or think that you are standing in the middle of a vast plain with majestic mountains in the distance ... Stand there quietly for a moment in preparation for your journey in time ... Feel a gentle breeze sweeping across the plain ... passing through your aura as it does ... clearing away anything that is not needed ... Experience the sun's rays shining on your head ... Become aware of your feet on the ground ... There is something very special about this place and you feel totally safe and secure here ... Invite your Higher Self to join you, and greet it when it does.

Begin to look around ... turning 360 degrees as you do, and relax even more ... Notice a circle of stones with a large stone at the center that is in a cleared area close to where you are standing ... This place calls to you ... and you have an inner knowing that this is a sacred place ... one that holds the memories of the past ... Walk over to the circle of stones with your Higher Self, who will be with you through this entire process ... Sense how your feet feel when they touch the earth as you walk ... Going deeper and deeper within with each step ... Counting, ... 1 ... 2 ... 3 ... 4 ... 5 ... 6 ... 7 ... 8 ... 9 ... 10 ... 11 ... 12 ... 13 ... 14 ... 15 ... 16 ... 17 ... 18 ... 19 ... 20 ... 21.

At the circle of stones now ... Walk around the outside perimeter ... As you walk past the stones, they seem to come alive ... You can feel their energy ... They feel very loving, supportive, and wise. After you have completely circled the stones, walk through the opening you see between the stones and continue on to the large stone at the center ... This stone is the control center of the circle and is an access point to the Akashic Hall of Records, where the records of all your past-lives are held ... If you are ready, it will allow you to access the memories of past-lives.

Place your hand on the center stone ... and it begins to open up, indicating that you are indeed ready for the next step ... As the stone continues to open, a bright, white light shines from within and becomes bigger and bigger until you and your Higher Self are completely enveloped by it ... You both walk into the center of the light and find yourself in a hall without walls or ceiling ... You are in the Hall of Records ... the place that houses the Akashic records ... Standing there in the hall, call to mind your intention once again ... When you have done that, you see an old man walking toward you with a large book ... 1 ... 2 ... 3 ... and he hands you the book ... You take it from him and thank him ... Now you and your Higher Self walk to a table nearby, sit down in a chair, and place the book on the table ... ready to find the record of the past-life you came here to review ... Before opening the book you look at the cover ... It has your soul name on it ... That name comes to your consciousness now ... Open the book, and it opens to just the right page for you ... Begin to read what it says ... It has all the information you desire ... As you continue to read, you go deeper and deeper into the story ... becoming a part of it only if you choose, yet reading or sensing, in some way, all the details and circumstances of that life that are meaningful for you to know ... then doing the spiritual work necessary to heal the soul wounding ... and sending the energy of the soul wounding into the Light for cleansing ... You know what to do, but you can call on your Higher Self for assistance if necessary .... Take all the time you need to transform what happened then.

Continue reading and notice how the vibration of that life's signature has been increased because of the soul development work you just did ... Recognize that it is now safe to come back into your body and feel ... Allow this to happen gradually as the physical and emotional come into alignment with the spiritual corrections you have made ... Feel how that feels ... Open the records to current time ... and read or sense how the past-life changes you made empower you to fully participate in your life in a way that creates healthy relationships with others ... and with yourself ... now able to feel emotions without being overwhelmed by them ... You release the need for additive substances of any kind ... having healed the soul wounding that first created the addictive patterns ... As you flip the pages to the future, you see that your new life is so much brighter and hopeful now.

When you are done, close the book, pick it up, get up from the chair with book in hand, and you and your Higher Self go back to the hallway ... The old man is waiting for you ... Hand him the book and thank him ... He leaves and you see the light beckoning you ... Go to it and return the way you came ... Instantly you and your Higher Self are back in front of the stone with your hand still on it ... The opening has closed ... In the future if you wish to return to this place to explore more of your records, all you have to do is close your eyes, set your intention, count from 1 to 10 ... and you will immediately be back here.

Walk back from the center and out through the opening in the circle now ... bringing everything back with you that you choose to bring back ... knowing that you have done the work that you came here to do ... Returning to the plain now ... Thank your Higher Self and prepare to return ... Continue walking back to current time, feeling wide awake, refreshed and relaxed ... 1 ... 2 ... 3 ... 4 ... 5 ... coming back ... 6 ... 7 ... 8 ... coming back even more ... 9 ... 10 ... All the way back now ... and when you are ready, open your eyes.

Life Lesson Regressions

As you read the "life-lesson" regressions, which were done using the addiction script, it will be easy to see how the lesson permeates a person's life, surfacing again and again to get that person's attention in order to effectuate change. What the participants discovered can, in some cases, be summed up in one word, but a word that conveys a multitude of variations, while others were woven into the very threads of their lives and in some way affected all aspects of it.

Although many of these patterns seem to be straightforward after we have learned what they are, they do not appear that way while we are living them. Perhaps these stories will shed light on your own lessons and encourage you to explore one or more of your adventures on this Earth.

SUSAN—GETTING IT RIGHT

Susan and I discussed the intention of her regression prior to starting. She mentioned a recurring dream — one that started a few years ago and sometimes appeared as often as once a week — a dream in which she felt that there was a camera focused on her. It "freaked her out" because it seemed to her as if someone were taping her as she was being watched and monitored. When she woke up, it felt as if it were still happening. It was just as real to her when she came to consciousness as it had been while she was sleeping. This dream panicked her and made her think that it had something to do with trust, and she knew that recurring dreams are an important message about something that needs to be addressed. She asked for guidance and received the word *judgment.* So she chose to explore a prior life related to the issues of trust and judgment.

Susan received her Akashic record book from the old man who is the Keeper of the Records. Her soul name as shown on the cover was difficult to pronounce but sounded something like Solio. The book opened to show her in a one room schoolhouse as a young girl. There were other children in the room. One of the first things she noticed was a ruler on her desk. The female teacher looked very stern and was tapping the ruler. Susan was afraid that the teacher was going to hit her with it. The teacher frequently hit the students with the ruler to make sure "they got it right." Susan felt that she could not do it right, and this made her fearful; she knew she would be hit. When Susan looked into the teacher's eyes to see if this was a person she knew in her current life, she said that they looked like her grandmother's eyes. She forgave the teacher for making her fearful and for planting the seed that she could not do it right.

I asked Susan where she was carrying the energy of "I can't do it right." It was in her shoulders. They were tense and felt like a rock, and the energy appeared to her to be a dark gray. Susan believed this was her own energy, not someone else's, that was being held in there. It was sent into the Light for purification to be reclaimed after that was completed. It seemed as if the energy was melting in her shoulders, and they felt much looser and more relaxed.

The next event she experienced in that life was being in a shed house. Her sister was trying to give birth, and she was assisting her as best she could. Her sister was screaming, and Susan was holding her but did not know what else to do. Her sister's husband was angry with her because she was unable to help. This energy, which was his, was being held in her stomach, and it was hot and orange-red. It was removed into the Light. She forgave him for judging her. She felt him completely changing his attitude, and he was relieved. She also forgave herself; she had done the very best she could for her sister.

Then we moved to her last day. As she was about to die, she felt very sad. Her dying thoughts were, "I have failed my family. I could never do enough." When her spirit left the body, she looked down on it and understood, "I am still a loving being. That is what mattered. I tried."

We discussed the recurring dream, which seemed to be triggered when she was feeling more vulnerable. At those times she **had a sense that she could not do enough.** There were several situations currently that made her feel that way. After we released the energy of "I can't do enough," Susan believed that she could now trust that it would be okay. She can let go now and be herself.

A short time later Susan reported that she had a dream about her grandma and recalled that one of the flashbacks during the "judgment" life had her grandmother in it as the teacher. This made sense to her as she and her grandmother had always been very close. Susan also recognizes that her grandmother is extremely judgmental and feels as if every move she makes is critiqued by her. She now believes that this may very well be a repeated soul pattern between them. The dream and the flashback to the teacher/school house are memories of that. When Susan recognizes that dynamic in their relationship, she can now lovingly and consciously change it.

CHRIS' MENTAL PRISON

Chris is a client who has done much work to change the addictive habits in her life. She has gone through rehab for alcoholism. She has also been in traditional counseling and experienced regression therapy not only for alcohol misuse but also for bulimia and depression. Chris committed to the healing process and has made great progress.

This regression was one of the many steps in her continuing walk toward recovery and wholeness, and it immediately followed a spiritual clearing session. What she discovered at first was darkness. It was cold. Moving further into the experience Chris realized that she, as a young boy of about eight, was in a well that was wet and cold. He was scared. The year was 1638, and it was in Switzerland.

The boy was pushed into the well by his older brother who was jealous of all the attention his sibling was receiving. The brother wanted to be the only child and left Chris in the well to die, which he did. No one could find him.

The final thoughts before leaving the body—the ones that have such a powerful ripple effect through all our lives—was, "I am not loved. I could not even rely on unconditional love (that was the love she had for her older brother as well as for her parents and the love her parents had for her). My love for my brother was not enough. He murdered me. It hurts to love." Because her parents had not been able to find her, Chris remembers thinking that their love could not save her and that even God was unable to hear their cries. As a result, she turned away from faith in God and spiritual help.

Before going into the Light she said, "I decided not to love; it hurts." Instead she chose to stifle her love in the future. The thought patterns that were energized as a result of the way she died created a soul wounding for Chris and has prevented her consciousness from fully entering the body since. The addictions keep her from feeling the emotions that she has not been able to handle until now. In looking at how this has affected her current life, Chris recognized that she has stifled loving herself. She put herself in her own prison with the behaviors of addiction.

The next step was the healing work. Reviewing the scene from above, she was able to see her parents. They were crying and in a lot of pain. She also discovered that her brother loved her; he was just troubled. The young boy had not known that. Chris forgave her brother and she saw him as being very happy. He even thanked her for forgiving him. She forgave herself for everything she had thought and said surrounding this death and the people involved. She also forgave herself for making the vow to stifle her love.

Then Chris envisioned a key to let herself out of the prison of addiction she had created. A pretty floral rope was brought down into the well by a cherub angel so that she could get out. Up till now she has always yearned for spiritual assistance. When the angel came, she knew that it was there. "That's the key. It is in your heart," the angel advised her.

The residual fears of being cold, hungry, and trapped in a well remained. She requested that her Higher Self remove them, and it was done. So that no one else would fall into the well, Chris filled it with white, gold, and iridescent light mixed with soil. It is now a loving tomb that will grow over with grass and flowers.

When the session ended, Chris felt at peace. She seemed very happy—happier than I had seen her before. She said this experience had been very freeing. This was not the end, but it was one more step on the path. She will continue to do what is needed to release the patterns that keep her from being who she truly is. A short time after the session she thanked me for sending her this valuable, life-transforming information that she had shared with loved ones. They found it to be very fitting with what they have seen about her personality characteristics.

JAN—
AN ATTRACTOR OF THE CHEMICALLY DEPENDENT

Jan chose to tackle an especially difficult problem for her very first regression. Her request for a session was driven by the desire to understand and change her life-long pattern of attracting chemically dependent people to her. Also, although her appearance belies it, she is a compulsive eater and grinds her teeth while sleeping.

Almost immediately, even before we began the session, Jan

began backpedaling. She was scared, and tears formed. We proceeded cautiously and gently.

Initially Jan saw her dad. He was smiling. She was very young when he died. Then she met her Higher Self who appeared to her as a large Native American man. He was sitting on her left shoulder pointing the way for her to go.

As the regression began, she was walking out into nothingness — out in space with nothing around her but grayish white. I instructed her to walk through it, to walk through this portal, which she did.

Jan first observed herself as a young woman in a white dress seated, laughing and watching. This was in current time. As she watched, the scene changed, and then she saw herself on the ground alone during an earlier, happier time. She was a young girl of about six who was part of a well-to-do family all who were dressed nicely. A picnic was being setup outside, and she wanted to participate.

This young girl was standing next to her mother looking up at her adoringly and marveling at her beauty. However, her mother had no bond with her. When I suggested that Jan look at this girl through her mother's eyes, she found that her mother only tolerated her. Jan believes that all her problems stem from her relationship with her mother.

As Jan went into a deeper trance, she experienced her father as being at one end of the spectrum and her mother at the other. She felt that her father was there to protect her. The nothingness at this point was so thick and dirty white that she could not see through. She felt as if she were in limbo, and it was not going to let her in. Her father was there, saying no. He did not want her to go in. "I belong to him. He does not want to share me," she told me. He was smiling.

At this point her neck became very tense and tight. Although she was still in the nothingness, she experienced herself running through the wilderness. It was uncomfortable, and her whole body was tense. I shifted the focus from a past-life experience to the issue of compulsive eating to ease her discomfort.

Jan has always eaten a lot but does it at night and does not eat during the day. She knows this replaces something. As we pursued the cause, she felt emptiness in her heart. That emptiness was created because she thought she had been abandoned by her father, who died so early in her life. Her heart believed he had broken their agreement to nurture her and to stay around.

I directed her back to their past-life that had formed the basis for the agreement. When she accessed this life, they were happy as they danced. The two were then husband and wife. Jan said she looked very feminine and happy as she twirled around in a long flowing dress.

This led back to the emptiness in her heart. Jan needed to understand why he had broken their agreement so she could forgive him and no longer try to fill the void with food. When she asked him why he left, he told her that things just had not worked out for him. It was not about her. Then she was able to forgive him for leaving earlier than planned. He smiled as a result, and that made her feel good. Her heart does not need food as nourishment. It needs love. She filled the emptiness with self-love, and her heart then felt full.

She spoke to her stomach asking not only about the amount of food she had been eating but also why she ate only at night. The stomach responded, "Give me a break!" Jan agreed to change her eating habits to ones that were beneficial to her. The stomach liked that. At this point she recognized that other people with addictions — the ones that were attracted to her — fed her emptiness. Because she has self-love now, they will no longer be attracted to her as she is now vibrating at a higher rate than they are. Her stomach also asked her to take some of the burden off of it and told her to take off weight. She made a contract with her stomach to eat less and to relax more. She hikes and does yoga sometimes, so she is going to do yoga more often. The stomach agreed to work with her and felt much better.

Her heart also needed release from tension. It needs for her to go within and spend time in the stillness. She made a commitment to do this for at least five minutes every day. An energetic shield was put around her heart to protect it in the future.

Then we asked the jaw why it needs to grind the teeth at night. It responded by telling her that it is processing what she goes through during the day. Exercise can replace the grinding of teeth. After connecting with her jaw, they came to an agreement that she would not only enter into the silence daily but also exercise and eat right so that her teeth no longer need to grind.

By this time the neck had loosened up. Jan acknowledged all the positive work she had done during this session. She recognized that she can let go, love, and be good to herself now. Her father's **love is eternal** whether he is in a body or not. This was a very powerful session for her, and its effects will continue to benefit her as she changes the patterns that have limited her up until now. Sometime later Jan wrote me that this regression had cleared up many things for her and it was as if a "huge weight/release has been lifted" from her.

CHRISTIAN'S SCIENTIFIC APPROACH

Christian is a young college student who believes he has a calling to be a healer by combining traditional medicine with spiritual knowledge. He has been profoundly affected by the writings/teachings of Dan Millman, author of *The Peaceful Warrior* and other books. In this regression Christian chose to explore the origin of this calling to assuage some of his skepticism because of the scientific lens through which he looks at the world.

As he read the book containing his Akashic records, Christian witnessed an event in 1842 that probably occurred in the United States. He saw a male in his forties or fifties sitting by a fire alone near a small cabin-like house surrounded by open space. The cabin was in the middle of a big valley surrounded by mountains and forests. Even though he was alone, it was not as quiet as Christian thought it would be. He discovered that the noise was coming from people sitting around other fires and preparing for battle with the Native Americans. Christian saw himself as a doctor. The doctor said, "I'd like to believe in God," but he was already prepared for what he was certain was to come.

As the life progressed, Christian saw the doctor in a tent where he and others were helping the people who were injured. He was not happy to see what had happened. This doctor loved the work he did, was very confident that he was good at his job, and was also very calm. However, as he worked, it did cause him to question whether there might be more than just a pumping heart and some organs to an individual. As Christian viewed this makeshift hospital from above it, he saw that every person had a glowing bluish-white light centered in one specific spot in his/her body. The doctor was treating a man whose light was flashing and alternating between bright and dim. When this person died, it was necessary for the doctor to walk away from the body to take care of someone else and not dwell on what happened to that person's soul. He did, however, see the light of one of those who had died travel up out of the body and sensed that it was a matter of focus. Whatever it was that a person focused on in his/her life, he/she had to let go of it. After death, it happens naturally as the person's essence goes home.

To bring this love of being a doctor into current time, Christian chose to awaken this memory of that life as a healer at a cellular level. Then he viewed the doctor in the moments before his death. He was very old and at home, and another doctor, a younger man, was there with him. It seems he knew the other doctor and loved him very much. As he was about to leave the body, he was just taking it all in and was not as afraid as he thought he would be. I guided him into the Light, and it was much vaster than he had imagined. Christian compared it to seeing many lights floating on top of the water. He felt the loving support around him and his connection to God's unconditional love.

As part of the transformation process he brought this feeling into his heart to awaken the memory of God's love for him, and then he merged it with his love for being a doctor. This will assist him in providing healing at all levels in his current lifetime. Finally, after these were combined, this energy of love was connected to his head with a golden cord that then went down to the throat so that he might speak his loving truth as a healer.

As the regression was coming to a close, Christian brought his focus back to his book of Akashic records to see how this reconnection is going to empower him to be the medical-spiritual healer he feels called to be. The changes that occurred as a result of having made this connection were that Christian realized he is "going to have to be a tougher cookie" with other people, especially the people he works with by being more compassionate towards himself. When he becomes a doctor/healer, Christian wants to have better rapport with his patients and a better sense of humor than he did as the doctor in the previous lifetime. Christian views this as a tradeoff because the doctor started out as being more serious, while Christian is more relaxed. He recognizes that he needs to incorporate the strength he had when he was a doctor. Christian can now see why he loves medicine and that the path has all been laid out for him. It was comforting for him to have this clarity. He can now see himself as a doctor even though he believes he is currently at a disadvantage in being accepted to medical school because of choices he has made.

Combining medicine with the spiritual seemed to be harder for him because he recognized that there is a big lesson in all of this for him. He seemed to be reluctant to tackle that lesson, whatever it is. The doctor had made a big commitment. Christian could see it on his face. It was also evident that the doctor had provided guidance for the younger doctor who was at his deathbed. "There is a lot of work to do," Christian said. He did, however, make the personal commitment to do the work that needs to be done and **ask for spiritual guidance** when he needs it.

Because of the lens through which he filters things, Christian was very skeptical of everything especially about what he called the irony of his being very spiritual and also scientific. He believes that they are somewhat contradictory and that there are a lot of gray areas between the two. As a scientist he agreed to be open to the possibility that there are things that he doesn't know and things that we cannot explain at this time. In the future, when he feels skeptical, he will use his new tools and reawaken the feeling of love in his heart—the love he had of being a doctor and healing others and of the connection with God that he felt when he was in the Light. This will help him answer his calling and walk a path that embraces both the scientific and the physical as he is an instrument of healing for others.

PATRICE'S PATTERN OF REJECTION

Patrice and I have done many different types of hypnotherapy and regressions sessions together so it was relatively easy to conduct the regression via an Internet webcam call. Throughout her life Patrice has had a pattern of being rejected, perceiving that she has been rejected, or both. Also she feels as if other people think she is different, eccentric, or odd, and has never fit in.

The safe place was created without effort. However, when Patrice asked her Higher Self to join her, she suddenly experienced a deep heaviness as if someone were sitting on her chest. After further questioning it was an earthbound soul—a young five-year-old girl who had been attached to Patrice for five to ten years. We assisted the child into the Light. The heaviness lifted, but a gray, dark fog then came up. Even though the fog was blown away by the wind, Patrice did not feel as if she had made the connection to her Higher Self. This was a reflection of her issue of being rejected so we continued on, knowing that her Higher Self was indeed there to guide her.

As she read in the Hall of Records from the beautiful leather book, hand-tooled with gold leaf, she saw a small hut-type house in Germany made from large round, rough stones. It had smooth plaster on the exterior and rough stone on the interior. Patrice saw herself as a ten-year-old girl with long, black, loose curls sitting outside in the cool night looking at the stars. It was hot inside, and she did not like the confines of being inside. Then the awareness came to Patrice that her family did not want her; they did not feel comfortable around her. This girl was different from them, more intelligent. The members of her family whispered behind her back. The girl "sees" things and it scared them. "I know things." Patrice said.

I then took her to a time in that life when she was abandoned, or thought she was abandoned, outside a medieval castle. It was 1793. This young girl was lost. There were many people at the outdoor market, and she somehow got lost walking in the crowd. She was scared because no one came to find her, and as evening approached, she was sitting on a low, flat rock crying. It became dark and cold, and everyone was gone. Finally, a man came who wanted her to come with him, and she did.

That event flipped her to a connected lifetime. She was outside again, also in Germany. It was a bright, sunny, warm day, and she was dancing in her bare feet with arms outstretched. This blond-haired girl wore a pretty blue rectangular shawl. It was a glorious day, and she was happy. As the sun set, she sat down to wait for someone, either her mother or father, to come for her. After a long wait, her mother arrived with a small wooden-plank donkey cart to take her home. The girl had gone to a festival by herself. Her family allowed her to do this because she was different. Her "kind of people" were at the festival—psychics. They also danced. Because she had to wait so long for someone to get her after the festival ended, she thought that her family did not want her back. The girl knew that the members of her family thought that she was odd, and she felt that she was not really one of them. She liked to daydream a lot; she just did not fit in. She had a higher vibration than her family and was on a higher plane. Even so, her mother had insisted to the others that she get the girl herself, which she did.

I instructed the German girl to go to the last day of that life. She was now old and frail and looked like a fortune-teller. Because of her abilities she had to live on the outskirts of town, isolated from others. It was lonely, and she felt sad. Somehow it seemed she believed she was bewitched or that others thought she was a witch.

After her spirit left the body and went into the Light, Patrice felt comforted with a sense of wholeness and of being accepted. Finally, she was able to connect with her Higher Self and they held hands. She smiled.

From that higher perspective she became sorry that she had not met her family's expectations. They did not appreciate who she was because they were just ignorant peasants. Patrice knew that she needed to walk a different path to be able to forgive them and to forgive herself for being "special." It felt very good for her to be loved and accepted. She felt filled with the golden light of God's grace. However, Patrice noticed that she had not fully forgiven herself. The difficulty resulted because she still experienced some sadness, and she started to cry. This sadness was given over to God who reached out to her. As it was released, she felt lighter. Then she took time to rest and to recharge her batteries in this loving place. When the session ended, Patrice was at peace. What she needed to do was complete.

TIM AND THE WATCHER

Tim, a former Army Ranger, had several problems that he hoped to address through a past-life regression — alcohol, tobacco, depression, and sleepwalking. He has been through re-

hab, had counseling, and worked with psychologists. I proceeded carefully and enlisted the assistance of a Reiki Master,
whom Tim knew and trusted, to work with me during the regression. She did Reiki on him prior to and during the session.

Because of the number of issues he presented and the seri-
ousness of some of them, I proceeded cautiously. I began by
having him create his safe place and then revisit a happy past-
life. Tim experienced himself as a male, about the same age as
him, in medieval times. It was spring in northern Italy, in
Palmanova, which was a walled city. He was in charge. He was
strong and free, and he thought it was nice that no one knew
him. This medieval man's nature was peaceful, but he still felt
torn between power/ destruction and peace.

Then I guided him to the life that would help him understand and begin to release him from his current problems. He
returned to the same general area as the happy life. Again he
was alone, always alone. As the "Watcher" or guardian, he
wore armor. This Watcher "knew" that it was eternal and that
this was the only life because all lives are one. He felt comfortable and safe on the hill lined with trees that overlooked the
city he was protecting. This male believed that he could control *everything* when he was alone. Control was the keyword
here. His mission was to protect life, and this was noble.

Connecting with the Watcher was necessary for Tim to make
the first steps in changing his behaviors. He recognized that he
had suffered a soul wounding of the mind and subsequently
closed off part of his mind in his current life. A floating head
came to his consciousness that felt more than paternal. It felt
familiar. It was this same "Guardian" or "Watcher" from the
prior incarnation, and he had also experienced it earlier in his
current life after doing a stretch of intensive meditation—but
without a spiritual ideal. He has been conscious of the Watcher
since that time, and Tim believed it was his Higher Self—up
till now. It has perpetuated his sense of having to be alone and
to be in control because it told him it had a higher purpose.

When I questioned him about what positive things the Watcher had done for him in his life, Tim was startled to recognize that it had done nothing positive. Instead of guiding him, Tim now understood that the Watcher was a thought form created during meditation, and he had been feeding it energy all this time. This was a real wake-up call for Tim. He committed to reexamining how it had governed his life and to make necessary changes. This is not going to solve all his problems, but it is an important start. If he continues to challenge his preconceived thoughts generated by the Watcher, the other issues may begin to recede as well as the Watcher itself.

NANCY—
TO BE SUPPORTED YOU MUST BE SUPPORTIVE

While writing this book I received guidance that I should have my own past-life regression to explore the origins of a pattern that has exhibited itself in relationships throughout my life. Although I recognized that a pattern existed, I was never quite able to put my finger on what it was, to articulate the core, the message of the pattern. It was time to learn what this life lesson was about and to put it to rest.

So, I set my intention to have a regression and choose Gayla Reiter as the regressionist. Gayla is a hypnotherapist and an IARRT (International Association of Research and Regression Therapies) Board member. I first met her in India at the 2006 IARRT World Congress and then again when I moved back to California from Virginia Beach.

In the days before the regression I sought more clarity about the life lesson. I had a brief flashback of a life in China in which I was the power behind the throne but did not get the recognition I had anticipated from this position. Somehow this expectation turned back on me. Additional guidance came that the pattern was about being blindsided and about entitlement. This struck home. Memories of the past came to mind that showed me how that had happened both in my personal and professional life. Before this I was not aware of how pervasive and deep the pattern was until I recognized how many times things took an immediate and often life-changing turn because I had been blindsided. As for the entitlement aspect, because of the nature of the relationship I had an expectation about what the other person's responsibilities were in the relationship. When that did not happen, I felt as if the shift had come out of nowhere. The rest was to be revealed during the regression.

Almost before my eyes closed I knew that I had just been born but had the awareness of an adult. There were several women looking down at me saying in disgust, "Oh, it's a girl." My mother was lying there with her face turned away in dismay because I was a girl. I didn't care; I had a mission. It was 763 [Gayla asked if it was BC or AD, and I answered that we don't know BC or AD and had no reference for what that meant. I referenced the Tang Dynasty.] The place was China in the Imperial City. The room was very large with windows covered by material or drapes to keep the sun out. The women were howling; everyone was disdainful. They bundled me up and took me away so that my mother did not have to look at me. I was very aware of their feelings, but I did not care very much, almost as if it were a joke. To me as the observer it seemed strange that I did not care. I told Gayla, "I am here, and it is too bad that they don't want me, but I do not care. I am stronger than they are. I don't need them. I have a strong sense of self."

I was very certain that I needed to be there in that specific time and place. It did not have a lot to do with the people in the family, but because I was born into a royal family, it was supposed to provide me with the circumstances to fulfill my mission. What was important, I thought, was the nature of the relationship itself, not the human connection.

Next I was aware of horses and a carriage for the funeral of my grandfather. I was outside the carriage in the royal gardens, but I was ignored because I was a female. He was going to be cremated. There was much activity because my father was now going to be emperor. I was six. There were many children around somewhere, probably brothers and sisters, but I was not connected to them. I had a different mission.

Then I saw my father. He tolerated me more than my mother. I made him laugh. I recognized my father as Frank, my husband in this life, who made me laugh often. After my grandfather died, the family situation changed due to my father's ascension to the throne. There was more separation because of his position. There were advisors around, and because I was a girl, they kept me in the background. They did not let me see him.

They were trying to teach me to be a lady [I laughed.]. I say, "I am so much more than that and they want to put me in a box. I have so much to say, and they won't hear me because I am a female. The message [my mission] has great urgency. This land cries out. There is too much population here, too many people. They are denuding the land, destroying its beauty and energy. There don't need to be so many souls on the earth at one time. If they keep inviting souls in before they are ready, the earth will be destroyed. They don't even know about these things. They think they need to keep having children until they have boys."

Gayla asked me if they killed the girls. My answer was, "Those who were peasants died through neglect and hard work." Perhaps some peasant girls were killed, but I did not know about it because we did not see it. We did not go outside of the royal city very much. I did not know if the royal family killed the female children, but I knew that I was alive even though I was female. If I had any sisters, I was not aware of them as they were not relevant to me.

The women all gathered together and gossiped during the day. They prettied themselves up but also listened to music and sang sometimes. They would sit by the pools in the gardens. I said that it was a lovely life, not very fulfilling, but a lovely life.

There were children in other parts of the palace, but I did not know why I was not with them.

I spent my time writing during the day. A teacher who recognized that I was "more" taught me to write. This was not done in the open so that others would not be aware of it. They didn't pay much attention to me anyway because I was an inconvenience. I recognized this teacher as Jack Elias, one of my main hypnotherapy teachers, who lives in Seattle in this life.

We moved forward to a significant event. I was sixteen, and it was my wedding. My husband was a noble; he did not work. He was a nice person. It was convenient as it would have been an embarrassment if I had stayed with my mother and father longer. I thought that he was pleasant enough if I had to marry, and maybe I could make my own way somehow and do what I wanted.

A few years later I found that I was a disappointment because I had not given birth. It was expected. Not that I cared. I did not have children because I blocked it energetically; I did not want any. My husband was embarrassed because he had no heirs. He had thought that marrying me would put him in an advantageous position, but I had not fulfilled the promise of a wife. Concubines were allowed but not multiple wives. I think he went off with the men, however, and diverted himself with drink perhaps to the point of alcoholism.

I spent my time writing poetry, writing about the earth, leaving messages about our relationship with the earth. The intention was to leave these messages for the people even though they would not be read while I was alive. The intention, and the mission, was that the poems be there for others to read after I had left the earth plane. At that time most people could not read, and they would not have read them anyway because I was a woman. If others in the palace knew I was writing, they did not care. To them I was just a barren woman.

Gayla asked me who the most important person in that life was to me. That was God. **God was in my heart, before me,**

around me, in direct connection. During the regression I knew that I have always had a relationship with God in all my lifetimes, although not as consciously as this one, but it has always been there. In this lifetime I was aware of God's presence even when I had just been birthed and was on the bed with the servants peering down at me. Perhaps that is why I did not care what they thought—I had a Divine mission.

Even though I always had an awareness of God in that lifetime, I did not receive direct messages. It was the consciousness of the connection that allowed me to feel independent. I came in with the message. That was what I was writing about. The message was intended to be left so that it might be read in later years.

I had no personal friends during that life. The connection with God was self-sustaining so I did not have a need for friends. However, that did not mean I did not enjoy companionship; I did enjoy my father's company.

The next major event, perhaps the most significant of my life, took place when the young princes found my writings and burned them. I was heartbroken. They ran in circles around me with the burning papers in their hands and the ashes flying, laughing at this old woman who wrote them. I felt that the message was lost, that no one would hear what I had to say, that my purpose for coming into the earth was subverted.

At this point in time I was further removed from the emperor than before because I was old and in a different part of the complex. [My father had died, so there was a new emperor.] I was quite elderly and alone. Divorce was not allowed. My husband was feeble, coughing because of smoking thin, little brown cigarettes. He had enjoyed life a lot and partied. His way was different from mine.

It was time for me to die because there was nothing more for me to do in that life. On the last day as I was dying, I was lying on a board or board bed dressed in white. There were a few old servants there. I did not draw much attention. I was ready to

leave; everyone else was gone. I was hardly there. I was ready
to go back home. That was the only emotion I had. My last
thoughts were that I would have to try again another time to
get the message across. And no, I was not depressed because I
had done the best I could.

After I left the physical body, I could see it while moving up
above it, going up quickly. I knew the way so nobody came to
accompany or greet me. I was an independent soul. Others
would have come to assist if I had needed them, but I knew I
would see them when I got "home."

During the life review I recognized that I could have been
more diplomatic. Being self-sufficient is good, but I could have
tried to connect more than I did and might have been heard
more in spite of the limitations of the circumstances. However,
the seed was planted, and that was all I needed to do. By energetically being on the Earth, by feeling the connection with the
Earth, and by allowing Mother Earth to know that I heard was
enough for that lifetime. That set up some type of energetic
system that would allow the seed to grow over time. It could
not be done in one lifetime. It could not be done in many lifetimes, but it had to be started somewhere. Nonetheless, I could
have been more gracious.

I had no carryover feeling of disappointment. I was sorry
the messages had been burned because I wanted to leave a
physical remembrance, not of me, but of this thought, this need
to wake up the souls on the earth. **There is always time for
this because there is no time.**

I expected a little more receptivity from others in the life.
Even from the first time I opened my mouth (as a newborn),
what I was saying was rejected. I expected to be able to have
someone hear the message I was bringing. Maybe because I
was so independent and I set it up to be so difficult, I made it
that way. Maybe I don't have to make it so difficult anymore —
so that the message is the important thing, not my ego about
how I can do something because I am a strong individual. The

connection with God was/is so strong that even though my guides are available, that connection is all that matters. At this point God laughed and patted me on the head. I need to soften up a little bit, and I know what I need to do. It is clear. I had no ambiguity or carryover need for forgiveness. These people were in their time and place doing what they knew to do. I had a higher purpose, but perhaps I could have set it up better so that the ego did not get in the way of the message. However, I did plant the seed, and it is coming to fruition now.

At this point in the review I literally saw alcohol going down the drain and knew that the familial pattern of alcoholism that has been interwoven through past and present lives was now healed. I felt that whatever work I needed to do regarding this ancestral pattern has now been completed.

As the regression was coming to an end, Gayla told me that she saw my face softening. One of the first things I said when coming to waking consciousness was that I was so focused on my own mission that I was blind to the mission of others.

Immediately I was able to recognize that this streak of independence, not caring about what others think, and wanting to do it all by myself has most definitely carried over to this current life. It has been only within the past few years that I have come to understand that anyone can make things difficult for herself. Making it easy is more in alignment with Spirit. I choose now to make it easy. Being so self-sufficient did not advance the message and may have hindered its delivery. This is something I need to look at. As we continue to do our spiritual work, more of our patterns come to the surface of our awareness to resolve. This was not the most pleasant picture of my personality, but this work is not always pleasant. We must allow the darker side of our nature to emerge so that we might change it in a way that is more in keeping with our true being.

The details of the regression were surprising. Based on the flashback just before the session, I had expected that the pattern of being blindsided would have played out as my being the power behind the throne but not receiving the expected benefits. At the start of the session when I was describing the issue and intention of the regression, Gayla, who is also a clairvoyant, had the feeling that I had been betrayed somehow. Although this exact word did not quite resonate with me, there was some energy to it.

After the regression was completed, I was not sure at first how this life represented the pattern of being blindsided in my current life but knew that it held the answer I sought if I dug deeply enough. I kept mulling it over in my mind searching for insight. Being barren in that life reminded me of how I had decided early in this life not to have any children. It seemed that I had always known that I had chosen this path. My sociology professor in college flashed into my mind. He had really brought home the message of the need for zero population growth [an effort to control the world's population by having the birth rate match the death rate as a result of parents having only two children], and this solidified my commitment not to have children.

That night I dreamed about the regression. The dream indicated that this needed to be cleared to allow me to open to future possibilities. However, the dream did not clarify how it related to my being blindsided.

Finally . . . I got it. In all the circumstances where I felt as if I were blindsided, I had an **expectation**, *based on the nature of the relationship*, of being supported in some way. That did not happen. The results were unanticipated and often traumatic to my psyche and well-being. What was the message? If I believed that I could do it all myself and did not need the support of others, then I would not receive that support!!! By not needing, wanting, or asking for support, that is exactly what was attracted to me — no support. The Universe responded by pulling the expected support out from under my feet, so to speak.

This regression helped me recognize that I must be conscious of my own expectations in a relationship of any kind and articulate these expectations to the other person. I must not assume that theirs and mine are the same.

I unexpectedly found the notes from the regression done at the A.R.E. Health Center and Spa in which I experienced a series of lives, one of which I reported on in Chapter 2. One of these provided further insight into the nature of our interconnectedness and need of mutual support. In that life I was a hermit living in a cave that had paintings of Buddha and other deities on the walls. People left food outside the cave for me. This was not as it might seem at first blush, that the hermit was dependent upon them or that he was unable to take care of himself. The hermit and those who took care of his needs had a symbiotic relationship. When they brought food to this man, they accessed higher energies. It was an exchange of energy, and the hermit and the people benefitted by helping each other. The lesson this life had for me was not to try to do it all alone and allow others to nurture me by accepting their help when it is offered. All are connected to Source. There are no dependencies, and we all benefit in this way.

Now it is clear. How could I have ever thought otherwise? There is more work for me to do, but now that I consciously recognize it, I will do just that—with the support and help of those around me. Even though this is not the most flattering portrait of me, I share it with you so that you might benefit in some way.

We each have come into this lifetime to work on several major issues and then use them as a launching pad for greater creativity and fulfillment. Do you know what yours are?

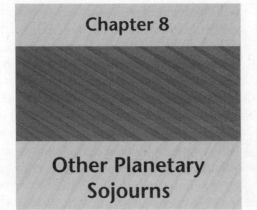

Chapter 8

Other Planetary Sojourns

Insights from Explorers of Other Realms

The Cayce readings indicate that our earthly bodies do not re-incarnate on other planets in this solar system, but rather we visit them as stages of consciousness. Each planet has its unique influences through which we must pass. We are told that some individuals see these stages as planes, some as steps, some as cycles, and some have even experienced them as places. Cayce informed us that our sojourns in other spheres of consciousness affect our urges—the latent forces within us as individuals. Although we may not incarnate elsewhere in an earthly human body, is it not possible that we might manifest in other places in the form that is most appropriate for that planet or system and that we can access those memories?

In the past-life regression and hypnotherapy field, many practitioners now have clients come to them who remember experiences and beings not of this Earth. Dolores Cannon, from whom I have taken past-life regression training, is one of these practitioners. She has been doing hypnotherapy for forty years. Her particular methodology leads clients into a very deep state of hypnosis in which they reveal not only past-lives on the Earth but also often very surprising lives on other planets—lives as other types of life forms in other energy systems, simultaneous lives, and even future lives. She is recognized worldwide for the results she has obtained and written about in her ten books. Dolores views her role as that of a reporter and not an analyzer. In her books *The Custodians, Keepers of the Garden*, and *The Convoluted Universe* series, she reports about client regressions in which they described UFO experiences, ET abductions, and "lives" in other forms, universes, and other dimensions. Not all practitioners doing past-life regressions of various types have had the same experience, however. One of those is Michael Newton, PhD, another well-known hypnotherapist who pioneered the regression method to access life between lives. Michael, who is the author of several books on soul groups, notes that he has never had a client who reported having a life on another planet between earthly incarnations.

In *The Omega Project* Kenneth Ring, PhD, one of the foremost authorities on near-death experiences, details a research study that compared parallels between the phenomena of UFO encounters, including abductions, and NDE's. His fascinating report suggests, among other things, that extraordinary encounters such as these are intended to open humanity up to an expanded reality. In a sense this is not unlike what Cayce said in one of his readings for Thomas Sugrue, author of *There is a River*—that when we have completed our cycle in this solar system, we may choose to pass on to another. If the soul encompasses ALL solar systems, as the readings indicate, is it not possible that we may be meeting aspects of the Universal Mind dressed in alien bodies or appearing as guides to take us to another plane when we have passed out of the body after death? Is it not possible that we and the aliens are one?

DEAN'S DREAM OF OUR DEPARTURE FROM EARTH

On occasion Dean has precognitive dreams, and it seemed that this dream was one. (This is the same Dean you have met in Chapter 1.) It was very special with its heightened sense of reality, very different from a normal dream. He sensed that it portends a future not unlike the one Teresa experienced in her

spiritual regression in which pilgrims from Earth will be settling on other planets, perhaps even in a different solar system.
After he had awakened, Dean had the feeling that he had experienced this before.

In the dream several hundred people, including Dean and
his wife, were together on another planet. The planet was very
Earth-like in appearance, but it had a different colored sky and
a non-oxygen based atmosphere. They were in an area with a
brilliant blue sea dotted with several islands covered with tropi-
cal vegetation. The islands had steep sides dropping down to
beaches. There were no signs of habitation.

The group had just arrived on this planet in two separate
craft. Dean was piloting one of them, and it seemed to be a
cargo or supply vessel. It was very large, and its shape was
reminiscent of a Zeppelin airship, but it possessed technology
that does not currently exist. It was full of containers whose
weight and balance were major concerns regarding the stabil-
ity of the craft. His wife and four or five others were with him.
The second craft was similarly shaped but was a passenger
transport with several layers of seating and traveling accom-
modations on board.

During an aerial tour of one of the larger islands, which they
were considering for habitation, both Dean and the pilot of the
other craft lost control of their airships. Dean attributed it to
an aberration in the planet's atmosphere. He was barely able to
control his craft, and everyone on his ship watched in horror as
the other ship plunged to the island in a steep dive and crashed.
There was a huge fireball at impact, and there were no survi-
vors.

His passengers had an understanding that the cause of the
crash was due to a change in the atmospheric properties of the
planet and an unaccountable loss of fuel. This atmospheric
change had also caused the same control problems with their
own ship. There was no panic, but they quickly stashed their
personal belongings and secured the equipment in order to

leave this place and return to Earth. The fuel gauges indicated
a gradual loss of fuel, and Dean expressed his concerns to everyone, but the general consensus was that they were okay.
Just as they are about to depart, he woke up.

Dean's dream may have been a view of the future, or it might have
been travel to another plane of consciousness, as Cayce suggested we
all do as part of our learning process. Regardless, it points to our ability
to explore our sojourns beyond this planet called Earth.

Create Your Own Trip to another Planet— Customizing the Script

If you would like to explore the possibility of a former life on or a
visit to another planet in consciousness, here are suggestions for some
of the questions you might want to investigate. Make changes or addi-
tions so that they are more closely suited to your personal reasons for
undertaking this regression. Consider asking your Higher Self, an en-
lightened spirit guide, or your guardian angel to accompany and assist
you in understanding this experience. If your incarnations have been
only earthly ones, you can suggest before you begin that your Higher
Self guide you into a profound sense of relaxation if that is the case.
Here are some things you can do to set the stage for the regression and
individualize it for yourself:

- Decide on the questions or things you would like to investigate
  while on another planet, although they may change based on
  what you are experiencing during the regression. Here are some
  possibilities:

  - What is the name of this planet/this place and its inhabitants?
  - When in time were you there before? One cycle or more?
  - How do you and the others travel? Communicate? Interrelate?
  - What form do you and the beings take, if any?
  - What are the communities like?

- What is this experience like?
- Is there anything you want to ask or explore that seems mean-ingful to you?
- What is your purpose in being there?
- What influence does this experience have on your current life?
- What soul lesson or lessons does this place represent for you?
- Why did you incarnate on the Earth after this?
- Is there something of value, perhaps some guidance, that you can bring back with you to benefit you in this life?

- Set the intention by giving yourself the suggestion that if you have ever lived on or visited a planet that was not Earth, you will travel back there now. You might want to add to the suggestion that if being on another planet has not been in your experience, you will either revisit a happy past-life or drift into a state of relaxation.

Life on Another Planet Regression Script

While you are comfortably seated or lying down . . . take a moment to breathe deeply and slowly . . . and as you exhale, you find that your eyes automatically close . . . and you just settle in . . . as your body unwinds . . . Slowly and gently breathing in and breathing out . . . Allow yourself to be in this place of easy relax-ation for awhile . . . sinking deeper and deeper . . . down into that in-between place . . . that place of letting go . . . no longer awake . . . yet not asleep . . . a peaceful place . . . *pause for several minutes.*

Now bring to mind your safe place . . . Ask your Higher Self or other guide to join you, and acknowledge its presence in some way.

When you are ready to continue, set your intention that **if** you have ever lived on another planet in a past-life or traveled there in consciousness that you go back to that time now . . . Then ask your Higher Self to guide you . . . It energeti-cally taps you on your third eye . . . Instantaneously you both are back on the path leading underneath the archway of trees . . . the path that will lead you back in time . . . Once again open all your senses to the beauty around you—the trees surrounded by colorful flowers, plants, and bushes . . . As you prepare to start walking down the path, hold your intention for this regression in your consciousness.

Now, with your Higher Self by your side, take the first step on the path of remembrance ... As you walk, begin counting backwards from 100, either out loud or silently to yourself ... placing one foot in front of the other ... Each step taking you further and further back in time ... Walking further and further back with each number ... Feeling more relaxed, more peaceful as you continue to walk this path ... having a sense of anticipation as you come closer and closer to that time ... Continue to walk down the path until you see or experience an open door to the past in front of you ... Discontinue counting when you do ... Walk with your Higher Self through the doorway into another place and time ...

When you have walked through the open door, take a moment to orient yourself ... First, notice if you have a body, and if so, what kind of body it is ... Next, become aware of anything else about yourself that is important ... Are there others here, and are they like you? ... How do you relate to each other?

Then take time to look at your surroundings ... Enlist all your senses so that you might fully experience this life and this place ... What is it like?

Are there buildings, and, if so, what are they like? ... Set out with your Higher Self and explore ... Perhaps you even hear or know your name ... Explore and discover everything about this place that you are interested in knowing.

When you are ready, ask your Higher Self to assist you in experiencing the significant events and beings of this life ... especially anything that pertains to your current one ... Ask all your questions about this place, this time, and perhaps even asking about your incarnation immediately following this one ... Spend as much time doing this as you choose ... and when you have learned all you desire to know, prepare to return.

With your Higher Self by your side, you easily find the doorway in time ... Walk back through it ... back through the archway of trees ... and back into your safe place ... If you choose, take a moment here to dialogue with your Higher Self about the experience ... Thank your Higher Self for its help, and say goodbye.

Slowly count from 1 to 5 as you breathe deeply and exhale slowly ... feeling your energies aligned and balanced ... remembering everything you choose to remember ... being able to recall this past-life any time you wish ... When you reach the number 5, slowly open your eyes and plant your feet solidly on the Earth.

Other Planetary Sojourn Regressions

In conducting the other planetary sojourn regressions and setting the intention, I was very careful not to plant a seed that these people had actually had experiences on another planet. They responded accordingly. [As you will read, several did describe their lives in other systems. Some went to a time before the Big Bang while others revisited themselves as spirits making excursions into the physical.] A few of these stories are reminiscent of what Edgar Cayce told us of our time *before the beginning.* As Sons of God we moved into the material in other realms of existence experiencing and expressing ourselves as spirit. We began injecting our beings into the physical on this planet and were initially able to move in and out. Gradually our vibrations became so dense that we almost became the material and were no longer able to come and go at will. Our mission is to reawaken our spiritual nature so that we may once again return *home.*

One person, however, just found the exercise to be relaxing. Most likely he had never incarnated in any place other than Earth and therefore traveled to no other system or planet. I have also included my personal experiences during a group regression. Wherever we went during these explorations (other than just being in a state of peace), the information we came back with was fascinating and uplifting.

STEPHANIE ON DARTIMUS

Stephanie followed her first mindwalking regression with this one in which she explored the possibility of life on another planet. During this recall she learned additional information about her gift of heart intelligence which she discovered in that initial session. This coincided with the spiritual guidance she was receiving on her own and helped her understand it in a multidimensional way.

As she began her investigation of this potential existence on somewhere other than Earth, Stephanie found herself on a mountainous, frozen planet of Dartimus in another galaxy. When I asked, "Why this planet?" she said that it played a special role in the evolutionary process. It was here that the reawakening of the consciousness of heart intelligence began.

The beings there called themselves Duwoks. Their form was similar to humans except that they were either dressed in fur or had fur, and they all looked the same. Their heart, which was a throbbing light, functioned for them as the brain does for us. They telecommunicated through their hearts and touched heart to heart as a group.

The Duwoks were a happy group and worked together in harmony. Due to their true sense of community, no one went without. They all had equal status and shared a purity of love that came as a result of their not judging one another. Their purpose was just to be — to be in joy and in community.

Stephanie's lesson in revisiting this place was for her personal soul growth so that she could experience *total acceptance* by others as she had never felt it this way in her current life. In fact, before this regression she could never have imagined that the unconditional acceptance she received on Dartimus was possible. This past-life memory was also meant to reawaken her own heart intelligence which was first birthed in her life on Dartimus. Here she felt the pure excitement and joy of life and learned that **love, joy, and heart guidance are truly all there is**.

She said that the knowledge she brought back to current time — knowledge she would not have had otherwise — was that the heart is growing vibrationally. There is an "amping up" of the vibrations of heart-healing ability, not only for Stephanie and all other humans but also for the Earth itself. She was told that she and others from Dartimus incarnated on the Earth to "bring heart intelligence to a heartless world." That brings to mind what Cayce told us when he said that it is through the spirit of love (which we hold in our heart) that we become aware of the closeness of our relationship to God. Love is a growing thing.

DONNA ON URANUS

Several times in the weeks prior to her regression, Donna, a homemaker and author, saw a whirling vortex in her room when she woke up in the morning and sensed that she had just emerged from it. When this happened, she had to figure out where she was because her mind was blank. It seemed to her that when the vortex sensed that she had seen it, it would disappear out the window. As both she and her husband had been experiencing health issues and several family concerns, the timing of these visitations somehow seemed to coincide with these challenges. The experiences were unnerving to her; that was until she received an explanation during this recall of a sojourn to another planet described below.

When Donna traveled back through time, she experienced herself standing on a purple planet which she thought may be Uranus. The form of the beings there was pure energy. They had no hands or faces and were more like cloud formations which stretched out and changed shape. The communities were energies whirling and floating around. These beings felt to her like mental vibrations, and they knew the thoughts of others.

She learned that she had lived in this place many times, specifically during the years 209, 1810, and 1936. As Donna explored the terrain, she started floating in the air around the paths and steps she saw carved in the sides of the hills. It was peaceful there. While floating, she saw a funnel/vortex similar to the one she observed in her bedroom and knew that her consciousness had been traveling through the vortex to this place for a needed rest.

The beings had such beautiful energy that she merged with one and felt total peace. The being soothed her like a baby, confirming Donna's sense that she goes there at different times to rest and reenergize her body and mind.

Her purpose in re-experiencing this place was to learn what **is** real. Donna discovered that after incarnating on this planet and being there for awhile, she had felt the need to return to the Earth to feel the body, even though being back in a physical body was always shocking. She made this choice because she believed that this is where she was supposed to be and that the body was "real." The beings on this planet told her, "**You always think of the body as something real, and what you think is real, is real to you**. That is why you always go back to the body. You go back to the Earth and live what you consider to be a real life in a body." There were many souls on this planet who no longer wished to incarnate in the physical, and Donna has the opportunity to stay there if and when she chooses. Donna received reassurance that she can go there for rest when things are really difficult for her and still come back to her body. She has not yet made the decision to remain.

As the regression ended and she was returning to waking consciousness, she touched her body, and it felt strange, foreign, to her. Her energy body seemed more real than the physical as she recalled the peacefulness of floating and merging with the other being. In fact, she had to pull on her arm to find out which of the two was real, the energy body or the physical body. Interestingly, she remembered almost nothing about her visit to another planet. She barely remembers me asking her to record her experiences immediately after she returned. I did not dialogue with her during the session because I was regressing both her and her husband, Ron, at the same time.

RON'S REFRESHING RELAXATION

Although Donna was able to access sojourns on another planet, both in her current life and in-between earthly incarnations, Ron, her husband, did not. Even though we had worked together previously, he was able to have a refreshing relaxation but received nothing more. This might indicate that merely giving the suggestion to re-experience life in an incarnation other than Earth does not plant the seed of a false lifetime, but it is not conclusive nor meant to be.

RHONDA ON "BEFORE THE BEGINNING"

In Rhonda's journey of discovery, she found herself without a body floating as part of the mist. When I asked about other beings and their form, she said, "We are the mist, the One, the many." It was **a place of no-place, yet everything**, before the beginning. She also said, "It is still us but always was," and she recited from Aldous Huxley's book *The Doors of Perception* the William Blake quote: "If the doors of perception were cleansed everything would appear to man as it is, infinite."[5] Rhonda was reporting on a time before differentiation. As for the influence on this, her current life, to her it is an example of what is real. "The Earth is a part of what is real because everything is connected; there is no separation. It is more of an effort to detach and create separation, individuals, worlds, and bodies than to see the reality of the unity."

She then progressed in time to a place where the light was yellow and the beings, called Flurries, had wings. This was before "life" as we know it existed and was among the first attempts to solidify.

Next, Rhonda found herself on the ground of some type where the beings were tall, willowy, and had bodies like sticks. At this point in the descent of beings into matter, she was among those who were learning to have a body and to move. "It is not easy to have a body, but it is still a good tool," she reported.

Finally she was on Earth but in the water. It was a chaotic period—a time of transformation and evolution. Incarnating on the Earth was just a step in that process. Rhonda has continued to be reborn on the Earth since then and has never lived on another planet.

After the regression ended, Rhonda told me that there were no words to describe the totality she experienced in her return

---

[5] Aldous Huxley, *The Doors of Perception and Heaven and Hell* (New York: Harper & Row, 2009), Dedication page.

to the beginning, that it is so simple yet so complex—"see the mist; be the mist; feel the mist, hear the mist."

For her, the importance of this experience was to know that **the Oneness still is**; it is not just a part of the past. In fact, she had been thinking about the quote from the Huxley book for several days before the session was even scheduled. As a result she felt calmness, serenity, and certainty when we finished. It reminded her not to take this "reality" too seriously.

NANCY ON ATLAS AND SATURN

At an A.R.E. workshop on interplanetary sojourns presented by Grayland and Julie Hilt, I participated in two planetary journey group regressions The first regression was to discover strengths, gifts, and talents that we brought with us from our soul's time on another planet, ones that we are currently using and testing. Although the Hilts' directions were to go to a planet in our galaxy, I found myself on Atlas in another solar system. The planet consisted of huge, tall, rigid, yet curved spires of ice of a metal blue color. This was such a solitary, lonely place—a place where I had to stand alone and show the way. I found myself in tears even after the regression was over. Atlas is a place of strength, and my experience there was meant to help me **stand for what I believe in**. It is necessary that I have this level of strength in my current life because of the spiritual work I am doing now. I have taken the road less traveled, a choice not always accepted by others.

The intention of the second regression they led us through was to gain insight into why individually we are here and to learn which planet is influencing us. I went to Saturn. As with Atlas, this was a very solitary experience for me. There were iron forgers everywhere, beating red-hot iron with hammers on their anvils to make the iron malleable and to reshape it. The process burned away all the dross to make a beautiful creature. It was hard work. After my "dross" was burned away, I became a part of that community of transformers and have continued our work in this incarnation on Earth.

This was very symbolic of the Cayce readings' suggestion that Saturn is the place of change where a soul goes for remodeling or remaking—an opportunity for an extreme makeover. He indicated that we are most influenced by the planet where our soul sojourned prior to coming to the earth plane. It also indicates our true calling. We can find this planet at or close to our midheaven, the highest point on the horizon at the time of birth. It was some time after this group regression that I learned Saturn is at my midheaven!

After visiting these two places, or planes of consciousness, it was clear that it was necessary for me to learn to be strong in my own right, especially because of the path I have chosen for this lifetime. Of course, there was (and continues to be) the need for me to transform those things that required changing for my personal spiritual development so I don't have to revisit Saturn!

JACQUELYN'S HOME—
THE PLEIADES, SEVEN SISTERS

You have read two of Jacquelyn's series of regressions in the physical and mindwalking chapters. This particular one promised to be even more interesting and enlightening as she has distinct memories of having lived on other planets and also has had numerous extraterrestrial encounters in this lifetime

Almost immediately after closing her eyes as the session began, Jacquelyn experienced herself dancing. There were other beings who looked like Grecian artists, dancing with her down the path leading to the portal to another planet. After dancing through the portal, she was back home in the Seven Sisters, the Pleiades. She had a light-body but could easily manipulate energy and create one that was humanlike. Although she lived there a long time ago, the memory of this place is in her cells. Therefore she can reconfigure her being and go there any time she chooses. **There is no time and space. She can always be**

there and it is peaceful.

In the Pleiades she was a dancer and creator showing others how to work with energy to manifest and bring it into the physical. Her lesson from that life is that she is a teacher, and this is all part of her growth process. During her Pleiades life she had a tendency to want to experience new things with a friend, but the lesson for her now is to learn more about community and sharing.

While on the Pleiades she had a choice to leave and go to Earth. Beings in this place and on other worlds had all received the call to assist in an important major shift on the Earth. She, along with her working partner who wrote and played music, answered the call as part of a big group. They all came down steps of some kind to get here. Jacquelyn and the other beings entered the earth plane over 200,000 years ago. This shift had to do with merging and bringing awareness of how to work with spiritual energies manifesting in the physical and bringing these energies to the outer. Since coming to Earth, Jacquelyn has had difficulty being in a body, as you read in her regression about her physical condition. She has found the heaviness of mass consciousness difficult.

There is another place/planet/plane she goes to now that is far away and called something that sounds like Nez. The beings there are very tall with light bulb shaped heads, and they have big hands and long fingers. In 1985, while receiving healing at United Research in North Carolina, she was in a colored light chamber and had her first encounter with one of these beings. Later that same day, she was praying in the upstairs dome when she was transported into one of their council meetings for a discussion of her contact with them. Their world became a healing place for her. She had another encounter with them after that in which they talked about a City of Light on Earth, and they let her see a music book with geometric-shaped (not rounded) notes. The beings kept showing her a book cover and talking about the City of Light. At first she did not understand but later found a painting that existed on the wall of the Light Center in North Carolina of this very City. She knows that they are watching over her.

Another time when she was aboard a space craft with a different space being, he showed her a golden grid and said he was monitoring the Earth. She asked if he ever wanted to come to Earth, and he shivered and said "NO."

What she wanted to share about the Pleiades is that it is a place of peace, love, and light, and also the knowledge that we can be as creative as we want to be. This includes creating and un-creating. Her group is working together to help change the feeling of heavy energy that has built up during centuries here on Earth. Some of them are here and others, elsewhere. The assignment is a group effort as they meld and blend together. In 1985, she joined a Galactic Committee that broadened her mission on earth and throughout the cosmos. The members shift into different levels within the group depending upon what job they are fulfilling. It is an experiment. They keep adapting. There are other beings that monitor and direct different levels of radiant light. The spiritual light work Jacquelyn is doing, alone, and in combination with other beings, nourishes her.

The guidance she received during the regression was to breathe in light-force. Also, she should practice movement with awareness. She can throw thought out from her being, embody it, then move and expand it. This will help keep her from being stuck in the mass consciousness of the body. Jacquelyn was also told that there are some kinks in her cell memory and that she should immerse her being in the elements, particularly water, to remove them. We did that on an energetic level. At the same time we included additional work to relieve some physical difficulties she had been having.

Jacquelyn also received information that some of the body problems she was experiencing were part of her teaching and learning experience. Now she is fully embodied in her light-self and understands that she still has a presence beyond the physical, which she was beginning to doubt. She was told, "Do not close in," and that she had graduated from one thing to the next at this point in time, but not what that was. When she asked for more clarity and awareness to help others, the answer was that it would come in the dream state and when she is in nature, specifically coming from water. Much of her guidance comes from these sources.

The message she was given about her working with transforming energy was SUCCESS. It will trigger a lot of people on their path. The lesson for us here on Earth is to share with other planets and galaxies. It is important for people to know that. It will help those in other places in a different way. And, most importantly — **there is no time. Time is an illusion.**

Revisiting her "home" turned a key for Jacquelyn, and she also experienced a sense of expansion in the physical, meaning that she felt more fully in her body than previously, and this was a good thing!

RIGDZIN ON GOING HOME

Rigdzin had complete certainty that he had sojourned on another planet so he looked forward to this spiritual adventure to uncover part of his soul's journey. He walked through the opening in time and stepped out into space, having no specific destination as his goal — just to go through the opening and be with whatever was there. He found himself standing in front of a huge, very bright sun receiving a blessing. There was nothing but white clouds around and a bright light. Everything but the sun was white, and light was coming through the clouds. No ground could be seen. It felt good.

Rigdzin experienced himself in a younger, humanlike form with a golden queue [a braid of hair hanging down the back of his neck]. In fact, he was gilded with gold but still alive. He had come here to visit and pay respects to the sun, just to be there with it. He asked his Higher Self if this was the destination and sensed that no matter where he went, this would still be the quality of the experience. The purpose for his returning to this particular place was a reminder "that this is what I am — pure light. I existed there from the beginning." (Rigdzin had been there before in a dream in which he was flying, but he was sent back. In that dream he wanted to go to the end of the blue, which he did and then took off. Everything got very bright. In the regression he was back there.)

When I asked him if he had lived on another planet, Rigdzin told me that there were too many other places and times for him to pick one of them. I suggested that he pick the most important one in relationship to this earthly incarnation, which he did. On this planet, which he did not name, there were beings like him who were also gilded with gold. They were somewhat ethereal although with humanoid bodies. These beings were able to communicate through pleasing thoughts, so it was unnecessary for them to talk. They did produce sound and sang for enjoyment.

He had been there for only one cycle and left after it was completed because there was an imbalance occurring in the universe. Rigdzin said, "We all chose to leave to restore balance." They turned into light that turned into form and then again into light and finally into multiple rays of light. Trillions of rays of light went out to the universe to correct imbalances and to manifest light in another form.

Even though he would love to return to this place of perfection, he cannot. He had vowed not to return until "all is good." In his current life he is here to help restore the "good." "It is my mission. I have no other choice. I made that choice then." [Rigdzin has taken a bodhisattva vow in this life to assist in the liberation of all sentient beings from *samsara,* the endless cycle of death and rebirth, and to delay his own enlightenment, or entering into *nirvana,* until we all enter *nirvana.*] He also told me, **"We are all perfect beings. We have just forgotten."** All beings must have this remembrance in order for him to return.

"It must be done no matter how long it takes." Rigdzin said that he personally has several methods to help the two-leggeds and some animals, although there are other methods. The ways he knows are very swift and are to be passed on to other beings.

Suddenly he was sent back to the present. There he was in the Light seeing the world he lived in [in no time], when unexpectedly the portal closed for him, and he came back to the present very quickly.

In the debriefing after the session, he added that being on Earth is a labor of love. "We will all manifest that light at some time and return to the nature of our being which is pure light." He told me that what he had described was when we began and the light was actually the Big Bang, the creation of the universe. This was where he went, not to Sirius where his conscious mind thought he would go. He thanked me for letting him visit home. This made him happy!

Is This Real?

Perhaps you are already a believer of the existence of life on other planets and no proof is necessary, but if you are a skeptic, that is good. It is wise to question and seek your own *knowing* and not take others' *truth* at face value, but at the same time it is good to be open to the potential that it is possible. Every day there are new discoveries that we would never have imagined just a few years ago. Even if none of the experiences of life on another planet or places of existence you have read is real, what is important are the messages that were brought back to us from the regressions: those messages of love, the concept of no-time, and a grander vision of the evolution of life. That in itself is reason enough to experience this type of past–life regression or to learn what others have found in their travels through the universes.

Chapter 9

Yes, Famous People Do Reincarnate

Reincarnation of famous people is a topic that sends skeptics scurrying to raise their red flags to warn us about the incredulity of prior existences. They claim that there are so many Cleopatra's running around that this makes the topic a joke. It is true that many people have been misled into believing they were someone other than they were in a past–life. Sometimes this identification with a historical figure is unintentional. They may have had a psychic reading in which the psychic incorrectly identified them as the famous person, rather than being *an associate of* the individual. It is also possible that those who have somehow experienced or been told they were a specific personality are tapping into aspects of an archetype or soul–pool, or even into a parallel life. In other cases, it is people's own need to have made a mark in the world or desire to be famous that leads them to believe that they were that historical person whose name has been known throughout time. This is a natural part of the human existence, but it hinders our understanding of the truth—that the soul (not the personality) never dies. The awareness of our eternal nature is necessary: individually, for

our personal spiritual growth and globally, for raising the consciousness of all the people of this planet

By focusing on why there are so many Cleopatra's, we are looking
through the wrong end of the lens. A better question to ask is **why
would people who had been famous *not* reincarnate?** Did their
personal soul development through incarnation on the Earth end with
that lifetime in which they were well-known? If they had a mission that
was not completed then, if they desire to expand on that mission or
explore new vistas, or if they have committed themselves in service to
the Source, they *would* seek the opportunity once more to be in a physical body and continue on. And if they had done harm, they might
choose to come back, change their ways, and atone for their actions. So
why would only people who live ordinary lives, perhaps remembered
by no one, be the only ones to reincarnate? Common sense tells us this
is not the case, and at least part of the purpose in writing this chapter is
to bring the discussion back into balance. To foster further dialogue,
opposing opinions about the value of past-life regression for identification of the reincarnation of the famous are also presented.

Edgar Cayce, for one, did attract souls of personages who were recorded in the history books. Many received life readings which dealt
with reincarnation. Life readings were given to those who asked about
their soul's history and past-lives. They learned not only details of those
prior appearances but also how they and their influences affected their
present experience. This was given so that they might build on their
strengths, overcome their weaknesses, and eventually become one with
the Creative Energy. Of the almost 15,000 total readings he gave, there
were about 2,000 life readings. Of the more than 10,000 prior lifetime
names given in these readings, less than 200 were the names of famous
people. They included Achilles (900-38), John Quincy Adams (sixth President of the United States) (2167-1), Alexander the Great (1208-1), Helen
of Troy (136-1), Alexander Hamilton (142-1), and Eli Whitney (2012-1).

Kevin Todeschi, Executive Director and CEO of the A.R.E., gave a short
sketch of seventy-two of those mentioned in the readings in his book
Edgar Cayce on the Reincarnation of Famous People. The readings of all seventy-two are available for everyone to see (and the reading numbers

are included in Todeschi's book). It is important to note that not all of the biographies were flattering, and some indicated that the individuals had much work yet to do to overcome patterns and actions they had initiated when they wielded great power and influence. One example of this was given in the reading for a young boy whose parents were told that in a prior life he had been Alexander the Great. This was a lifetime in which his soul lost ground in its spiritual development because of Alexander's indulgences during which he used his military conquests for his own personal "exaltations."

Walter Semkiw, John Adams, and Societal Evolution

Walter Semkiw, MD, MPH, is a Board Certified Occupational Medicine physician and practices in San Francisco. He has served as the Assistant Chief of Occupational Medicine at a major medical center in San Francisco and was a Medical Director for Unocal 76. Walter has authored several books about reincarnation including *Return of the Revolutionaries* and *Born Again*. He is a founder of the Institute for the Integration of Science, Intuition and Spirit (IISIS), which is dedicated to researching reincarnation, soul evolution, and related phenomena scientifically. This organization has many objectives including the promotion of social transformation through objective evidence of reincarnation.

I interviewed Walter in September 2009 to discuss the topic of reincarnation of famous people. As we both belong to IARRT, our paths have crossed several times. One of those was during IARRT's World Congress held in India in 2006 (the setting for my past-life experience in India told in Chapter 7 on life lessons).

Although Walter has been trained to do past-life regressions, this work is not his focus. Rather his passion is research to provide evidence of reincarnation to transform society as a whole and make the world a better place. Walter spoke of the research conducted by the late Dr. Ian Stevenson and now continued by Jim Tucker, MD, both of the University of Virginia. Their findings have provided the most solid evidence of reincarnation to date.

Dr. Stevenson is known around the world for the meticulous research he did investigating possible cases of reincarnation and other evidence of survival after death and in identifying recurring patterns related to this. If there was anything about a case he thought was a falsification or it was not strong enough, he rejected it. He founded the Division of Personality Studies, now The Division of Perceptual Studies, at the University of Virginia, which continues to study previous life memories, near-death experiences, and apparent paranormal phenomena using scientific methods. His research found that violent or sudden death was one of the patterns frequently present in children who remembered their most current past-life. He also wrote a two-volume report on birth defects and unusual birthmarks of children that were consistent with the wounds they had suffered in the prior life. Walter said that Stevenson originally focused on birthmarks but later began to study facial architecture and their similarity between the current and prior incarnation. Dr. Stevenson himself was highly skeptical about information received regarding prior lifetimes that was obtained through hypnosis and past-life regression. Apparently he also kept a file on those who had sent him claims they were famous people reincarnated and joked about it.

Walter's personal transformation began in 1984 when a friend suggested that he see a medium who was working in a local bookstore. Walter's parents were from the Ukraine; his background was science, and he was in residency training in Chicago. Perhaps for these reasons he did not believe in psychics or mediums, but he was intellectually interested in spirituality and went. Walter was careful not to share any personal information with the trance medium (one who allows a spirit or spirits to control his/her body and speak through him/her). One of the two guides who came through the medium gave Walter very detailed information about himself that was accurate, and he questioned how these two guides could know the things they did. He was told about two former lives, and it was suggested that he study the life of John Adams, the second President of the United States. At first Walter thought that they meant he was somehow associated with Adams, but they said no. When he asked if he was John Adams, they said, "This is truth." The other lifetime given was during the time of Louis XIV of

France. In that French incarnation he was the economic minister who helped develop systems that created the modern state. Before that it had been a feudal state.

Since this session with the trance medium made no sense to Walter, he dismissed it and did nothing about the information for twelve years. Then he went on a business trip to Hawaii. He was standing there in Hawaii in broad daylight when out of nowhere a booming voice within his head said, "Study the lifetime of Adams." It was as if someone had a megaphone inside his head, and he could not deny it happened. It was bizarre, but it caused him to buy books and start to read about Adams. He discovered they had similar personality traits, both good and bad. He found a portrait of Adams that has the same facial features as Walter. (You can see it at www.johnadams.net) People in Adams' life that he discovered through this research also seemed to be in Walter's.

He pursued his search for two years before going to Massachusetts and to the Quincy Historical Society. There, in a shoebox, he found a picture of Peter Adams, brother of John, and Peter's wife. Walter said that they are dead-ringers for his (Walter's) brother and his brother's wife. All of these things started to come together for him in such a way that he began to believe he had been Adams, but he was afraid of talking about it in public. He was conflicted. He had started out in psychiatry and was very aware about delusions and delusions of grandeur, but he recognized that if this is how reincarnation works, it could be of value to people. However, he also knew that if he went around telling people that he was the reincarnation of John Adams, people could easily think he was crazy and he could lose his job.

During the John Adams research, Walter went to about a dozen different psychics in the San Francisco area to ask if it was true and if they could help him with other cases. His personal story made him research reincarnation seriously, and he put up a Web site about his work. People began writing to him about hypothesized cases. Also, he was looking for someone who could help him evaluate his and other proposed cases. Regarding the question of whether he was John Adams, the psychics he went to all said he was, but he did not know if he could trust them. "How do I know they are right? They could not demonstrate that they could discriminate valid cases from erroneous ones," he told me. In this process he met Kevin Ryerson. Kevin is an expert intuitive and trance channeler who became famous after appearing in Shirley MacLaine's *Out on a Limb*. One of the spirit guides Kevin channels to receive information is Atun-Re. Kevin's Web site, www.kevinryerson.com, reports that "Atun-Re is an ancestor of Nubian descent and an Egyptian priest who lived during the time of Akhnathen."

Walter had a number of proposed matches between current and prior incarnations he had accumulated through six years of researching on his own. About sixty proposed cases were related to the John Adams' soul group. Walter went over each of them with Atun-Re and was told which were right and wrong conclusions. Yes, he was told, he was Adams. There were also cases of people whom Walter suspected were part of the Revolutionary soul group, but he had no idea of who they may have been in Revolutionary times. Walter found that Atun-Re could tell who these people were in past lives. Often these cases involved individuals that Walter had never heard of or people who were very obscure. Yet when Walter did research, he found that Atun-Re was correct; the individuals found had the same facial features, personality traits, thought patterns, and passions as they did in contemporary times. These findings include the cases of Ralph Nader, Carl Sagan, and Neale Donald Walsch, which can also be reviewed at www.johnadams.net. These cases demonstrated to Walter that Atun-Re could make accurate reincarnation matches, and over time in working with Kevin, Walter has found Atun-Re to be a key resource and ally.

In 1998–99 Walter started to make presentations about facial similarities because he had found a number of independent confirmations. One of the cases was that of C. Norman Shealy, MD, PhD, alternative medicine physician, founder and first president of the American Holistic Medical Association, and speaker at many A.R.E. conferences. Dr. Shealy was identified as the reincarnation of John Elliotson, a British physician in the nineteenth century who operated on people while they were mesmerized. Another confirming breakthrough occurred in the year 2000 when two cases researched by Dr. Stevenson were made public that demonstrated the same finding—that facial features remain the same from one incarnation to another. These cases involved Suzanne Ghanem and Daniel Jurdi, both of whom live in Lebanon. Walter viewed these cases as a bonanza because they provided additional credibility for his claims.

The body of evidence about the truth of reincarnation has been growing over the years. Many cases of past-life remembrances are now being reported in the West where formerly they had primarily been in Eastern countries. Walter mentioned three types of research he is currently involved in. The first are the independently researched cases that stand on their own. The second are those he "solved" and continues to solve through Kevin Ryerson and Atun-Re. They have sessions at least once a month and have accumulated a huge database of over 2,000 cases. The third type is past-life regression. Walter was on the Board of Directors of IAART and is very supportive of regression therapy to help overcome trauma and to change behaviors. However, he warns that there is danger of delusion as it is a natural part of the ego to want to be important. Therefore, it is easy to fall into a false belief system that you were somebody famous.

He gave the example of someone believing he/she had been Cleopatra and how a misconception might occur. Here's the scenario he provided: A client who is deathly afraid of snakes goes to a regression therapist and sees a past-lifetime that appears to be Egypt. "You see a place. You see Cleopatra, and you see the Court, the Nile, and other scenes. Then you see you are bitten by a snake and die. All of that could have been historically correct, but you could have been somebody other than Cleopatra. You may have known her and worked in her palace, been just an ordinary person such as the maid, stable boy, or advisor. When you try to identify who you were, you go to the most famous person. In this case it was Cleopatra." Walter calls these *landmark associations*. That is where a famous person acts as a landmark for that incarnation. He believes this happens with psychics, too, where a psychic says, "I see you had a life in Egypt; I see you died by snakebite. Oh, I think you must have been Cleopatra. And then the client goes away thinking she was Cleopatra." That is why he does not do regressions himself. He believes there are other ways to access information more accurately.

Walter acknowledges, however, that regressions can bring accurate in-formation and can help people therapeutically. On the other hand, he warns that they can be the source of false identifications.

Everyone tends to have a passion about a certain area of life. Atun-Re has informed him that each soul was created with a particular en-ergy structure that stays with it forever. That energy pattern is who we are. Lifetime to lifetime we tend to replicate patterns of career and what we pursue because that is what we are good at and like. For example, artists tend to come back as artists or painters or musicians, all in the artistic field. When we incarnate, we follow the patterns based on our own energy structure. Due to these similar life patterns, we can even be naturally drawn to who we were before. Walter calls these *affinity cases*. As an example, his research points to the finding that Halle Berry is the reincarnation of Dorothy Dandridge. Halle went to great lengths to make a movie about Dandridge. In contemporary times Halle fulfilled the ambitions and dreams of Dandridge, who was discriminated against in Hollywood due to race. This case is also detailed on his Web site.

Walter thinks there must be an energy body or soul that contains who we are. He believes that the soul projects an energetic template into the fetus. The body then shapes around it. This template includes our unique facial structure and appearance. The energetic connection to the soul is also how we are able to download information and ex-plains how we can have child prodigies. There has to be some kind of energetic container that holds our experience from lifetime to lifetime, according to Walter. This container can be called the soul or something else. We reincarnate because the soul comes back to learn, and this belief is very much in keeping with the Cayce readings.

Walter has analyzed his own past lifetimes, as he knows several of them. He knows that his soul is interested in social evolution. Adams was a social scientist who pushed people to vote for independence be-cause he saw how it could create a whole new social system. Walter has the same passion as Adams had for creating a better society. He does not anticipate being as famous as Adams but is still interested in the same things. This research is not an ego trip for Walter, and he is some-what reluctant to talk about his being John Adams. He wants to be a spokesperson for other, more important, cases.

Walter said, "Think of how huge the universal acceptance of reincarnation would be." To that end he has founded IISIS, the Institute for the Integration of Science, Intuition and Spirit. On the Web site that is being created, IISIS will present compelling, solid cases from around the world that will be translated into many languages. Walter is doing this because he says, "When you read the evidence, your whole framework changes. No one religion has the exclusive truth. When you realize that you can reincarnate practicing different religions, it takes all that conflict away. If you know that you can be Muslim in one lifetime and Jewish or Christian in another, that concept takes away the whole ideological basis of *jihad*." With this Web site he wants to create something that will last beyond his life. That is why the information there will be published in every language possible to help bring the world together.

His focus is set on the social change that this can bring about although he thinks it will take decades. "The people who are going to bring about the change are the young people who are open. The path to making this a better world is for people to realize that reincarnation is real. It makes us think about how we behave, what we do. Our destiny is in our own hands."

As you can tell, transformative societal effect is what excites Walter the most; clearly he is looking at the macro view. The way it works, according to Walter's research, is that you have to reincarnate into the culture you detest. If you have hatred toward a group of people, you will incarnate into that culture to learn about it! Walter cites the very important case of Barbro Karlen, who has had memories since childhood of being Anne Frank. Barbro was a child prodigy writer, like Anne, and she has the same facial features. Anne Frank was persecuted as a Jew, while Barbro was born into a Christian family. Walter told me, "If the Germans knew that you could be born Jewish in one lifetime and Christian in another, as the Barbro Karlen case demonstrates, the Holocaust could never have happened." From a social perspective he challenges us to imagine the impact if we knew, really believed, that we change religion, ethnicity, nationality during different lifetimes. Understanding this can help stop conflicts such as the long-standing ones that continue to rage in our world!

Donald Norsic/Tsar Nicholas II of Russia

It is a rare occurrence for a past-life regressionist to work with the incarnation of a famous person. Of the many regressionists I know, some of whom are quite well-known, none of them has had that opportunity. In my own work, I have regressed a few people whose names might be found in the history books, but they were only minor players in their time. The following case which has been shared with me is one of the rare exceptions.

Donald Norsic was an Art Director for large advertising firms in Chicago. Despite his youth his career was progressing faster than most, and he was enjoying a good life, even becoming a member of the prestigious Columbia Yacht Club where he raced his sloop *Westerly*.

That was until he saw the movie *Dr. Zhivago* with some friends. Life has not been the same nor as friendly since going public with his experience. While watching the movie, he was horrified to witness the upheaval of the Russian revolution and the destruction of the society that occurred as a result. Up to this point, he knew almost nothing of Russian history and had no reason to be swept into what was happening there. As the movie played out, Donald suffered turbulent emotions of shock and revulsion. He felt as if someone were squeezing his stomach and was surprised to learn later that none of his friends who had accompanied him had experienced anything similar.

That night he dreamed of fragments of experiences of Russia, but unrelated to the movie, and it seemed as if something sprung open that had previously been shut. These dreams continued, at first nightly, and then less frequently, but became more precisely definitive and included vivid details about Russia and events of the life of the Tsar. As this change happened, another dream began occurring in tandem with the others, one very insidious—a murder nightmare in which his very life was being threatened. This murder nightmare happened ever more frequently and intensified to become so frightening that as it continued, Donald feared suffering a heart attack. The murder nightmare was so emotionally and physically exhausting he decided to try to find a way to stop it.

He first shared his dream experiences with another Art Director who suggested that he see a hypnotist for a past-life regression. Donald did not believe in reincarnation, and the idea of seeing a hypnotist was abhorrent to him. His friend's persistence and persuasion caused him to give it try. His first experience was a disaster, and he immediately put the thought of pursuing a regression out of his mind. But the unrelenting recurrence and intensity of the murder nightmare drove him to look for another hypnotist.

A newspaper article about a hypnotist specializing in past-life regression caught his attention, and Donald gave him a call. Deciding to proceed cautiously, he chose instead to participate in a less threatening group regression. During the group workshop the hypnotist gave the suggestion that they move to the day in which they had achieved their highest rank in any lifetime. He then asked them to visualize themselves on that day. As the hypnotist continued to give them suggestions about things to recall, Donald began to relive various experiences of Tsar Nicholas II: as a child, as a youth, and as a man. Then the hypnotist suggested that they go to the last day of that life, although this is usually not done in a group regression. Donald thrashed his way to consciousness after experiencing the horror of his family and him being shot to death. When the regression ended and he was asked to report back to the group, he extremely reluctantly told them that he had been the Tsar of Russia. The hypnotist, intrigued by what Donald had uncovered, suggested that he and Donald explore it in more detail. A date was set for an individual session, and Donald was asked to refrain from reading or investigating anything about Nicholas or Russia before the appointment.

That first extensive regression provided many details of Donald's life as Tsar: details about places, names, and events that were not known to him consciously. The hypnotist also knew little about Russian history, evident in many of his questions. His lack of knowledge caused them to miss many significant events worth exploring but accidently caused them to stumble upon other things that were astonishing in what they revealed. What came out of this blind probing was remarkable.

A subsequent session was scheduled to explore further this prior incarnation. An interesting consequence of this exploration was that once he began this investigation, the murder nightmare never again occurred. Donald says that it seems the nightmares were meant to awaken him and launch him on what was to ensue.

The first session had taken him in historical time from the beginning of his reign to 1911. The second session began with the onset of World War I and continued up to the time just prior to his death. It provided many more details of that life, and those, along with the rest of his story, are reported in his book, *To Save Russia*.

Because of Donald's professional responsibilities as well as the hypnotist's prior engagements, it was some time before they were able to schedule any further exploration. When they finally did, they settled on the only available option, an intense series of sessions covering two full days. In fact, Donald was regressed three times the first day. During this series the questions covered a wide variety of subjects, and Donald was impressed by the intimate details of Nicholas' life, some important and others inconsequential, that he was able to access. This included the surprising details of the first party he gave for his future wife in an unlikely place outside of the capital where it traditionally would have been held. In the last regression they succeeded in getting to the actual murder of Nicholas and his family. The circumstances he revealed were quite different from what the history books have recorded.

The information Donald recovered in the regressions caused him to begin researching what he experienced about Tsar Nicholas II's life and death, at first to convince himself of the validity of his having been Tsar. Nothing that he had said during the sessions turned out to be erroneous after additional investigation, no matter how illogical it seemed at the time. Then he further researched, in great depth and also analytically, so that he might educate the world to the real truths about those times, and the information proved to be accurate by the results of more than thirty years of research. He told me this is not his opinion but well-recorded facts that can be confirmed in any library. They include the variant details of the murder of the royal family. Confirmation of the validity of the material was also necessary to enable him be fully convinced that he indeed had been this famous person. He finally was forced to accept the inevitable by the overwhelming and increasing indications of confirmation of it as well as revelations that began coming from sources outside of his own mind, including a handwriting analysis done by a well-known and respected analyst that confirmed sameness of intellect, a first of its kind.

I learned about Donald Norsic and his story when a friend who knows Donald sent me, *To Save Russia*. What I read rang true to me, and not too far into the book I felt a compulsion to meet this man who believed he was the incarnation of Tsar Nicholas II. After talking to him on the phone, I decided to do just that on my next trip to Chicago.

We arranged to meet at a public location downtown. Having arrived early, I was standing in the lobby when I noticed a man get into the elevator on the other side of the lobby. It was Donald, and I recognized him instantly, although we had never previously met. He looked like the pictures I have seen of Tsar Nicholas II, not only facially but also in height. Similarity of facial features incarnation to incarnation is very much in keeping with the findings of Drs. Stevenson and Walter Semkiw, as you have read. Also, although many of the Tsars were very tall, Tsar Nicholas II, officially reported to be 5'7," was probably shorter than that. Donald is about the same height.

Our meeting and subsequent conversations furthered my conviction that he had indeed been who he knew himself to be. Whether I believe that Donald is the reincarnation of Tsar Nicholas II is inconsequential. What is important is the impact that knowledge has had on him and the world, and what he has done with the information in this life. Donald firmly believes that he was born in this place and time in this current life for a purpose. That purpose was to remove from the Russian people the evils placed upon them by Lenin and to use his talents to energetically set in motion the forces to eliminate the government of the Soviet Union. He told me, "Egotism and ego have utterly nothing to do with my experience. I have been motivated entirely by the desire to free the Russian people and to correct the injustices of the untruths of those times."

Following the spiritual principles of "mind is the builder" (261-27) and "thoughts are things" (105-2), he created a step-by-step scenario, in essence a blueprint, of how to free Russia and presented it in the form of a novel, *Clouds of Glory*. The vision he presented was based on his incarnating in Russia in his next life, and how he would be instrumental in overthrowing that government. Even though this was written as a novel, it was always his intention that it was ultimately to serve as a course of action that *would be fulfilled*. Whether you subscribe to his postulation or not, it is difficult to escape the fascinating fact that for sixty-five years until the spring of 1983 (when he started to create *Clouds of Glory*), nothing had changed in the Soviet Union. After spring of 1984 (when he completed *Clouds of Glory*), nothing *ceased* changing in the Soviet Union until Communism was destroyed.

Donald felt elation at the freedom of his people and his country and believes that the creation of the plan/blueprint presented in *Clouds of Glory* became the reality of what has taken place—that the thought form took on a life of its own and had such power that it caused the events to occur. He continues the research that began many years ago to discover the true facts and record them for posterity. He has dedicated himself to creating a document that "goes beyond the lies and Soviet propaganda generally accepted" and reveals the real truth about everything that happened leading up to the fall of the Russian dynasty. His intention is "for the edification of Russia as well as the misled nations of the West." He is driven by the need "to vindicate himself/Nicholas from the unfair and false judgment of history as well as to exonerate the Romanov Dynasty to prove there was no mismanagement in Tsarist Russia's stewardship; this management was proving so successful that Russia was rapidly beginning to overtake all of the advanced nations of the world, including the United States, with every indication of surpassing them, as its arts had already done in every field. Most of this information contemporary Russians are unaware of because of Soviet concealment of it. There is, therefore, a real need to reacquaint them with the greatness their country has attained and for them to be justifiably proud of and inspired by that achievement." That is Donald's mission.

As we look at Donald's life and the sacrifices he has made, which are many more than I have described, we see a person who seeks the truth, no matter the personal cost. In his words, "Righting a wrong, addressing a challenge, saying *No* to the majority has never been questionable or difficult for me. There has never been *a test*. There has only been the *right way* to handle a problem, easy or not."

What If You Believe That You Were Once Someone Famous?

When people ask Walter Semkiw for advice after they were told or think they were famous, he tells his story. He also asks, "What do you want to do with it? If it helps you psychologically, that is fine. " Walter cautions, though that "If you want to make it public, be sure that you have objective evidence to validate your conclusion. Otherwise, people will think you are crazy."

If you do believe that you were once famous and it seems important to know if it is true, consider doing research and comparing your findings to the information you already have, but even more importantly from the soul's perspective, ask your inner guidance, your Higher Self not only for validation but also for the higher purpose in knowing this.

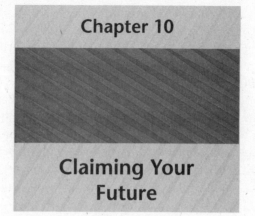

Chapter 10

Claiming Your Future

Where We Want to Be

Creating a vision of the future we desire is a time for dreaming, capturing imaginatively those things that have always fascinated us and pulled a hidden string inside that makes us smile. This life is not meant to be all drudgery, in fact, just the opposite. Even though our tasks may be difficult, we can embrace the adventures we have had, even if they were a momentary diversion from our final destination. We are here to learn, and there is all the time we need. Quantum physics informs us that time as we know it is an illusion. It is only a concept available to us to become aware of the infinite, according to Edgar Cayce. Linear time exists only in our minds. That is why, when we change something in one life—past, present, or future—it changes them all, and our futures open up to new potentials. Imagine the opportunity that presents for living our heart's desire.

The earthly experience is not intended to be a punishment where we pay off our bad karma, correct our behavior, and then are released. So much focus is placed on reforming our bad habits that we often lose sight of our co-creative destiny *and* the link between the lessons and creation. The archetype of the wounded healer, defined here as one who has undergone and been transformed by suffering and pain, transcended the wounding, and then becomes of service by being a healer to others who are encountering similar difficulties, is a personification of that combination. Some easy examples are prior addicts who counsel those who are still addicted; former victims who shed that role and aid others who are being abused, and even those people who create loving relationships with family members in situations that previously were dysfunctional. We know within ourselves what our true calling is, even if we can't put a label on it. It whispers to us in our dreams. In order that we might manifest that destiny in our lives, it has to move from fantasy to an idea of how we can live it—a vision that is palpable and invites the participation of Spirit. Action is required when we work in cooperation with the Creative Forces in order to live our life's purpose in a joyful way. Aligned with Spirit in this joint effort, however, does not mean that we turn over the reins of our lives and become helpless. That is the victim mentality and hinders the results we hope for. The Cayce readings give us to understand that we are to be active participants in this process of creation with the Divine. It is not intended that we be bystanders watching our lives go by and wondering what strings God is going to pull next. Instead, life is meant to be a wonderful interplay of our spirit dancing with God's and creating something beautiful and unique as we each realize our destiny.

Where We Are

Nothing is impossible when we are on the path we set for ourselves before coming into this life. The resources of the Universe are put at our disposal to accomplish this mission; we have all we need. In the denseness of this environment we may get bogged down in the earthly adventure and forget our purpose. Because of this, it becomes easier for us to accept the idea that we will fail rather than to believe we will succeed. There can be any number of reasons for this, including early childhood situations and conditioning, past-life memories and/or karma, imprints from previous "failures," etc. Whatever the reason, this mindset impedes our ability to achieve what we desire, even though our destiny continues to tug at our sleeve until we address it.

What Holds Us Back?

Fear is what holds us back, keeps us from putting our toe in the water as the wave glides onto the sand. It comes in many different permutations: fear that we are not good enough, not worthy, or even fear of how powerful we are and what might happen if we unleash that power. Fear surrounds us not only in the media and global events, happened or imagined, but also in our own myopic view of the world and personal options. Many of us are afraid of what others will think or how the security of our life situations, no matter how uncomfortable, may change if we shift direction. We are convinced that it has to be difficult, when it may not be. Most insidious is the fear that makes us believe that change must be all or nothing. The walls come up, and we can see only one possible path ahead with no deviation, almost as if we are racing down a track on a bobsled with no brakes and no ability to maneuver. Where did this fear originate? Are the current circumstances truly like those that created this emotion, or are they remnants of a past that no longer exists? A journey to a prior time might just hold the answer and the remedy. It might open us up to the recognition that there is a continuum of possibilities between the choices of maintaining the *status quo* and doing radical surgery on our lives. Then we can choose an option within that range of opportunities that will allow us to pursue something we love.

Bringing the Past to the Future

To help us actualize our destiny we can even reclaim beneficial resources through past-life remembrance, carrying to the surface those talents that have spoken to us through our interests and passions. Retrieving skills from a prior time does not mean going back to the Stone Age and learning how to make fire. Our abilities and talents are much greater than that. When we first incarnated on the Earth, we were aware

of our connection to Source and recognized ourselves as spiritual beings. We were able to manipulate energy in our creative process, and
we each possessed distinctive talents and gifts—some that were then
adapted to life in the physical and honed through successive lifetimes.
Those special abilities never left us. They are waiting there just beneath
the surface of our consciousness to be retrieved.

This is a time of melding of modalities where the old rules no longer
apply, and we are freer to express ourselves in ways that lift our hearts
and that bring hope and healing to the world. For example, you may
have been a healer in one life, and someone who gathered herbs in
another. These could be combined in any number of different ways
today, such as naturopathy, homeopathy, herbal medicine, aroma-
therapy, massage, or a synthesis of these healing arts. Perhaps you were
a baker of bread in former times, filling the basic need for food of the
townspeople, and in another one you were a designer. In this life you
could create a gourmet cake recipe and design a gift box, then bake the
cake, put it in the gift box, and sell it online using your computer skills.
We *can* use our abilities in nontraditional ways. There are no limits to
what we can do by using our imagination and listening to our heart. By
following the thread of something that calls us, perhaps first when we
were a child, we can find those treasures from the past that are being
held in safekeeping for us.

Bringing the Future to the Present

If the future is always out there in front of us in time, that is where it
will remain. It will be that elusive something that we can't quite grasp.
This is when we need to use our tool of time in a very different way
than we normally do and embrace the concept of no-time. First, we
must identify what it is that we want at a heart level. Then, we can
begin picturing how it will look with all it details, involving all the
senses, yet without putting so many constraints on it that it limits the
possibilities of what we cannot imagine. All the resources necessary to
actualize it are available to us if we ask in faith that they will be provided. This does not mean that we pray to God and ask to win the

lottery so that we might quit our jobs and spend our lives surfing. Rather, it is coming to the understanding that if this direction is in concert with our mission in this life, all that is needed will be given. Spiritual guidance is there for the asking, but we must ask because we have free will. The power of the law of attraction can be put to work by adding our energy, thoughts, and emotion to this visualization. Add to that a quick trip to the past to gather up our necessary gifts. Then jumpstart the process by traveling into the future with them and carrying the new future back with us into the now. Just like that, our new life is beginning!

Past-Life/Future Life Regression

The memory of our special gifts is stored within our being, in our cells, waiting to be awakened and used to assist us in achieving our destiny and to create the future we desire. In using the *Past-Life Gifts to Create Your Future* regression, you will first revisit the past to reclaim your unique talents in present time. The second half is a journey forward in time to experience these very abilities being used in your new destiny. This future view will inform the present you of what steps are needed for this to occur and put you on the right track to accomplish your dreams. If there is something about how this plays out that you do not like, you can, as the author of your destiny, rewrite the script and change it as you desire. Your Higher Self will assist in the process.

Past-Life Gifts to Create Your Future Script

Close your eyes ... Get as comfortable as possible ... Take a deep breath ... and just let go ... Take another deep breath ... and this time bring energy into your body ... and with your mind ... send the energy of the breath to every cell of your body ... And now with a third breath ... send energy to each of the seven major chakra centers ... Visualize and feel each center opening and clearing, allowing it to spin at its optimum rate ... so that each of them is smoothly spinning unimpeded ... The chakras becoming fine-tuned ... activating and recharging your entire system ... As you do this now, all of the centers come into synchronization ... balanced and in harmony ... Experience that happening ...

Feel yourself revitalized, centered, and in tune with universal energy ... You are now vibrating in harmony with the energy of the universe ... and it is an easy thing for you to slip into a deep altered state and to once again get in touch with your Higher Self.

Now turn your attention to relaxing your physical body ... Start with the toes ... Allow the relaxation to move through your feet up through your calves to your knees and then to your thighs ... Feel them becoming totally relaxed ... The relaxation continues to move up, now to your hips and lower torso ... Experience your hips and lower torso relaxing ... Now it flows through your chest and upper body ... moving up to your shoulders ... and down through your arms, hands, and fingers ... relaxing your shoulders and your arms out to the very end of your fingers ... Relaxation now moving into your neck and head and relaxing them completely ... Your whole body relaxed.

Feel your breathing becoming slow and deep ... Focus your attention on your breathing ... As you inhale, feel the air pass into the nostrils ... up through the upper nasal passages ... down through the large and small airways ... and all the way to the bottom of your lungs ... Be present to this process as it reverses itself when you exhale ... Feel the air in the bottom of your lungs move upward ... up through the nasal passages ... out through your nostrils ... Each breath revitalizing you, soothing and smoothing your physical, mental, and emotional bodies.

Allow yourself to sink even deeper into a state of pure relaxation as you count from 1 to 10 ... Each count helps you unwind even more ... 1 ... 2 ... 3 ... 4 ... 5 ... 6 ... 7 ... 8 ... 9 ... 10 ... So deeply relaxed now that your mind begins to daydream ... and your conscious mind gives way to your subconscious ... As your mind wanders, you find yourself in a classroom seated in one of the chairs there ... surrounded by other classmates ... Look at each of them and see if there are any whom you recognize ... Notice that there is a teacher standing at the blackboard in the front of the room ... Written on the board is the title of the class—*Past-Life History: The Key to Creating Your Future* ... Experience the teacher instructing you to pick up the history book lying on your desk and then telling you to open it to the past life that contains your special gifts ... those that will aid you in creating the future of your destiny.

Pick up the book and open it now ... When you do, you discover that it is an interactive electronic book ... All you have to do is press the start button on the left to turn on the book ...Press it now, keeping in mind your goal ...to retrieve those highly-developed gifts, skills, and talents you mastered in the past and that will aid you in fulfilling your destiny in this life.

The book turns on ...Use the directional arrow buttons to quickly scroll down through the pages that are blank ...Continue scrolling and watch as the pages gradually come to life ...At first the colors are dim and the images fuzzy ...Now becoming brighter and more lifelike, clearer and more defined ...as they become more energized ...The image is clear now and you see another place and time displayed on the page of the book ... Before turning on the interactive function, the button on the right ...take a close look at what you see on that page before you ...Pay close attention to the topography, buildings, people and their dress, time of year, and anything else that you notice ...Whatever details or impressions you observe will assist you in this retrieval process.

Using the interactive button on the right you are easily able to place an image of yourself in this picture ...Do that and then merge your consciousness with this image ...When you are in the picture, look around and make note of how you appear in this life ...Take time to discover the important details such as your gender, age, nationality, unique characteristics, and just how you fit into this scene.

Continue to interact with the scene to see or experience yourself using your special gifts and talents, the ones that you are highly skilled in ...or scroll forward or backward to move through that life until you do ...Perhaps your gift is exhibited in your life's work, that may be as a parent, sheep herder, teacher, healer, or a person who can listen at the heart level to another, or anything else that is spirit-filled ...Whatever your special gifts, be open to the possibilities ...Ask your Higher Self for assistance or clarification, if necessary ...When you are ready to create your future, accept these gifts as your own now ...This awakens the memory within the cells of your body and brings these abilities into your current life ... Then watch as the picture changes and you are now in your present-life combining these skills with those you are already using in a way that is unique to you and benefits you and others ...Take in all the details.

Begin scrolling forward in time to a couple of years from now ... into your new future ...the future you are creating by using your reclaimed gifts ...Interact with this future if there are details that you wish to alter ... As you do that, they change to be more in keeping with your soul's destiny ...Consult with your

Higher Self to ask if committing to this new path is for your highest benefit ...
and then accept it or make additional modifications according to the feedback
you receive ... Become aware of all of the circumstances of this choice ... When
you have finished designing the future, announce to the Universe that this is
what you desire ... Now, with the support of your Higher Self, your conscious
mind becomes aware of each step necessary for you to take to manifest that
choice ... Note any additional information of importance ... Knowing that you
are able to keep and have full access to the knowledge and resources you have
contacted when you return to consciousness.

Thank your Higher Self, and you find yourself back in the classroom ... You
have retrieved your special gifts, awakened them in your current life, and know
how to use them to create your future destiny in a way that will bring you fulfillment ... Thank the teacher, and then turn off the book as you prepare to come
back to the current time.

Once again focus on your breathing, breathing in deeply and exhaling slowly
... Allow your body to gently come back to the place you are in, feeling very
alive, energized, and excited about using your special talents ... When you are
ready, open your eyes to a bright new future.

Past-Life—Future-Life Regressions

The following regressions will give you a flavor of the types of prior
life gifts that can be retrieved and also how these individuals envision
using theirs in the future.

IMELDA—ENGINEERING BEAUTIFUL HOMES

Imelda had been caring for her husband's ailing grandmother
in addition to raising their young son. As she considered her
future and the changes to her daily schedule which would come
when she was no longer a caregiver, she chose to explore on a
spiritual level what her options might be for the future—what
she might do that would give her joy and a sense of purpose
and fulfillment. First, we went to the past to retrieve her special skills that will benefit her in creating what she desires, then
carried them into the near future to see how their use will be

played out, and finally brought them into the present to provide guidance for the choices she must make for this future to actualize.

The journey began when Imelda crossed a rainbow bridge, with her Higher Self beside her, back into her prior life in 1768. She saw herself as a female dressed in a long robe and sandals with straps and holding a basket of fruit. She had only one functioning eye.

This woman worked in a tent next to a stream making swords and armor. Part of her process was to smooth their edges on a lathe. A long line of people watched her. It was great entertainment for them, and she enjoyed it immensely especially because of her limited sight.

This transitioned into her painting a picture of a flower that was tied with a beautiful bow. She also made decorations with flowers. One of her paintings was a Chinese Tree of Life with purple flowers and included a purple butterfly. This seemed very symbolic of her creating beautiful things in her life.

Unexpectedly she lifted over the scene and began seeing with the sightless eye. What she observed were various types of symbols—a white box above her heart and a white table on her chest which represented giving and sharing what she had in the box, her giving and sharing from the heart. Then she saw a large, purple butterfly absorbing rust, cleansing, rejuvenating so that the final product might be displayed. This made her feel happy. She took her **two gifts—one of sharing, and the other, rejuvenating things to make them beautiful by her giving to others from the heart**—with her into the future, into 2012.

When Imelda moved forward to 2012, she found herself in a large house filled with the elderly. She was on the terrace observing all the various elements of it, including the fountain, garden, and the structure of the house itself. The people who lived there were very happy, and that made her happy as a result.

Looking back from 2012 to current time (2009), she identified the steps necessary to live this potential future. She saw
herself going to the local college and graduating with a certificate in her hands. It was an engineering [architectural design]
certificate, and she liked this idea. Although she continually
looks at how homes are designed and their architectural aspects such as arches, she had never really acknowledged before how their engineering was something that really spoke to
her. She shares this love with her father who taught technical
engineering in Uganda, and when she was younger, she accompanied him during his building inspections as the General
Inspector of Schools.

Imelda liked the idea of pursuing this vision. With great joy
and compassion she cared for her husband's elderly grandmother who was ill. Her nature of sharing and caring along
with her love of housing design can perhaps be combined to
create engineering, or architectural, plans for homes for seniors
that are beautiful and in which they can be happy. This seems a
natural utilization of her abilities and interests. She will hold
this vision and expand upon it so that she might take action
and acquire the necessary skills when the opportunity is presented.

JULIO AND THE ENERGY OF NOTES

As we prepared for this regression (You have read several others of Julio's.), Julio talked about how art and music were
woven into him, but he had always pushed them away.

When the images became clear on his electronic book, he
saw a scene in Britain prior to England's becoming an organized state. It was a nice day in the countryside, and the peasants were at the Saturday market milling about and conducting
their business. There were no buildings, but there were pigs,
dogs, and chickens freely roaming around. Ducks were hanging in the stalls waiting to be sold.

Julio revisited this life in Britain at the point when he was a
young male in his teens. He was a Saxon and had very white

skin and rosy cheeks. This young man was a street performer who played the mandolin and entertained the people. He was very good at this, especially the entertaining. When he played, there was a personal connection with every individual there. Julio recognized that the skills he developed in that life were two-fold: (1) to play a stringed instrument well, expressing himself by playing the wonderful music he created, and (2) making people laugh and smile as an expression of his inner being. Bringing others joy was a side benefit.

An additional talent that was developed in this life was being adept with a bow and arrow. They were used when he hunted for food. However, he preferred playing the mandolin. He hunted only because he had to and did not like killing.

When these gifts were taken into the future a few years from now, Julio saw himself as a guitar teacher. "I like to teach." He was playing to entertain and to make people laugh and smile once again.

The use of the bow and arrow indicated a darker future for the world, he thought, because it will be used to hunt for food and also for protection. Julio has always been a very good shot with a bow and arrow in his current life, but had not had much experience using them. Until this regression he had never recognized that being accurate when shooting at a target was much of a skill because that ability was innate. Now he knows why he has that ability and why others do not which frustrates them. Julio chose to work with his Higher Self to select a more positive future in which the world was a happier place. Then he found himself instead using the bow and arrow for practice in order to maintain the skill he had mastered when he was a Saxon.

Mandolin was a word Julio had never before used to describe a stringed instrument. As he talked, he recognized that during the Saxon life as a performer playing the mandolin, he made a connection at the individual and at the group level, and even more importantly, at the soul level from where energy

comes. Making that energetic connection would make performing meaningful for him now. He recognized that there is
more to it than entertaining, and that something more is an
exchange of energy.

In his career, Julio has taught many things. He taught others how to drive. He was even offered a teaching position in
telecommunications at a nearby college at one time but had to
decline because of other commitments. Teaching comes naturally to him, and he enjoys it.

This energetic connection is what will motivate him to teach
in the future. For him to look up at the person while playing
and see this energy connection is very satisfying. This regression helped Julio to recognize that this connection, or recognition of it, may have been what was missing in his art and music
and why he had pushed it away till now.

He said that the results of this regression were totally unex-
pected. Since childhood he has felt that there was something
ready to burst from him. He has loved music, especially because of the notes and the tone of the music. He referred to the
Philosophy section of *There is a River,* the story of Edgar Cayce
written by Tom Sugrue. In it Sugrue described God's projecting from Himself the cosmos and souls. The power of the
changing of the wave length and the rate of vibration of the
primary wave sent out from God created the law of diversity
"which supplied endless designs for the pattern."[6] Sugrue lik-
ened this to a person playing on a piano, arranging the melodies he produced into a symphony. In this comparison
evolution is to be accomplished by movement or change. When
several notes are struck on a piano at the same time they "unite
to make a chord; chords in turn become phrases; phrases become melodies; melodies intermingle and move back and forth,
across and between and around each other, to make a symphony. **The music ends as it began, leaving emptiness, but**

[6]Thomas Sugrue. *There Is a River.* (Virginia Beach, VA: A.R.E. Press, 2007), 363.

between the beginning and the finish there has been glorious beauty and a great experience."[7] That is how Julio feels about the sound of the notes.

NATALIE CONTRIBUTES TO THE SHIFT IN CONSCIOUSNESS

When Natalie, a professional manager, was laid off, she was quite pleased. Although she has done many different types of things in her career life, she has never found her vocation. She likes the more relaxed lifestyle she has now, loves the company of animals, and enjoys writing and editing with a purpose. What she truly desires is to contribute to the coming shift in consciousness. A past-life/future-life regression seemed perfect to help her find clarity for the next step.

As Natalie viewed the page in the interactive book, she saw herself as a Native American male about thirty-five-years-old, dressed in full regalia sitting on a white horse. It was daytime in 1792. She was alone, very pensive looking out across the plain. There was a mist on the horizon. She was the chief of what sounded like the Uwok. Natalie observed that she as the chief had no unique characteristics.

The next page of the book showed her on her horse circling the village to see what was coming so that she could protect them. Her job was knowing, protecting, and predicting psychically. The information came sometimes in visions, but mostly she just had a knowing. Her special gifts were as a seer, as a guide. She was a kind person. Her Higher Self added the talents of being a negotiator and peacemaker to the list Natalie had already recognized.

As the chief walked through the village, he visited with people. He made them laugh and put them at ease. They felt camaraderie. Natalie acknowledged that this may also be one of her gifts.

---

[7]Thomas Sugrue. *There Is a River.* (Virginia Beach, VA: A.R.E. Press, 2007), 363–64.

The thought of being a seer was scary. Natalie felt it in her third chakra. She described that feeling as being long and thin like a needle. When I asked who put that needle there, she said the townspeople. "They thought I was a witch." [This was a different lifetime.] We removed the energetic needle, but an aching wound remained. She and I discussed the need for her to forgive them. She saw the souls of the townspeople but had to work at forgiving them. This was not easy. Then her Higher Self showed her that **it is all just a play, all a dream**. After realizing that, just a small wound was left. Natalie said it will take some time to complete the forgiveness process as some of those souls have also affected her in this lifetime. She continued striving to come to a place of forgiveness and recognized that holding onto these negative emotions does not serve her. The residual was sent into the Light. The wound was healing and will continue to heal until it is complete.

After this work was done, Natalie felt respectful of the gift of being a seer. She was able to accept it in current time in a way that is appropriate. Some concern remained about how to utilize the gift of clear seeing properly and about her being responsible for its use because of the way others react. She set her intention to use it properly, and the picture changed as she viewed herself using this ability in the future. Her concerns persisted and created resistance in the form of a heavy mist as she rode the horse into the future. Sunlight was brought in to dissipate the mist.

What she looked at then was a beautiful building that was perhaps a church where spiritual people were working on projects. Natalie decided to walk inside to see what was happening. The people were using computers and talking to each other. There was a sense of cooperation and joy. They were **doing good things for the world—working toward peace, communication, and collaboration.**

Initially, Natalie saw herself as working with them as a peer. She also had a computer. When she turned it on, she felt that she needed to write something. Her dog was there, and its job was to bring joy. Then she discovered that she was a supervisor. She did not want that. It would be okay to be responsible for the work but not for the people. Using the interactive book, she changed it so that she will not supervise others. Being responsible just for the work itself felt much better to her.

Fear in the third chakra made itself known again. This time it was a rounder pain shaped like a lemon but having no color. Natalie realized that it was her own energy of self-judgment, so it was sent into the Light for cleansing to be returned later to be reclaimed in the present.

Her mind thought this scenario was good, but her heart felt that there was no freedom in this future. She changed it so that it was not necessary for her to be in this building or place in order for the work to be done, although she liked the people. In her creation, Natalie added traveling all over the planet to meet with like-minded people. There was no pressure, no judgment. It was all based on respect. There were other dogs walking through the building bringing joy. Most importantly, her work will make a difference.

The new future was not yet complete. More windows and light were added to the building. There will be more free time to be outside and not much material pressure from the outside. Natalie added more creatures to the picture and experienced complete harmony.

The next steps to creating this new future included not giving up, being peaceful at home, and also interacting with others. She must believe it will happen — allowing for the possibility, meditating, and holding the vision. When she asked how soon this would manifest, she was told three months. The future she is destined to live is very near for her.

Claim Your Destiny

The future has many possibilities based on the choices we make, even though it may seem as if we are on a highway that has no exits or alternative routes. As seen in Natalie's regression, there were elements of her potential life she did not like, so she changed them and collapsed the wave of possibilities to the outcome she desires. We have the power to do that in spite of our fear that change means we have to start from scratch in order to move in a new direction. These regressions show that this is often not necessary. Resources we have already acquired can be retrieved from the past, combined with our present-day skills, and developed in a new, creative way in current time to provide the foundation we need. When we reawaken our inherent talents, we can choose to use them to shift course and create a new future that we may not have previously thought possible.

As we begin to move in a new trajectory, it is important to recognize and accommodate the tension of the pull from what we have been and from what we will be. Past-life work can help us clear the path to unlock our present and manifest a new today and tomorrow that is more in keeping with our life's purpose. This time right now is a time of possibility as the future is still fluid. There are more choices available to us after we have explored our past with an eye to our new destiny. There is momentum. That momentum can lead us in a brighter, more conscious direction as we use our awakened spiritual gifts. All we need do is claim that future.

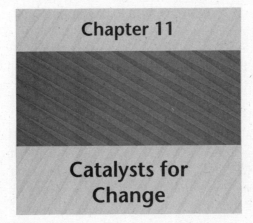

Chapter 11

Catalysts for Change

For each entity in the earth is what it is because of what it has been! And each moment is dependent upon another moment. So a sojourn in the earth, as indicated, is as a lesson in the school of life and experience. 2823-3

In these changing times when old patterns, old institutions are falling away and higher consciousness is beginning to emerge, there is a lot of fear and confusion. What we thought were solid foundations have, in many cases, turned to sand. The shift does not come easily as we move through this period of transition. We feel the pressure for us to evolve or be left behind because the change is imminent. Although it does not seem like it from our human perspective, there is all the time we need to become the fit companions and co-creators with God that we are destined to be. If we choose to remain stuck in our old ways, the opportunity will be presented again, in this life or another.

The knowledge that we are eternal beings whose souls incarnate life after life can become more real to us and less hypothetical when we relive our own past-lives, either through regression, mindwalking, or other means. Delving into our former incarnations provides us with a rich opportunity to look deep within and make discoveries, often surprising, about ourselves. Past-life exploration can provide a wellspring of information for us to use in our journey, and it can often be joyful. It does not always have to be difficult or anguishing.

Many of us choose to explore our past lives, however, because we are suffering in some way—in the physical, mental, emotional, or spiritual. Our suffering may express itself dramatically in our daily lives; it may just be a gnawing, elusive feeling that there is something more to life than the *status quo*; or it may be a longing to return home. Although we may not be comfortable with who we are in this world or with how we interact with others, the fear and pain of change often prevents us from doing anything differently than we have always known to do. We make parts of ourselves inaccessible as a means of protection. These parts stay stuck in the past and in the drama, and we are unaware of their existence—until we choose to remember. To come to a state of wholeness, we must first become conscious of all of the various aspects of ourselves and then acknowledge and own them.

Just knowing information about a past-life is not sufficient. If we merely understand it intellectually and do not apply what we know, transformation does not happen. Regression and mindwalking are very efficient tools for catalyzing all the various elements into something new, something positive. They allow us to clear negative thought forms and old vows and agreements that are not in keeping with our spiritual ideal. By revisiting a life we can uncover the initial cause of our difficulties. Then corrections can be made quickly as we bring to the surface of our consciousness those things we need to alter. Of utmost importance is that we forgive others as well as ourselves. This releases us from repeating these patterns in a future life by removing the karmic seed so that it will not sprout again. This can be very healing in alleviating our limiting conditions. We can unlock the potential of the present and future by first rewriting the past and then applying what we know. Each layer of negative patterning that is released, each energy block that is cleared opens the circuits to the flow of higher vibrational energy. By healing the past we raise our vibrations. Our new, amped-up vibrational frequency is sent out through our interconnected web and comes back to us multiplied. That energy, in turn, brings us more and more in tune, more in at-one-ment, with the Universal Forces. It allows us to look to our present and future with new eyes focused on fulfilling our purpose. We can then live our lives with hope, grace, and love while we move to our next lesson and beyond. No part of us is unaffected.

Discovering past lives provides us with opportunities for soul development so that we might fulfill our destiny that was set when our souls were first brought into being. Through exploration of the inter-life and the pre-birth planning process, we can learn why we chose our current bodies, life circumstances, and lessons—what their purpose is in our soul development. When we recognize that we are the cause of our life situations, we can respond in ways that are more in keeping with our higher understanding.

Past-life work is like exploring an untapped gold mine with many riches waiting to be uncovered. Some veins hold our learning opportunities from the past, while others possess all the resources we need to accomplish what we set out to do when we put this life's template into place. In a regression or mindwalking journey, we are also afforded the experience of our spirit leaving the body in a former life and traveling back into the Light. That reconnection lets us know on a soul level that we are not separate. We are not alone. We are all linked one to the other and to the Divine.

P.M.H. Atwater, after her own three NDE's, recognized "reincarnation as the refinement and recovery of memory that has taken shape in the world of form."[8] The memory she refers to is "that part of the central vision that we are capable of developing and carrying out—our potential."[9] As we learn our life lessons, we can use the knowledge we acquire to live our soul's purpose. Then we have a greater freedom to be— freedom to become co-creators as individuals, as members of our soul groups, and as builders of a greater consciousness. We each can expand the limits of our capabilities in a way that brings peace and harmony to our world and to the universe.

It is great time to be alive, to be fully immersed in this physical life,

---

[8]P. M. H. Atwater, *We Live Forever: The Real Truth About Death* (Virginia Beach, VA: A.R.E. Press, 2004), 43.

[9]Ibid.

and yet always aware that this is a place of learning and testing. Earth is a stopping point in our evolution but not our ending place. Through past–life remembrance we can come to recognize that we are eternal souls and that the death of one physical body is the birth of another. When we recognize that this is not the only life that we live, we can unleash the tremendous healing potential of past–life regression and mindwalking as catalysts for change to rewrite our pasts and create our futures.

Bibliography
Works Cited

Alexandra, David-Neel. *Magic and Mystery in Tibet*. New York: Dover Publications, 1971. Print.

Allen, Eula. *Before the Beginning*. Virginia Beach, VA: A.R.E. Press, 1963. Print.

Arntz, William, Betsy Chasse, Matthew Hoffman, Mark Vicente. *What the Bleep Do We Know!?* Directed by William Arntz, Betsy Chasse, and Mark Vicente. Los Angeles, CA: 20th Century Fox, 2005. DVD.

Atwater, P.M.H. *We Live Forever: The Real Truth About Death*. Virginia Beach, VA: A.R.E. Press, 2004. Print.

Cataldo, Gerald J. *A Dictionary: Definitions and Comments from the Edgar Cayce Readings*. Virginia Beach, VA: A.R.E. Press, 1973. Print.

Eubel, Nancy. "Love Manifested at the Taj Mahal." *Venture Inward* (July/August 2007): 35–38. Magazine.

Gammon, Margaret. *Edgar Cayce's Astrology for the Soul*. Virginia Beach, VA: A.R.E. Press, 1998. Print.

Hilt, Grayland and Julie. *Interplanetary Sojourns & Soul Groups*. Handout from an A.R.E. seminar held at the Finnish American Heritage Association in Sonoma, California, May 3, 2008. Print.

Huxley, Aldous. *The Doors of Perception and Heaven and Hell*. New York: Harper & Row, 2009. Print

Irion, J. Everett. "The 40-Day Prayer." *Venture Inward* (September/October 1985): 8–9. Magazine.

Karma of Physical Ailments & Abnormalities. Circulating File. Virginia Beach, VA: Edgar Cayce Foundation, 1971. Print.

Ledwith, DD, LLD, Míċeál and Klaus Heinemann, PhD. *The Orb Project*. New York, NY: Atria/Beyond Words, 2007. Print.

McKay, Matthew and David Harp. *Neural Path Therapy: How to Change Your Brain's Response to Anger, Fear, Pain, and Desire*. Minneapolis: New Harbinger Publications, 2005. Print.

Newton, PhD, Michael. *Destiny of Souls: New Case Studies of Life between Lives*. St. Paul, Minnesota: Llewellyn Publications, 2000. Print.

——— *Journey of Souls: Case Studies of Life between Lives*. St. Paul, Minnesota: Llewellyn, 1994. Print.

——— *Life Between Lives*. St. Paul, Minnesota: Llewellyn Publications, 2005. Print.

Norsic, Donald. *To Save Russia: The Reincarnation of Nicholas II*. Grand Rapids, IA: Sunstar Publishing, 1997. Print.

Reincarnation and Planetary Cycles. Circulating File. Virginia Beach, VA: Edgar Cayce Foundation, 1971. Print.

Semkiw, MD, Walter. *Born Again: Reincarnation Cases Involving International Celebrities, India's Political Legends and Film Stars*. New Delhi: Ritana Books, 2006. Print.

——— *Origin of the Soul and the Purpose of Reincarnation*. New Delhi: Ritana Books, 2008. Print.

——— *Return of the Revolutionaries: The Case for Reincarnation and Soul Groups Reunited*. Charlottesville, VA: Hampton Roads Publishing Company, 2003. Print.

Sugrue, Thomas. *There Is a River*. Virginia Beach, VA, A.R.E. Press, 2007. Print.

Todeschi, Kevin J. *Edgar Cayce on the Reincarnation of Famous People:* Virginia Beach, VA: A.R.E. Press, 1998. Print.

Web sites and Contact Information

Association for Research and Enlightenment, Inc. (A.R.E.)	http://www.edgarcayce.org
Cannon, Dolores	http://www.ozarkmt.com
Chips, DCH, Allen	http://www.holistictree.com
Elias, Jack	http://www.findingtruemagic.com
Eubel, Nancy L.	http://www.nancyeubel.com
Foundation for Shamanic Studies (FSS)	http://www.shamanism.org
Hilt, Julie	juliehilt@gmail.com
Institute for the Integration of Science, Intuition and Spirit	http://www.iisis.net
International Association for Near-Death Studies, Inc. (IANDS)	http://www.iands.org
International Association for Regression Research & Therapies (IARRT)	http://www.iarrt.org
National Association of Trans-personal Hypnotherapists (NATH)	http://www.holistictree.com
Reiter, Gayla	http://www.gaylareiter.com
Ryerson, Kevin	http://www.kevinryerson.com
Semkiw, MD, Walter	http://www.johnadams.net
Society for Shamanic Practitioners (SSP)	http://www.shamansociety.org

About The Author

Nancy L. Eubel is a former Executive Director of the A.R.E. and a master clinical hypnotherapist who has a private hypnotherapy/past-life regression practice in the San Francisco Bay area. Nancy taught the Dreams and Meditation Class for the Cayce/Reilly School of Massotherapy and was also a hypnotherapist at the A.R.E. Health Spa in Virginia Beach. She is a frequent speaker at A.R.E. programs across the country and is a mentor for several of A.R.E.'s online spiritual eGroups.

She has traveled extensively, including such places as India, China, Nepal, and Tibet. She has also led an A.R.E. Tour to Tibet. Her places of study include Loyola University of Chicago, the Tibetan Nyingma Institute, and the Berkeley Psychic Institute.

Prior to her work with the A.R.E., Nancy was a corporate controller and has an MBA in accounting and was a Certified Management Accountant (CMA).

Believing balance and service to be important, Nancy volunteers not only for the Scrutineering Crew for the San Francisco Region of Sports Car Club of America but also for local A.R.E. activities.

Mindwalking: Rewriting Your Past to Create Your Future is Nancy's first book. If you would like to contact Nancy, please visit her Web site: www.nancyeubel.com.

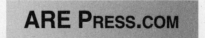

EDGAR CAYCE'S A.R.E.

What Is A.R.E.?

The Association for Research and Enlightenment, Inc., (A.R.E.®) was founded in 1931 to research and make available information on psychic development, dreams, holistic health, meditation, and life after death. As an open-membership research organization, the A.R.E. continues to study and publish such information, to initiate research, and to promote conferences, distance learning, and regional events. Edgar Cayce, the most documented psychic of our time, was the moving force in the establishment of A.R.E.

Who Was Edgar Cayce?

Edgar Cayce (1877–1945) was born on a farm near Hopkinsville, Ky. He was an average individual in most respects. Yet, throughout his life, he manifested one of the most remarkable psychic talents of all time. As a young man, he found that he was able to enter into a self-induced trance state, which enabled him to place his mind in contact with an unlimited source of information. While asleep, he could answer questions or give accurate discourses on any topic. These discourses, more than 14,000 in number, were transcribed as he spoke and are called "readings."

Given the name and location of an individual anywhere in the world, he could correctly describe a person's condition and outline a regimen of treatment. The consistent accuracy of his diagnoses and the effectiveness of the treatments he prescribed made him a medical phenomenon, and he came to be called the "father of holistic medicine."

Eventually, the scope of Cayce's readings expanded to include such subjects as world religions, philosophy, psychology, parapsychology, dreams, history, the missing years of Jesus, ancient civilizations, soul growth, psychic development, prophecy, and reincarnation.

A.R.E. Membership

People from all walks of life have discovered meaningful and life-transforming insights through membership in A.R.E. To learn more about Edgar Cayce's A.R.E. and how membership in the A.R.E. can enhance your life, visit our Web site at EdgarCayce.org, or call us toll-free at 800-333-4499.

Edgar Cayce's A.R.E.
215 67th Street
Virginia Beach, VA 23451–2061

EDGARCAYCE.ORG